# A GUIDE TO THE
# SKI AREAS
## OF NEW ZEALAND

# A GUIDE TO THE SKI AREAS OF NEW ZEALAND

## Marty Sharpe

RANDOM HOUSE NEW ZEALAND LTD

*This book is for Monica,
Toby, and my parents*

Random House New Zealand Ltd
(An imprint of the Random House Group)

18 Poland Road
Glenfield
Auckland 10
NEW ZEALAND

Sydney   New York   Toronto
London   Auckland   Johannesburg
and agencies throughout the world

First published 1995
Copyright © Marty Sharpe 1995

Front cover photograph supplied by Joanna Savage
Back cover photograph of snowboarder by
Sheena Hayward/Snowpix
Designed by Graeme Leather

ISBN 1 86941 252 4
Printed in Australia by Griffin Paperbacks

All rights reserved. No part of this publication may be reproduced or
transmitted in any form or by any means, electronic or mechanical,
including photocopying, recording, storage in any information retrieval
system or otherwise, without the written permission of the publisher.

# Contents

*List of Ski Areas* — 6
*List of Resorts* — 7
*From the author* — 8
*Introduction* — 9

## North Island
Central Plateau — *21*
Taranaki — *73*

## South Island
Nelson–Marlborough — *87*
North Canterbury — *107*
Central Canterbury — *127*
South Canterbury–North Otago — *223*
Central Otago — *261*

## Heliskiing — *329*

# List of Ski Areas

| | |
|---|---:|
| Amuri* | 109 |
| Awakino* | 225 |
| Broken River* | 129 |
| Cardrona | 263 |
| Coronet Peak | 272 |
| Craigieburn Valley* | 135 |
| Erewhon* | 142 |
| Fox Peak* | 233 |
| Manganui* | 75 |
| Mount Cheeseman* | 149 |
| Mount Dobson | 240 |
| Mount Hutt | 156 |
| Mount Lyford | 115 |
| Mount Olympus* | 165 |
| Mount Robert* | 89 |
| Ohau | 246 |
| Porter Heights | 172 |
| Rainbow Valley | 96 |
| Temple Basin* | 179 |
| The Remarkables | 280 |
| Treble Cone | 288 |
| Tukino* | 23 |
| Turoa | 30 |
| Waiorau Nordic | 295 |
| Whakapapa | 39 |

Those areas marked with an asterisk (*) are run by clubs; all other areas are commercially run.

# LIST OF RESORTS

| | |
|---|---:|
| Arthurs Pass | 186 |
| Christchurch | 188 |
| Fairlie | 254 |
| Hanmer Springs | 122 |
| Kurow | 259 |
| Methven | 212 |
| National Park | 50 |
| New Plymouth | 82 |
| Ohakune | 59 |
| Queenstown | 301 |
| Saint Arnaud | 104 |
| Springfield | 220 |
| Wanaka | 318 |
| Whakapapa Village | 50 |

# FROM THE AUTHOR

For helping to get things started I'd like to thank the staff of the Christchurch Polytechnic's Ski Area Management Programme: Robin Armstrong, Alison Kuiper and Fane Shearsby. Thanks also to Isa Moynihan for hours of reading and invaluable advice.

Without the assistance of ski area managers, and ski club members throughout the country, this book would simply not have been possible. My thanks to the following: Anne Begbie, Mark Carswell, Mike Davies, Peter and Shelley Foote, Barry Gerard, Gordon Hassell, Gerald Hood, Suz Kelly, Linda Kestle, Mary Lee, Ray Lee, Scott Lee, Royce McGlashen, Bruce McGregor, Fiona McNab, Mike Morrison, Mike Nielson, Peter Quinn, Tom Richards, Dave Robinson, Joanna Savage, Doug and Jenny Simpson, Lawrence Smith, Murray Strong, Martin Toon, Arthur Tschepp, Debbie Thomson, Peter Thompson, Duncan Veall and Pam Whetnall.

I was ably assisted in the skiing part of my research by the following: Andy Boyd, Pete Deuart, Duncan Dunbar, Paddy and Joy Helmore, Kevin O'Sullivan, Fi Prout and Neil Wiggins.

Thanks to everyone who shared numbers 10 and 11 Peacock Street with me – Jo, Nerm, Jack, Tim, Bell, Tussock, Andy and others – for their moments of patience, and for facing my pasta dishes with commendable fortitude.

# Introduction

## The Land

New Zealand is a country of islands in the South Pacific Ocean between latitudes 34° and 47° south. The three largest islands are the North Island, the South Island and Stewart Island.

These islands are the result of the meeting of two tectonic masses – the Australian and Pacific plates. In a process that is continuing today, the Australian plate is being lifted upward as the Pacific plate forces its way beneath. Some parts of the mountains of the South Island are rising as much as 20 millimetres per year, although erosion is wearing them down at about the same rate.

The main mountain ranges, like the country, run in a southwest–northeast direction. The highest peaks are found in the Southern Alps of the South Island; the country's highest, Mount Cook, reaching a height of 3754 metres.

As well as the main southwest–northeast mountain ranges, there are also a number of smaller ranges. About 85 per cent of the land is above 200 metres, with 20 per cent above 1000 metres. There are also valleys, plains, glaciers and geothermal areas, and even a desert. Generally speaking, though, New Zealand is a land of coast and mountains in which you will never be more than 160 kilometres from the sea.

Of the South Island's 21 ski areas, the vast majority lie in the Southern Alps. All four ski areas in the North Island lie on two volcanic peaks – Ruapehu and Taranaki.

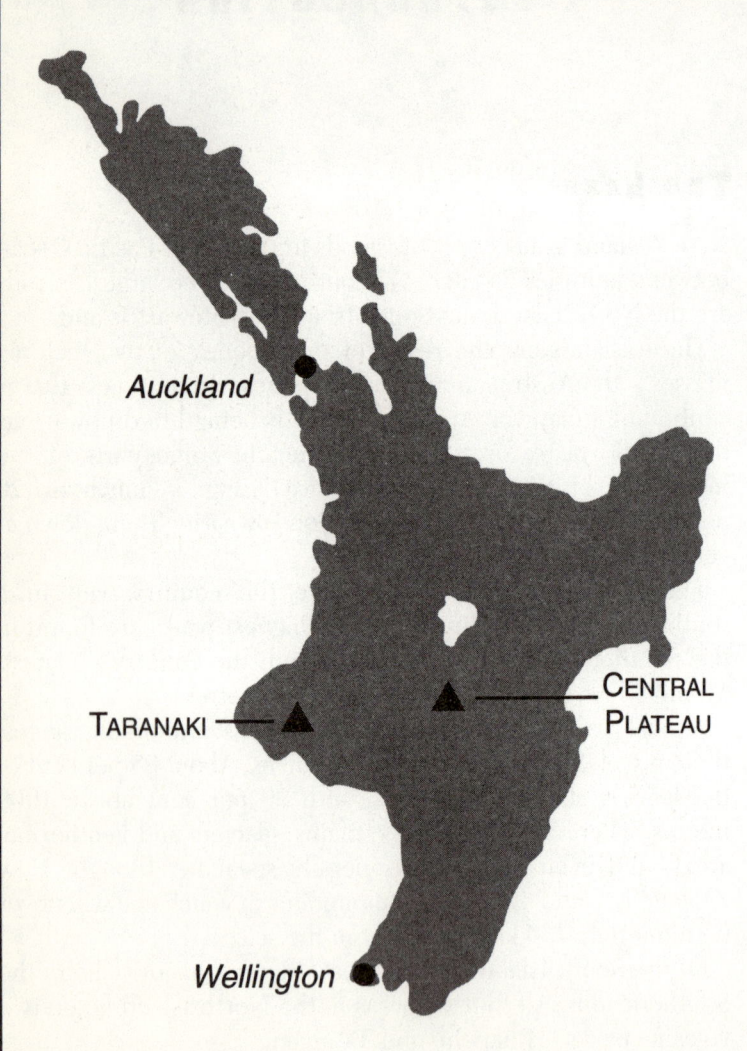

# SKI AREAS

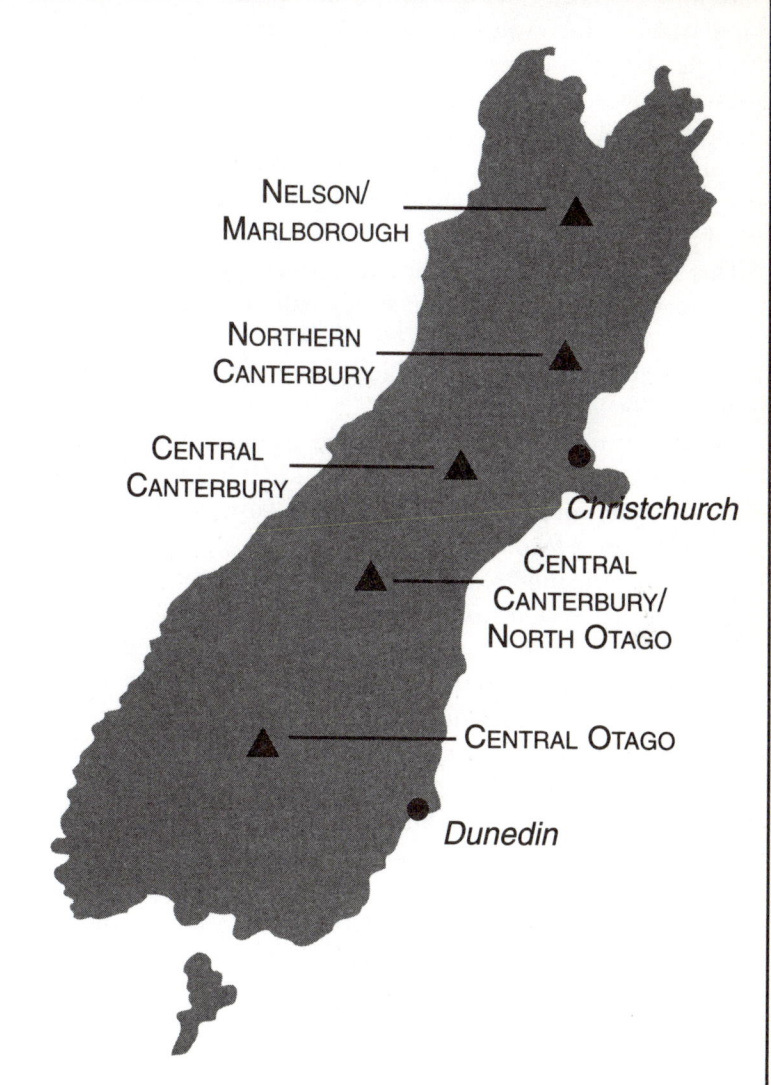

With New Zealand a long and thin country, and with the nearest large land mass (Australia) 1600 kilometres to the west, the climate is almost entirely influenced by the sea.

Weather comes from the west, usually as high-pressure zones (anticyclones) followed by low-pressure zones (depressions or troughs) and normally in three- to seven-day cycles. The high-pressure zones, which tend to pass over the north of the country in spring and over the south in autumn, bring warm, fine weather with light winds. Low-pressure zones tend to pass over the south of the country and bring cold, windy and often wet conditions.

This weather hits the southwest–northeast mountain barrier and creates a distinct difference in weather patterns between the east and west sides of New Zealand, particularly in the South Island with its higher and more extensive mountain range.

As wet air from the west hits these mountains, it rises and cools, falling as rain or snow in the west and in the mountains. The resulting dry air then continues east, warming as it descends to give *foehn* winds.

Consequently, the areas lying to the west of the main range tend to be cooler and wetter than the east. On the West Coast of the South Island, for example, rainfall often exceeds 8000 millimetres per year, but in parts of Central Otago on the eastern side, the mean annual rainfall is a mere 300 millimetres.

Winter and spring will usually bring snow down to about 1500 metres in the North Island, and to between 1000 and 1300 metres in the South Island. Snowfall at sea-level is very rare.

The Southern Alps of the South Island receive regular snow. In the North Island, most snow falls on the central volcanic plateau area that includes Mount Ruapehu, Mount Tongariro and Mount Ngauruhoe.

# HISTORY OF SKIING

The early history of skiing in New Zealand is a story of enthusiasts enjoying their sport and volunteering to build and maintain huts on their local slopes.

The first New Zealand ski championships were held on Ball Glacier, near Mount Cook, in 1933. As well as the orthodox events, there were also two novelty contests: pair-skiing, with the couple strapped together, and the Gelandesprung, with skiers hurtling down a slope and over a bump to see who could travel the farthest before landing.

The first successful rope tow on a New Zealand ski area was a portable one that began operating on Mount Ruapehu in 1946. The lift was over 200 metres long and proved to be very popular. In the same season, rope tows began operating on Mount Egmont (now called Mount Taranaki) and at Coronet Peak in the South Island.

Four more rope tows were installed at Whakapapa (Mount Ruapehu) in 1949 and 1950, then four years later the first chairlift opened on Whakapapa's Rock Garden slope.

With great terrain, five rope tows, a chairlift and an access road, Whakapapa had become the 'Queen' of New Zealand's ski areas. New Zealand first competed in the 1952 Winter Olympics in Oslo. No small feat for a country with one chairlift and only eight rope tows! In 1955, the country's first T-bar was installed on Whakapapa's Staircase slope.

Professional instructors from Europe and North America started teaching on New Zealand's slopes in the 1960s, and the idea of taking a ski-lesson started to catch on, attracting more people to what was fast becoming a fashionable new sport.

Skiing continued to flourish throughout the 1960s and 70s. Along with the larger ski areas of Whakapapa and Coronet Peak, other smaller areas began to develop, and lifts were starting to appear all over the country. More and more New Zealanders were heading to the snow in winter.

New Zealand's first double chairlift was installed on the Shirt

Front slope of Coronet Peak in 1964. It was really in this year that Queenstown, with its new airfield and its bus services running to Coronet Peak, evolved into the country's first real ski resort. The Coronet Peak ski area developed further in 1967 with the installation of New Zealand's first platter lift and, in 1973, with the country's first triple chairlift.

By 1980, New Zealand was recognised worldwide as a worthy ski destination, and the country's winter tourism, due largely to the ski areas, had increased considerably. In the mid-1980s, after years of sporadic progress, a rush of development occurred. Four quad chairlifts were installed in the South Island in 1985, two at the new Remarkables ski area, and two at the fast-developing Cardrona ski area.

Possibly the most significant advance in the last decade was the hosting of the 1990 World Cup Giant Slalom race on Mount Hutt, the first time a world cup event had been held in the Southern hemisphere, and broadcast live around the world.

In 1992, at Albertville, France, Annelise Coberger won New Zealand's first Winter Olympic medal to become the first person from the Southern Hemisphere to win a winter Olympic medal. Gaining silver in the slalom event, it was the best performance by a New Zealand skier since the 1984 Olympics in Sarajevo, when Marcus Hubrich came fourteenth in the giant slalom event.

Disabled skiing is a well-established and growing sport. Patrick Cooper, perhaps New Zealand's most accomplished racer, is a disabled skier who has won five Paralympic medals – a silver in 1988, two golds in 1992, and a gold and bronze in 1994. In the 1993 and 1994 seasons, Cooper often finished in the top ten on the New Zealand able-bodied ski circuit.

In 1992, the number of skier visits to New Zealand ski areas reached one million (a skier visit is defined as one person visiting one ski area once). Not really a large figure considering that some overseas ski areas can receive that amount alone. However, few countries, if any, can boast that their number of skier visits amount to almost one-third of the entire population.

# On the snow today

Like other skiing nations around the world, the current snow scene in New Zealand has its own certain peculiarities which it is best to know about.

First, there are two types of ski area operation – commercial and club. The commercial areas are run by companies as fully commercial businesses, whereas the club ski areas, of which there are 12, are non-profit organisations run by club committees.

Facilities at the commercial areas tend to be larger and more comprehensive than those at the club areas. For example, there are no club areas with chairlifts, but some do have T-bars or platter lifts. The most common lift on club areas is the rope tow, requiring a tow belt and a 'nut-cracker'. The belt, which you wear about your waist, is attached by a short piece of rope to a steel unit (resembling a nut-cracker). Skiers manually attach and detach this unit to the rope tow. The apparatus is simple to use, completely safe, and offers the fastest trip to the slopes of all lifts. No commercial areas use the nut-cracker tows.

It's really only on the commercial areas that you can buy hot meals and sandwiches. The clubs vary from area to area (and day to day), but they all have a small store selling things like coffee, chocolate bars, potato chips, and so on.

All ski areas have full first-aid facilities and a team of qualified ski patrollers. On the club areas most of the lift operators, and many of the ski patrollers are club members working on a volunteer basis.

Road access to the ski areas is generally good, although some roads are not particularly well sign-posted, and can be easily missed. It is always advisable to carry chains for the tyres of your car. These can be hired from ski shops and some petrol stations (most of the commercial areas hire chains out on their access road). There is no charge for parking vehicles in the parking areas provided, and only on an exceptionally rare occasion will a ski area's car park be full.

In most areas, the snow usually starts falling in late May and ends sometime in October. Snow-making machines, which are used on some areas, have solved the problem of unreliable early winter snow, meaning the ski season often begins in early June. Some ski areas will remain open until early November, and sometimes even as late as early January on Mount Ruapehu. A lack of customers, rather than a lack of snow, is almost always the reason for an area closing its season.

All ski areas are open between the hours of 9 am and 4 pm, although most of the club areas seem to work to their own timetable, and will often operate for a few extra hours. Night skiing is also available at some areas.

Long-range forecasting in New Zealand is difficult as the weather can change quite rapidly, particularly in the mountains. It is wise to listen to the daily ski reports on morning radio, or phone the ski areas' snowphones. With most ski areas doing their own forecasts, these are usually quite accurate. Experience has shown that it's important to always be prepared for the worst weather, regardless of how great the day starts.

While there is a wonderful range of skiable terrain, there is only one specialist cross-country area – The Waiorau Nordic ski area in the South Island. New Zealand usually gets more snow than the European Alps but little reaches the floors of the valleys. For people who are especially fit, and who are keen to explore the more remote mountainous areas, ski touring is available, mainly in the South Island. Unless you have had a lot of experience in alpine terrain, it's a good idea to rely on guides who know the region. The easy and less-exhausting alternative is, of course, heliskiing.

The rest of this book includes sections on each of the 25 ski areas in New Zealand, covering such aspects as the area's beginnings and development, the best way of getting there, the facilities it has to offer once you are there, and a description of its slopes. A trail map for each area appears in the coloured section in the middle of the book.

When describing the slopes and terrain, the terms 'to your right' and 'to your left' are used. In all such cases, it is assumed that you have reached the top of the ski lift and are looking down the slopes. The terms 'ski', 'skier', 'skiing' have been used as an alternative to writing 'ski/snowboard', and so on.

The prices given for transport, ski schools, and equipment hire and repair, were accurate at the time of writing. A general pricing guide has been given for other costs.

**Ski lifts** *(based on an adult day pass)*
- Low         $25 and under
- Moderate    $26 to $40
- High        $41 and over

**Accommodation** *(per person per night)*
- Budget      $15 and under
- Low         $16 to $29
- Moderate    $30 to $50
- High        $51 and over

**Restaurants** *(cost of main courses)*
- Low         $9 and under
- Moderate    $10 to $20
- High        $21 and over

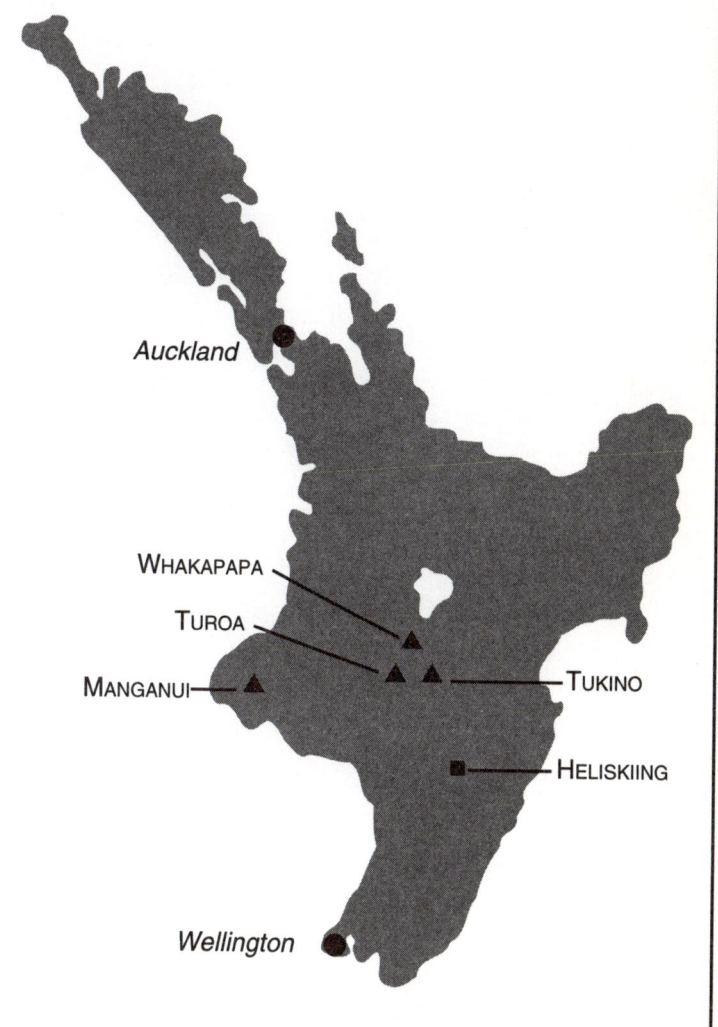

# Central Plateau

## Ski Areas

Tukino 23
Turoa 30
Whakapapa 39

## Resorts

National Park and Whakapapa 50
Ohakune 59

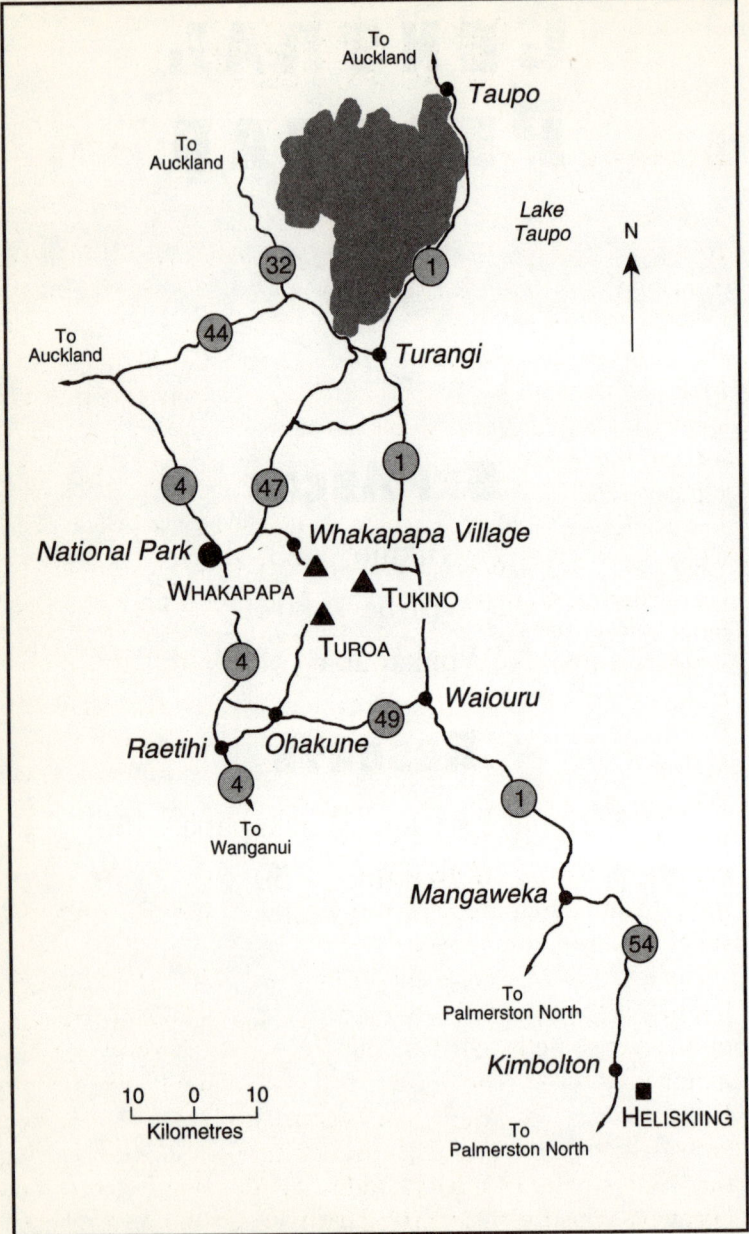

# TUKINO

## HISTORY

This ski area is named after the Maori chief of the Tuwharetoa tribe, Te Heuheu Tukino IV Horonuku, who gifted the Tongariro area to the Crown as a protected National Park.

Skiing on the eastern side of Mount Ruapehu first occurred in the early 1940s, when soldiers based at Waiouru Military Camp took jeeps across the Rangipo Desert and climbed up to the snow. In 1952, a group of enthusiasts from the military camp formed the Waiouru Alpine and Ski Club, and started making regular trips to Tukino. By 1962, club members had built a rough road through the desert up to an altitude of 1650 metres, where they had erected a Nissen hut (a long semicircular, corrugated-iron hut – like a huge 44-gallon drum cut in half lengthwise).

Meanwhile, members of the Wellington-based Aorangi Ski Club, which had a lodge on the Whakapapa ski area, decided to look into the possibility of developing a ski area elsewhere on Mount Ruapehu. In the late 1950s and early 1960s, facilities on Whakapapa had become overcrowded, and demand by members on the club's lodge was getting out of control. The club sent parties of experienced members to Ruapehu's northwestern, southwestern and eastern slopes in search of a suitable area.

The eastern slopes were chosen as being most suitable, largely because of the already established access road, but also because of the consistently good amount of snow that side of the mountain receives. The Tongariro National Park Board, and the Department of Conservation, whose land the access road crosses, granted the club permission to proceed in 1963. During the 1963 winter, members conducted snow-level studies and began planning the first working party for the summer holidays.

A nationwide search for a vehicle capable of carrying club members up the access road turned up a 1943 Chevrolet 4x4 truck. Named 'Marmaduke', after a Marmon Harrington vehicle the club had considered buying, the truck went into action on Boxing Day 1963, taking the first working party up to the Nissen hut. The site selected for the club's lodge was on a small plateau at 1770 metres, members climbing to the site from the Nissen hut each morning.

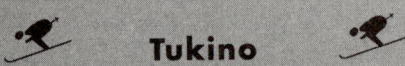

## Tukino

*Location:* 66 km from Ohakune.
101 km from National Park (via Ohakune).

*Season:* Open on weekends from early July until late October. Open midweek during August.

*Elevation:* The top of Aorangi tow is at 1890 metres and the base of the Wangaehu Tow is at about 1650 metres.
The lodges are at about 1700 metres.

*Vertical drop:* 240 metres.

*Terrain:* Beginner 75%, Intermediate 20%, Advanced 5%.

*Snowmaking:* None.

*Grooming:* None.

*Road toll:* None.

*Lifts:* Three rope tows. Low charge.

*Ski hire:* None.

*Specials:* Group bulk booking deals may be arranged with the three member clubs. A weekend stay, including transport from base camp to lodges, two nights' accommodation, lift passes, one ski lesson per day, breakfast and lunches, plus an evening meal on

With the roof and walls of the lodge completed in time for the 1964 season, members made regular trips to Tukino from their Whakapapa lodge to continue snow-depth studies. By early 1965, the lodge was nearly completed and the club, having obtained a Volkswagen engine and tow parts, began constructing a rope tow. Heavy snowfalls early in the season caused a few problems but, in September, the Aorangi rope tow was operational and the Tukino ski area had begun.

## Tukino

Saturday costs $180 for an adult; $90 for a child. Reduced mid-week rates on tow fees and ski lessons also possible for groups.

*Ski school:* A group lesson (maximum six people) for 90 minutes is $25 for an adult; $15 for a child. Private lessons cost $40 per hour.

*Ski weeks:* Frequent mid-week ski weeks (transport from base camp, a five-day ski pass, five lessons, ski races, five nights' accommodation and all meals): $370 (Adult); $195 (Child). For further details, contact one of the member clubs.

*Accomm:* All three club lodges – Aorangi, Christiana and Desert Alpine – are modern and have all the standard facilities. You may be able to organise an overnight stay by phoning one of the clubs.

*Address:* Aorangi Ski Club, PO Box 1945, Wellington: 0-4-478 0116. Christiana Ski Club, PO Box 367, Hamilton: 0-7-855 4402. Desert Alpine Club, 11 Grendon Road, Titirangi, Auckland: 0-9- 817 8987.

*Snow reports:* Phone the ski area: 0-6-387 6294.

The Tukino Lodge was officially opened in April 1966. Two years later the Auckland-based Desert Alpine Club built a lodge at Tukino, and constructed a small beginners tow on a slope near the road end. In 1974, members of the Hamilton-based Christiania Ski Club, experiencing the same frustrations in their Whakapapa lodge as Aorangi Club members had earlier, became the third club to build a lodge at the 'Tukino Village'.

A year later, the three clubs got together to form the Tukino Mountain Clubs Association (TMCA), bringing a more co-ordinated approach to developments on the ski area. The TMCA, consisting of members from each of the clubs, took control of all ski tow operations on Tukino, with ownership of both tows being handed over to the association. In 1977, the association dismantled the beginners' tow and built the

## GETTING THERE

**From Ohakune**
*By car*
Head west on Highway 49 towards Waiouru, a 22-kilometre drive. From Waiouru, head north on Highway 1 (the Desert Road). After 23 kilometres you'll arrive at a sign on the road marked 'Tukino Ski Village – Four-Wheel-Drive Access' pointing west. From here it's nine kilometres to a car park. A standard two-wheel-drive car will make it this far, but between here and the village requires a four-wheel drive equipped with chains. Phone the mountain before attempting the drive.

*Hitching*
This certainly won't be easy. You should aim to be on Highway 49 heading west no later than 7:30 am. Very few people travel between Ohakune and Tukino, and you're more likely to get two separate rides – one to

Wangaehu Tow, suitable for beginners, below the Aorangi Tow. A portable beginners' tow was later constructed on the slopes accessed by the Wangaehu Tow.

In 1977, the Tongariro National Park Board decided to restrict the development of Tukino by stipulating that only three more lodges could be built in Tukino Village. It also stated that the access road must remain passable only by four-wheel-drive vehicles, thus limiting the number of day visitors and minimising the environmental impact of both the ski area and its road. The development of Turoa on Ruapehu's southwestern slopes, and the effect it was expected to have on Whakapapa's overcrowding is likely to have been a contributing factor in this decision. Four years later, in 1981, the Nissen hut built by members of the army some 30 years previously was removed.

---

Waiouru and another from there to the ski area turn-off on Highway 1. The best idea is to call the club a day or two before you're going and see if many members are likely to be heading to the area on the day you are. If there are, your chances of getting a lift from Highway 1 to the area are improved. The middle of the Desert Road is not a great place to get stuck!

*By shuttle*
Snowliner Shuttle may run a trip to Tukino if Turoa is closed. Return fares are $34 (Adult); $32 (Child). To check if it's running, phone 0–6–385 8573 or 025–435 550.

**From National Park**
No shuttle companies operate between National Park and Tukino. If you're driving, or hitching, head south on Highway 4 to Ohakune and follow the directions above.

Today, Tukino has established a firm niche in the North Island's skiing experience as a small and friendly club-operated ski area that is not particularly accessible. While at Tukino, it is hard to believe that only a few kilometres separate you from two of New Zealand's busiest ski areas.

## THE SKI AREA

Tukino is the smallest of the North Island's ski areas. It is also the least accessible. The access road is 17 kilometres long. The first nine kilometres to 'Base Camp' (a car park) are a relatively easy drive along a dirt road. The eight kilometres from Base Camp to the ski area are impassable to anything but a four-wheel-drive vehicle with a high base clearance. Snow chains, a shovel and a torch must also be carried. Don't even think about going further than the base camp with anything less. The club vehicles may make trips between the car park and the ski area in the mornings and afternoons of ski weeks and weekends. Call the ski area to arrange this.

The area you drive through to get to Tukino is the Rangipo Desert, close to an area in which the army, based in Waiouru, runs training exercises. A short way along the access road you come to a sign that warns you to stick to the road and to expect the occasional explosive sound.

Having negotiated the access road, you will arrive at Tukino Village, consisting of the three lodges of the Aorangi, Christiana, and Desert Alpine ski clubs. Once here, start looking for a club member or someone who appears to know what they're doing. They'll be able to tell you where to get a tow belt, and you can ask them about basing yourself in one of the lodges for the day. If you're up for the weekend, or a week, this will have all been organised for you.

The views from the village are magnificent. The slopes and peaks of Mount Ruapehu (2797 metres) tower above you. To the north is Mount Ngauruhoe, with Lake Taupo 40 kilometres away, and to the east, looking over the Rangipo Desert, is the

Kaimanawa mountain range. The ever-present isolation factor inherent to Tukino is unique for a North Island ski area.

The area has three rope tows – the Beginners, the Wangaehu and the Aorangi. The Wangaehu accesses a large, and arguably the North Island's best, learners' slope. The Beginners Tow is also located here. There are three reasons why this slope is excellent for beginners: there are never any queues; the slope is long and wide; and the gradient is ideal, with a vertical drop of 90 metres over a distance of 800 metres. The Wangaehu Tow is also very user-friendly.

Intermediate and advanced skiers are likely to most enjoy the Aorangi Tow's slopes. To get to the Aorangi from the lodges requires first going up Wangaehu tow and then making a high traverse to the left. A very short climb is also sometimes required between Wangaehu and Aorangi.

Aorangi Tow is 700 metres long with a vertical drop of 150 metres. The terrain accessed is typical of that found on a volcano. There are plenty of rolls, dips, cornices and rocky buttresses, etc. The runs either to the immediate left or right of the tow are the smoothest and least interrupted by these terrain features. To the left of the tow, there's a cornice that is worth checking out; a short run but worth the jump. Also try going out to the right of Aorangi where there's some interesting terrain and a short, steep pitch just before coming on to the learners' slope.

What Tukino lacks is long runs. For an advanced skier the beauty of the area is really the varying terrain features accessible by the Aorangi Tow.

The ski-touring potential from Tukino is huge and advanced skiers are well advised to bring touring gear. The prominent peak above the Aorangi Tow is the 2728-metre Te Heuheu, and its eastern and northern slopes offer some excellent skiing. For an advanced skier the temptation to climb the peak and ski these slopes can become overwhelming.

# TUROA

## HISTORY

In the early 1900s, the North Island's main trunk railway line, which skirts the southern and western slopes of Mount Ruapehu, was under construction. The Government foresaw a need for a route up the mountain and commissioned a report on the feasibility of a road from the township of Ohakune. Climbing and tramping were already popular pastimes and a track up the mountain, with a new train station built at Ohakune, was likely to be well used.

The main trunk railway line was completed in 1909, the same year that a young T. A. 'Joe' Blyth arrived in Ohakune to teach at the town's school. Blyth became immediately interested in Mount Ruapehu and its access, and was the first to start cutting a track through the dense forest on the mountain's southern approaches. The track became known as 'Blyth's Track'.

The Ohakune Ruapehu Alpine Club was formed in 1910 and began taking guided tours in the park. Bernard Drake and William Mead, who would later become the first to ski in the park and form the Ruapehu Ski Club, were founder members of this club. To make Blyth Track an easier walk for visitors, club members widened it for some distance from the railway station.

Mead and Drake made their famous ski trip to the northeastern slopes of Ruapehu in August 1913, marking the beginning of skiing in the park. Although Mead believed that the southern slopes of the mountain would offer good skiing terrain, it was easier at that time to access the snow areas on the eastern side. The gentle terrain on the east is also likely to have been more suited to their skiing abilities.

With World War One taking many of the country's climbers and trampers abroad the following year, skiing in the park didn't really get a chance to take off. However, a little tramping still took place around Ohakune.

In 1920, a year after he returned from the war, Blyth, along with the Ohakune Ruapehu Alpine Club and the Ruapehu Ski Club, started building the Mangawhero Hut 14 kilometres along the track from Ohakune (the hut was renamed Blyth Hut, following his death in 1940). The hut, completed in 1922, began attracting more climbing parties and the occasional skier to the region. During the 1920s and 1930s, the Tongariro National Park Board spent money on improving the track, though most of the Board's attention at that time was concentrated on the more popular Whakapapa side of the mountain.

In the late 1940s, the Government commissioned an engineer's report on possible routes for a road up Ruapehu's southern slopes. However, the Government declined to release the report, claiming that a road would cost too much. So, in 1952, the Ohakune community got together, formed the Mountain Road Association and submitted its own road plan to the Park Board.

Ohakune had been experiencing an economic decline since the 1930s and, having seen the success of Whakapapa, the community decided that a ski area could be a new economic base for the township. Founders of the association aimed to build a mile of the road a year and began by using voluntary labour on weekends during the summer and autumn of 1952.

By 1963, the road had reached the 12-kilometre mark. There had been help from the army in building the bridge over Reid River, and a Government grant, but most of the progress was due to local fund-raising and volunteer labour. The Ministry of Works constructed a further five kilometres to the present car park the following year.

In 1962, two brothers, Rodney and Peter Winchcombe, built and operated a rope tow at the site of the present base area. Three years later, they sold their licence to Robin Reid who built another ski tow. In 1967, John Broadbent took up a second licence and ran a lift on the area now called Broadbents Flat.

##  Turoa

- *Location:* 20 km from Ohakune.
  54 km from National Park.

- *Season:* Usually open by early/mid-June and closed by mid-October.

- *Elevation:* Turoa is on the southern slopes of Mount Ruapehu, which is 2797 metres high.
  The highest lift, the Bacardi T-bar, has its top station at 2322 metres.
  The car park and base buildings are at 1600 metres.

- *Vertical drop:* 720 metres.

- *Terrain:* Beginner 20%, Intermediate 55%, Advanced 25%.

- *Snowmaking:* On Alpine Meadow beginners' slopes.

- *Groomers:* Six.

- *Road toll:* None.

- *Lifts:* Two quad chairlifts, two triple chairlifts, three T-bars and four platter lifts.
  High charge, though low for beginners' lifts, young people and the over 70s.

- *Ski hire:* Full set $25 (Adult) $15 (Youth).
  Snowboard and boots
  (full day) $35 (Adult) $35 (Youth).
  (per hour) $10 (Adult) $10 (Youth).

- *Specials:* A 'Turoa Card' can be bought for $46 ($23 students). With this card, a day pass will cost you only $39.

  Multi-day passes:
  | | | |
  |---|---|---|
  | 3 Day Anytime | $129 (Adult) | $64 (Youth). |
  | 5 Day Anytime | $199 (Adult) | $99 (Youth). |
  | 8 Day Anytime | $310 (Adult) | $155 (Youth). |

#  Turoa

A Learn To Ski Package (an Alpine Meadows Lift pass, ski hire, and a lesson) is $42 (Adult); $24 (Youth).

A Learn To Snowboard Package (an All Lifts Pass, hire and a lesson) is $86 (Adult); $68 (Youth).

An All Lifts and ski hire (no lesson) package is $64 (Adult); $32 (Youth).

An All lifts, ski hire and lesson package is $84 (Adult); $42 (Youth).

*Ski school:* The Turoa Ski School runs a number of special programmes and clinics. To find out more about these contact the ski area at the address below, or phone 0-6-385 8456, or fax 0-6-385 8992.

Lessons:
| | | |
|---|---|---|
| Beginners (90 mins) | (10:00, 10:30, 12:00, 2:00) | $20. |
| Group (2 hours) | (10:30, 2:00) | $25. |
| Group (2 x 2 hours) | (10:30, 2:00) | $40. |
| Private (1 hour) | (9:00, 9:30, 12:30) | $60. |

Each additional person $15.

*Address:* Turoa Ski Resort, PO Box 846, Ohakune: 0-6-385 8456.

*Snow reports:* Phone the Turoa Snowphone on 0900-99444 (costs 99c per minute), or listen to any local radio station, or contact any ski shop in Ohakune.

By the late 1960s, things were getting quite crowded on the Whakapapa ski area, and the Park Board was concerned about the environmental impact brought about by the pressure placed on the area's facilities and the large number of huts appearing on the mountain. Recognising the potential of a ski area on

## GETTING THERE

**From Ohakune**
*By car*
Simply get to Ohakune Junction. When you're at the corner of the Powderkeg Bar, take the road that has the railway bridge above it. Stay on this road and after 17 kilometres you'll arrive at the car park. The road is sealed the whole way. It's a large car park, so the sooner you get there, the shorter the walk.

*Hitching*
Get to the Powderkeg corner, walk under the railway bridge, and from there you shouldn't have too much trouble catching a ride. A good time to start is 8:30 am.

*Shuttles and buses*
Dempsey Mountain Transport picks up from around Ohakune every half an hour, depending on demand. An adult return fare is $12; student is $12; youth is $10. To book, phone 0–6–385 4022.

Snowliner Shuttles make daily trips on demand. An adult return fare is $15; a student (13–18) is $14; a child is $11. To book, phone 0–6–385 8573 or 025–435 550.

**From National Park and Whakapapa Village**
*By car*
Get to Highway 4. You can't miss it from National Park

Turoa, and the subsequent pressure relief this would provide Whakapapa, the Board issued an international prospectus in 1970, asking for applications from interested developers. The prospectus attracted considerable interest, but it wasn't until 1975 that the Board granted a concession to a Swiss company,

as it's the only road to the place. From Whakapapa Village, drive west on Highway 48 for six kilometres, then southwest for another nine to get to National Park and Highway 4. From National Park, along Highway 4, it's a 26-kilometre drive south to the Highway 49A turn-off to the east. From the turn-off it's nine kilometres to Ohakune, and a further 20 kilometres to Turoa.

*Hitching*
Try to be on Highway 4 by 8:00 am. Any car with skis on it is likely to be going either to Turoa or through Ohakune. It's not always easy catching a ride to Turoa from National Park.

*By shuttle*
The Ruapehu Ski Shuttle makes a daily trip from Whakapapa Village and National Park to Turoa. It departs from the Whakapapa Visitors Centre at 8:00 am, making pick-ups en route, and arriving at Turoa by 10:00 am. It leaves Turoa at 4:30 pm. Adult return fares cost from $25. To book a seat, phone 0–7–892 2854 or 025–965 027.

There are a few shuttle operators who run trips to Turoa from other centres around the North Island, such as Wellington, Auckland, Taupo and Turangi. To find out about these, as operators seem to change or cease from time to time, contact your nearest visitors information centre.

Populaire Investments Ltd. Populaire, however, chose not to go ahead with development.

Finally, in 1977, the hopes of the Mountain Road Association, which had started the road 25 years earlier, and which had seen Ohakune's population slowly decline, were realised. Alex Harvey Industries (AHI), having conducted a feasibility study, confirmed its intention to develop the Turoa ski area and was granted a licence in November. AHI's director at the time, Tony Wright, later indicated that the most significant contribution in creating the base for Turoa's development had been the access road already constructed by the Mountain Road Association.

Development of the ski area began over the summer of 1977–78, and it was opened on a limited basis for the 1978 season with two triple chairlifts, base buildings, and a snow groomer. A high-level T-bar was installed the following summer, and Turoa was officially opened in the 1979 season. Whakapapa had already established a large following of skiers in the North Island, so it wasn't long before Turoa was 'discovered'. As a consequence, it has probably been the fastest-developed ski area in New Zealand.

Today, with 11 lifts on Ruapehu's southern slopes, and about 200,000 skiers visiting Turoa every year, Ohakune has virtually changed beyond recognition. Many visitors choose it as a base to ski both Turoa and Whakapapa. The Mountain Road Association and residents of Ohakune couldn't have hoped for more.

## THE SKI AREA

Turoa is the second-largest ski area in New Zealand and its 720-metre vertical drop is the country's largest. Ideally, a couple of days are required to ski the whole area.

The access road is about 17 kilometres long from Ohakune Junction to the car park and is sealed the whole way. It's a great drive through thick native bush, which becomes thinner and thinner, petering out as you approach the ski area.

The ski area is covered with gullies, bowls, walls, and wide smooth slopes; the type of terrain found only on a volcano. This can vary incredibly, however, from year to year, depending on the amount of snow cover. Gullies and bowls become shallower, rises become bigger, and walls become skiable. Consequently, different skiers hold different opinions on the skiing at Turoa, all largely based on the amount of snow present when it was skied. Few, if any, opinions of Turoa are poor. It is simply too large and too varied for there not to be something for every skier.

For absolute beginners there is the Alpine Meadow area beside the car park. The cafeteria is right beside it, so it's never too far to go for a bit of warmth or a hot drink (or a bit of shade, and a cold drink for that matter!). Alpine Meadow is a large area served by two platter lifts. The Wintergarden area at the top of the Parklane Triple Chairlift is also an excellent learners' area, though a beginners' pass does not cover the use of the platters there.

The first thing advanced skiers should do is get to the top of the Bacardi T-bar. From here you can appreciate the scope of the place and get an idea of where you'd like to ski. The runs out to your right (Limit, Solitude and Layback) are long runs in wide, open spaces where the thrill of skiing down an active volcano can be fully realised. The runs way out to your left (Speedtrack, Main Face and Triangle) are a little steeper and may require too much attention for you to get the full benefit of the 'active volcano' sensation.

There is nowhere on Turoa where the urge to climb Ruapehu's peak is stronger than when viewing Mangaheuheu Glacier from the Glacier Entrance run. If you want to climb to the top, check with ski patrol on the best route, and do not go without informing them. They'll also appreciate it if you can report to them on your return. It doesn't matter which route you take from the peak back down to the ski area; they are 475 of the most unforgettable vertical metres in New Zealand.

On powder days, which do not occur with great frequency in

the North Island, Turoa's walls and gullies can be the dauntless skier's bliss. There's nothing quite like skiing off Clays Leap or the Mangawhero Headwall and landing in the safe hands of powder.

The runs marked on the trail map are really of little more than aesthetic value. There are countless possible routes and, like Whakapapa on the other side of the mountain, the beauty of skiing at Turoa is finding these. Also like Whakapapa is the potential danger when skiing in poor visibility, and this is when it's best to stick to the marked trails.

Because the area is so large, and conditions can vary so much, it is justifiably worthwhile spending time in the bars of Ohakune Junction, meeting the locals and finding out where the current best spots are. Besides, a trip to Turoa is virtually incomplete without at least a quick visit to the Junction!

# WHAKAPAPA

## HISTORY

The mountains on the Central Plateau – Mounts Ruapehu, Tongariro and Ngauruhoe – are tapu (sacred) to the Maori. In the early nineteenth century the local tribe, Ngati Tuwharetoa, sought to prevent anyone from climbing the three peaks. However, with the steady flow of Europeans coming to the country, this became increasingly more difficult and, in 1839, Mount Ngauruhoe was scaled by the botanist and explorer, John Bidwell. Mount Ruapehu was climbed in 1851 by Sir George Grey, and again in 1879 by George Beetham.

By the 1880s there were too many botanists, explorers and geologists in the area for the Tuwharetoa to stop. The tribe's chief, Te Heuheu Tukino IV Horonuku, was greatly concerned about the treatment of the land. The Land Wars of 1845–1872 had been mainly Maori versus European, but they had also pitched tribe against tribe, and many of the anti-European tribes had had their land confiscated by the Government. So it wasn't only the Europeans who concerned the chief, but also rival Maori tribes who were after the land for themselves.

Chief Horonuku, a man of great vision, handed his tribe's land over to the Crown in September 1887, on agreement that it remain preserved and protected. In 1894 this land became a National Park, the country's first and only the world's fourth.

The Desert Road between Waiouru and Tokaanu was constructed in 1893. A hut was built near Waihohonu Stream on the eastern side of the mountains in 1901. Eight years later, the main trunk railroad was finished on the western side, passing through Ohakune and Waimarino (now called National Park). With these developments the park became easily accessible and tourists began visiting the area, mainly in the summer for walking and climbing.

Bill Mead and Bernard Drake were two young railway engineers based in Ohakune. Both were keen climbers and, in 1910, they attempted their first winter ascent of Mount Ruapehu. The frustration of moving at a snail's pace through deep snow got the better of them, and they returned to Ohakune unsuccessful. Fortuitously, they met Captain Bernard Head, an English guide at Mt Cook, who advised them to 'procure skis and travel over the snow instead of through it'. They took his advice and promptly imported skis from Switzerland.

In July 1913, armed with the only English skiing textbook (*The Ski Runner* by E. C. Richardson), they took a coach into Waihohonu Hut and spent four days 'on ski'. After a day's practice, they climbed to the Tama Lakes and skied back down. On the third day they climbed to about 2500 metres on Mount Ruapehu, noting then that the Whakapapa area was better than any other for skiing. ('Whakapapa' in Maori means 'to lay out flat', referring to a tribal battle when the slain victims were laid out flat before a cannibal feast.) They spent that night below the slopes of Whakapapa in an old shepherds' hut, the 'Haunted Whare', returning to Waihohonu the following day.

Before leaving Waihohonu Hut, they left a note informing visitors that they were organising the Ruapehu Ski Club and that anyone interested should contact them. Few New Zealanders in those days knew what a ski was, and this note would surely have perplexed its share of readers. Nevertheless, this note was the first step in establishing the country's first ski club.

As well as leaving the note, the pair contacted fellow climbers and enrolled them in the new club. Bill Meads was club president, and his brother, Arthur, became the secretary. A subsequent ski trip was made in December, and another planned for August 1914. However, World War One duty took seven of the 12 members booked on the trip. Although the majority of members eventually ended up abroad on service, skiing continued throughout the war.

From 1915 to 1920 the Government began constructing a road between Tokaanu and Waimarino using prison labour. In 1919, club members Bill Salt and T. W. Downes convinced the Government to put a cart track from the new road into the Whakapapa area. They received a £500 grant and completed the track early the following year. Now, when skiers arrived in Waimarino by train, they could use the new road and track to get to the Haunted Whare. It was 19 kilometres and most people walked. Only the larger parties used a coach from Waimarino.

Once Salt and Downes finished the track, the club built a hut at the end of it. A few other huts were built here, and by 1926 the site was known as Whakapapa Village. Nearly all skiing occurred on the lower Scoria Flat, well below where the present ski area lies, and it was a six-kilometre walk from the Village to the skiing. In 1923, the Ruapehu Ski Club built Glacier Hut, on Hut Flat, at 1760 metres.

The track was upgraded to a road by the newly formed Tongariro National Park Board in 1925. It was named Bruce Road after Mr C. Bruce, a local farmer and naturalist whose estate had contributed to the park's development.

By 1928, with a rapidly increasing demand on the village huts, it was decided by all concerned parties – the ski club, tramping clubs, National Park Board and Government – that some form of hostel was required. Arguments ensued over where the hostel should be located, and the whole proposal became deadlocked.

Rudolph Wigley, owner of the Mount Cook Transport Company and operator of the Hermitage Lodge at Mount Cook, got wind of the hostel predicament and put his entrepreneurial skills into action for the first time in the North Island. He formed the Tongariro Park Tourist Company Ltd and designed an elegant four-storey luxury Georgian hotel to be built near Whakapapa Village. The idea of this huge hotel alongside their old wooden huts astounded the skiing and tramping fraternity, who met the proposal with mixed feelings.

# Whakapapa

*Location:* 7 km from Whakapapa Village.
22 km from National Park.
57 km from Ohakune.

*Season:* Usually opens in early June and closes early November. If snow allows, also opens over Xmas and New Year period.

*Elevation:* Mount Ruapehu is 2797 metres high.
The top of the Far West T-bar is at 2300 metres.
The Top o' the Bruce (base area) is at 1625 metres.

*Vertical drop:* 675 metres.

*Terrain:* Beginner 30%, Intermediate 45%, Advanced 25%.

*Snowmaking:* In Happy Valley beginners' area.

*Groomers:* Six.

*Road toll:* None

*Lifts:* One express quad chairlift, one quad chairlift, four double chairlifts, four T-bars, four platters, and 11 rope tows.
High charge, with reduced student and youth rates; moderate charge for lower mountain lifts. Children under four and adults over 70, free.
5 day Anytime: $207 (Adult); $189 (Student); $104 (Youth).

*Ski hire:* Full set: All day: $25 (Adult/Youth); $15 (under 16).
Half day: $18 (Adult/Youth); $11 (under 16).
5 days: $85 (Adult/Youth); $53 (under 16).
Executive gear (full set): $45.
Snowboard and boots (full day): $45 (Adult/Youth); $30 (under 16).
Clothing can also be hired.

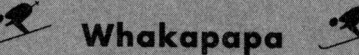

# Whakapapa

*Specials:* A First Timers' Pack (Happy Valley Lifts Pass, full day's hire and a 90-minute lesson): $46 (Adult/Student); $25 (Youth).

'Ski Ruapehu Passes' (valid at Whakapapa and Turoa ):
'Ski 4 out of 5 Day Pass': $156 (Adult); $78 (Youth).
'Ski 5 out of 7 Day Pass': $198 (Adult); $98 (Youth).

*Ski school:* Many clinics and programmes during the season. For details, contact the ski school at the address below or phone 0–7–892 3738.

One Group Lesson: $20.

Five Group lessons: $80.

Private:  One hour:  $60 (each extra person $25).
Half day:  $105 (each extra person $35).
Full day:  $170 (each extra person $45).

*Accomm:* There are 52 Ski Club lodges on Whakapapa. Unlike the South Island clubs, however, these are used by members and invited guests only.

*Address:* Ruapehu Alpine Lifts, Private Bag, Mount Ruapehu. Phone: 0–7–892 3738. Fax: 0–7–8923732.

*Snow reports:* Listen to any local radio station, or phone 0–7–892 2833 or 0900–99333 (99c per minute).

Construction of the Château Tongariro began in January 1929, and it was open for guests by August. During the Depression of the 1930s the Tongariro Park Tourist Company was wound up, and the Tourist Department of the Government took over the Château.

In 1931, the first public on-mountain day lodge – the Salt

## GETTING THERE

**From National Park and Whakapapa Village**
*By car*
From Whakapapa Village, just drive up the Bruce Road. From National Park you should get on to Highway 4, head south for about 100 metres, then turn east on Highway 47. After ten kilometres you'll arrive at the Bruce Road on your right.

*Hitching*
From Whakapapa Village, it's easy to catch a lift. It's not too difficult from National Park either. It's best to make the short walk to Highway 47 and hitch from there, as cars coming from the north or south must take this road.

*By shuttle*
The Ruapehu Ski Shuttle makes pick-ups from hotels in National Park and the Village at 8:00 and 9:00 am. Shuttles depart from the ski area at 4:00 and 4:30 pm. A return fare is $10. Bookings are essential, so phone 0–7–892 2854 or 025–965 027.

The Whakapapa Shuttle operates from the Tavern car park in Whakapapa Village. It makes trips on demand from 8:00 am. An adult return fare is $10; a child return is $5. Bookings are not required.

Memorial Hut – in memory of Bill Salt who had died in 1929 – was built at 1550 metres, where the Top o' the Bruce buildings are today. A mountain road up to the hut was started in 1930 and worked on by relief workers during the Depression, and then prison labour until its completion in 1939.

The 1930s saw a boom on Whakapapa. Overseas instructors

---

**From Ohakune**

*By car*

Head west on Highway 49A, then north on Highway 4 for 26 kilometres where you'll arrive at the turn-off (Highway 47) on your right. Ten kilometres down this road you'll come to the Bruce Road on your right. It's about a 45-minute drive from Ohakune to the Top o' the Bruce car park.

*Hitching*

It's not difficult catching a lift to Whakapapa but, ideally, you should be on Highway 49A by 8:00 am.

*By shuttle*

Dempsey Mountain Transport makes trips on demand. An adult return fare is $14; a child return is $10. Bookings are essential, so phone 0–6–385 4022.

Snowliner Shuttle makes a daily trip, making pick-ups at 8:00 am. An adult return fare is $27; a child return is $25. Bookings are essential, so phone 0–6–385 8573 or 025–435 550.

There are a few shuttle operators who run trips to Whakapapa from other centres in the North Island, such as Wellington, Auckland, Taupo and Turangi. To find out about these, as operators seem to change or cease, from time to time, contact your nearest visitor information centre.

came and taught the locals, ski racing began and, in 1938, the first rope tow was installed. Built by the Public Works Department, at the request of the Tourist Department, this tow worked for only a few hours before breaking down and never going again. It was, however, the first ski tow in New Zealand. Ruapehu Ski Club built another hut on Hut Flat in 1936. Regarded as being somewhat luxurious by having a stove and a sink, it was called 'Pansy Palace'.

Things quietened down again during World War Two. The Château was used as a psychiatric hospital from 1942 until 1945 when, between August and November, Mount Ruapehu erupted. The heavy ash it sprayed out so disrupted the Château's water supply that it wasn't opened to the public again until 1948.

In June 1947, Ted Pearse and Sam Wathen built and installed the Salt Run rope tow. In August 1949, Pearse and Bill Hamilton (who had designed Coronet Peak's rope tows) installed another tow above Pansy Palace on the Staircase Run.

Climbing and tramping clubs throughout the North Island were catching on to the idea of skiing, and in 1948 some of these clubs built huts on the slopes. By 1950, there were ten huts in the area (now there are 52) which had become known as Iwikau Village. With all these people coming to ski, the demands on the small rope tows were huge, and the next logical step was to improve the mountain's lifting capacity.

Bryan Todd, a keen Whakapapa skier, and Walter Haensli, a Swiss ski instructor who ran the ski school for several years in the 1950s, were instrumental in forming the Ruapehu Alpine Lifts (RAL) Company in 1953. The company's initial capital of £63,000 was almost wholly subscribed for by skiers who bought shares and debentures in the company. In 1954, RAL installed the Rock Garden chairlift, the first in the country. Another chairlift and a T-bar were installed the following year.

Conveniently located halfway between Auckland and Wellington, Whakapapa was attracting people from all over the North Island. By 1963 the area had three chairlifts, a T-bar, a platter lift and two rope tows, making it by far the most developed ski area in New Zealand. (At that stage, Whakapapa had the only chairlifts in the country.) In the 1966 season, 170,000 people visited Whakapapa.

The 1970s and 1980s saw the boom continue. The development of the Turoa ski area on Ruapehu's southwestern slopes in 1978 helped alleviate the crowding of Whakapapa. Even so, it still remains the busiest ski area in the country.

With so much of New Zealand's skiing being in the South Island it's easily forgotten that Whakapapa is the country's largest area and was the site of some of the earliest skiing, the first ski club, and the first ski lifts.

## THE SKI AREA

Whakapapa, located on the northern slopes of Mount Ruapehu, is New Zealand's largest and busiest ski area. It also has one of the longest seasons, often having enough snow to allow skiing over the Christmas and New Year period.

From Whakapapa Village (or the Château) it's a seven-kilometre drive up a sealed, two-lane access road, probably the best in the country. There is room for 2000 vehicles in six car parks on the mountain, so if you're driving, bear in mind that the earlier you arrive, the closer you'll be to the base buildings. A courtesy coach operates from the lower car parks.

Whakapapa is the only ski area in New Zealand on which carrying a trail map is almost a necessity. The map is handy for choosing where you'd like to ski, but more importantly it identifies the various bluffs and drop-offs in the area. If you're skiing off-*piste* it can be in your best interests to know where these are!

Naturally, in an area the size of, and with the terrain of, Whakapapa, there is going to be good skiing for everyone. For the beginner and the 'never-ever' skiers, there's the Happy Valley area, where the slopes have a perfect gradient for learning and improving the basics. Happy Valley is unquestionably New Zealand's best-serviced learners' area with its own cafeteria, ski-hire building, and free chairlift access (Happy Valley is located below the base building area). The valley is also totally secluded from the rest of the mountain and is consequently used only by learners; faster skiers are elsewhere.

Like Turoa on the other side of Mount Ruapehu, there are countless routes down the mountain. Advanced skiers are likely to feel drawn, to some extent, to the steep slopes and chutes of The Pinnacles, the huge face on the eastern side of the ski area. There are some fairly hair-raising runs over there and skiers of less than advanced ability should think twice before heading over. The Pinnacles are best skied in spring or fresh snow conditions. If they're icy it's best that you really know what you're doing!

If you spend any time around regular Whakapapa skiers you'll hear the term 'out west' used with some frequency. This refers to the area on the left of the Far West T-bar (although it can include the area to the right of the T-bar, too). The runs here are in the 'Black Magic Area', which is outside the ski area boundary and has no signs, fencing, or avalanche control undertaken in it. The skiing out west is on steep, ungroomed, and less crowded slopes. It's best suited to advanced skiers.

The huge area between the Waterfall T-bar and the West Ridge Chairlift holds some awesome terrain, which can, and should, take hours of exploring. If you're at Whakapapa for a short time only, try finding someone who knows the mountain, and glean as much information on this area as you can. Alternatively, just follow a group that appears to know where they're going. If you're not familiar with the mountain, and visibility is not good, ski cautiously.

From the top of the Far West T-bar it's a 20-minute walk up to the rim of the crater lake. It's a fantastic ski from here back down to the ski area, while the views of the lake and looking north are superb. There are plenty of routes down, but one of the best runs from the rim is down the slope above the Valley

T-bar. It's a long, wide expanse of snow that just asks to be skied.

The ski-touring potential from Whakapapa is great. It's possible to traverse around the mountain to the ski areas of Turoa on its southern slopes, or Tukino on its eastern slopes.

The weather on Mount Ruapehu can change at an incredible speed (you won't believe it until you've seen it), so if you're touring be prepared, and let ski patrol know your intentions.

# NATIONAL PARK AND WHAKAPAPA

The village of National Park, originally called Waimarino, started as a tiny railway settlement on the main trunk railway line. Prior to the completion of the railway, very few people visited the western side of Mount Ruapehu. The Desert Road had been completed on the eastern side in 1893.

In the late 1800s, a popular tourist route involved sailing from Wellington to Wanganui on a coastal steamer, then travelling up the Wanganui River on a river boat (which would be winched through the rapids) as far as Pipiriki. The following day would be spent travelling by stage coach from Pipiriki to Raetihi, then on to Waiouru, and along a track through the Rangipo Desert to the Waihohonu Hut. From there, tourists would continue by coach to Lake Taupo, cross the lake on a steamboat, and catch another coach to the thermal resort of Rotorua.

The railway, finished in 1908, brought more visitors to the western side of Mount Ruapehu, but it wasn't until a road was built between Tokaanu and Waimarino in 1919 that the area started to become popular. In the same year, members of the Ruapehu Ski Club constructed a cart track from the new road up to an area on the mountain called Whakapapa.

The ski club built a few huts at Whakapapa, and these became known as Whakapapa Village. Trampers, climbers, skiers and sightseers began coming to the village, and it soon surpassed Waimarino as the most popular place to stay. (Waimarino's name was changed because it had become best known as the arrival and departure point for the Tongariro National Park.) Accommodating visitors, mostly skiers, became a problem during the 1920s, and it became apparent that a hostel of some sort was required. The solution actually came in the form of a luxurious Georgian hotel, the Château Tongariro, built in 1929.

The appearance of the Château really marked the beginning of steady development. The popularity of skiing on Mount Ruapehu grew and grew. So, too, although on a much smaller scale, did Whakapapa Village and National Park. Today, they're both reasonably small places and neither really has a nightlife comparable to the resort of Ohakune, at the base of the Turoa slopes, although there are occasions in the two bars – 'Trails' and 'Schnapps', when this is questionable. The lack of nightlife is largely due to the fact that many people skiing at Whakapapa belong to one of the clubs with lodges on the ski area, and spend the whole time up there. National Park and Whakapapa Village being separated by 15 kilometres doesn't help either.

# Arrival

*By train*
The train station is in National Park so, if you're staying there, it will be a five- to ten-minute walk to your hostel or hotel (by phoning the hostel/hotel, you may be able to arrange a pick-up shuttle). If you're staying in Whakapapa Village, you will have to arrange for a shuttle from the hostel/hotel to pick you up. Don't even think about walking, and hitching would take too long.

*By bus*
The only company running regular trips to National Park is Intercity/Ritchies, which has depots in Ski Haus and Howards Lodge. Again, if you need to get to Whakapapa Village, you'll have to arrange for a shuttle pick-up.

*By car*
National Park is right beside Highway 4 and impossible to miss. On the south, a turn-off to the east (Highway 47) takes you to Whakapapa. If you've come from Taupo or Turangi, you'll have come along Highway 47 to get to National Park.

# Ski and snowboard shops

**Eivans** has two shops in National Park, both beside Highway 4. One is a retail shop; the other a hire shop. The hire shop (0–7–892 2843) is on the intersection of Highways 4 and 47.

*Hire charges:*
Full ski set:  Adults     $20 (day); $36 (two days); $84 (week).
              Children   $14 (day); $25 (two days); $58 (week).
Snowboards:    $35 (day).
Executive skis: from $25 (day).
Also hires out clothing, roof racks, sledges and chains.

The retail shop (0–7–892 2844), 300 metres north of the hire shop, has an excellent range of ski equipment and clothing, but no snowboards yet.

*Repair charges:*
Full tune: $45.     Edge and wax: $15.     Wax: $5.

**Frozen Wave** (0–7–892 2801) at 3 Carrol Street, National Park, is primarily a hire shop, but also does some repairs:
Full tune: from $15.     Wax: $6.

*Hire charges:*
Full set:
Adult   $20 (day); $36 (two days); $56 (four days); $84 (week).
Child   $14 (day); $25 (two days); $39 (four days); $58 (week).
Snowboard and boots: $35 (day); a weekly rate is negotiable.
Also hired out are clothing, roof racks, mountain bikes and some touring equipment.

**Howards Lodge** (0–7–892 2827), also on Carrol Street, hires out ski equipment.

*Hire charges:*
Full set: $20 (day).
Pants and jackets: $10 each per day.
Multi-day discounts are negotiable.

**Roy Turners Ski Shop** (0–7–892 2757) is on Buddo Street. This shop, along with the Eivans retail shop, has the largest range of skis and ski equipment for sale in National Park. There are also a few snowboards for sale.

*Hire charges:*
Full ski set:   Adult $20 (day); $40 (weekend); $96 (week).
                Child $16 (day); $28 (weekend); $63 (week).
Snowboard and boots: $35 (day); $50 (weekend); $115 (week).

There are discount rates for midweek hire of longer than one day; prices for longer hire can be discussed upon application.
*Repair charges:*
Edge sharpen, base grind and wax: $25.
Wax: $5 ($10 snowboard).
Serious work: $25 per hour.

**Ski Biz** (0–7–892 2717) is on Carroll Street, across the road from the dairy and takeaway shop. It's really just a hire and repair shop with ski clothing and accessories for sale.

*Hire charges:*
Full ski set for one day: $20 (Adult); $14 (Child).
Midweek concessions:
   Two days: $36 (Adult); $25 (Child).
   Up to seven days: $83 (Adult); $52 (Child).
Executive skis: $25 (day).
Snowboards: $30 to $40 (day).
Also hired out are clothing, chains, roof racks and sledges.

*Repair charges:*
Wax: $5.   Edge sharpening: $5.
Crystal glide: $15.

**Edge to Edge** (0–7–892 3867), in the basement of the Skotel in Whakapapa, doesn't deal in retail equipment, but does sometimes sell second-hand gear. There's a huge range of rental gear.

*Hire charges:*
Full ski set:   One day  $25 (Adult); $15 (Child).
                Seven days  $105 (Adult; $63 (Child).
                Group discounts for ten or more.
Snowboards:   Day  $40 (Adult); $30 (Child).
                Seven days  $160 (Adult); $115 (Child).
Executive equipment:  Day  $40 (Adult); $30 (Child).
                Seven days  $160 (Adult); $115 (Child).
Also hired out are clothing, climbing gear, ski touring equipment and toboggans.
*Repair charges:*
Wax: $5.    Full tune: $25.

## Places to stay

*National Park*
For value for money, and a friendly atmosphere, **Howards Lodge** (0–7–892 2827) on Carroll Street is hard to beat. A bunk in the backpackers' dormitory is in the budget range. A double room is moderately priced; a quad is high. The rooms are tidy, there are good kitchen and laundry facilities, and a large warm lounge with a log burner and a (free) pool table. Meals are available for a small extra charge. There's a drying room, and a great spa pool ($2 to use). They hire ski equipment, and mountain transport is also available. It's an idea to book ahead.

**The Ski Haus** (0–7–892 2854), also on Carroll Street, offers both bed and breakfast, and self-catering accommodation. There are double, twin or dormitory-style rooms available, with a very comfortable lounge/bar area with an enormous open fire, pool table and TV. Adjoining the lounge is a restaurant, serving good, very reasonably priced food (see Places to eat). There is also is a fully equipped kitchen for guests' use and a laundry, drying room and spa pool. It's a great place to stay, particularly for the relaxed and very sociable atmosphere, ever present in the lounge. It's possible to hire skis and arrange mountain transport from the lodge. Bed and breakfast in a dormitory is moderately priced; high in a double or twin room. Self-catering accommodation is slightly cheaper.

**Pipers Ski Lodge**, on Millar Street, is run by Pipers Ski Tours, an Auckland-based company. Book on 0–9–480 2095 or 025–922 020. Though mainly occupied by tour groups, anyone is welcome to stay in the lodge. It is particularly popular with the 18–35 age group. The organised parties every Saturday night are legendary throughout National Park and Whakapapa, and Pipers is not really the place to stay if you prefer the quieter things in life. The lodge has an in-house bar, a large lounge with an open fire and pool table, a laundry, drying room, three spa pools, and complimentary tea and coffee. It runs transport to the mountains daily. There are double, twin and dormitory rooms available, and all accommodation is based on a dinner, bed and breakfast basis. The cost ranges from low to high.

The **Chalet on the Rocks** (0–7–892 3719) on Ruapehu Drive consists of two converted railway houses. Both houses have three bedrooms, and can sleep two–six people in each. They're comfortable places, very much like a 'home away from home'. The kitchens are fully equipped, and there's a log-burner, TV and stereo in both lounges. There's a laundry, and linen is supplied. For families or groups, these places are perfect. The cost is in the low range, with generous reductions for children under 10.

*Whakapapa Village*
On entering the **Château** (0–7–892 3809 or 0800–733 944, toll-free), one could be excused for feeling instantly overcome by a pervading sense of decadence. From the enormous lobby with open fire, grand piano, full-size snooker table and chandeliers, to its luxurious rooms, the Château is the absolute height of elegance. The in-house bar is in the lobby, from where the restaurant, 'The Ruapehu Room' (see Places to eat), can be

entered. The Château has a sauna, heated pool, gymnasium and games room. There are single, double and twin rooms, each with en suite, mini-bar, fridge, and tea- and coffee-making facilities. Prices – from $180 to $400 a night – match quality.

A short way up the Whakapapa Mountain Road (turn left after the Château) is the **Skotel** (0–7–892 3719). It's a large modern hotel, offering a range of accommodation – hostel, standard and deluxe rooms, as well as a number of chalets. The hostel rooms are twins or doubles, with a communal kitchen/dining area. The other rooms sleep two–six people, and come with a TV, radio, fridge, and tea- and coffee-making facilities. The hotel has a spa pool, sauna, games room, laundry and drying room, an in-house bar, which serves rather exquisite cocktails, and a restaurant ('Heathers') with a very good wine list (mains are in the high price range). The rooms, even in the hostel section, are quite luxurious, and most have superb views down the mountain (the Skotel is apparently the highest hotel in the country). Prices are in the high range, from $81–$171 per room. A chalet, fully contained and sleeping up to six is $225 a night.

## PLACES TO EAT

The **Ski Haus Restaurant** (0–7–892 2854) in the Ski Haus on Carroll Street offers good-sized meals at moderate prices in a pleasant informal setting. A good relaxing place to dine, it's licensed and open from 5:00 pm until late. Book ahead.

For those who choose not to stay in the **Château** (0–7–892 3809), it's possible to experience the charm of the place by dining in its restaurant, 'The Ruapehu Room'. The menu reads like poetry, and once read is hard to forget in a hurry. The service is superb, the decor daunting, and the wine list wonderful. Most mains are in the high price range. It's licensed, and open from 5:30 pm. Bookings are essential.

**Fergusons Café** (book at the Château reception) is over the road from the Château. As well as serving good coffee, this café also serves light meals (pasta, nachos, etc) for a moderate price. It's BYO, and open from 8:30 am until 9:00 pm. The Continental or cooked breakfasts are filling, and in the low price range. A few historical photos of Whakapapa adorn the walls.

## Happening places

**Schnapps Bar** (0–7–892 2788) beside Highway 4 is where it all happens in National Park. It's a large open-plan bar, usually packed with people, and caters to most types (provided you can tolerate a bit of noise). Part of the bar is taken up by a large open fire surrounded by comfortable sofas, while for entertainment (when there's not live music) there is table hockey, a pool table and, occasionally, a ping-pong table. A games evening is held every Wednesday. Quite sizeable bar meals are in the low price range, while the food at an adjoining à la carte restaurant is in the high price range.

In Whakapapa Village, it's the **Trails Bar** (just down from the Château) where it all happens. It too is a large, open-plan room which, following a day's skiing, can become what could be best termed 'the New Zealand equivalent to a Bavarian beer hall'. It has a popular juke box, a pool table, dart board and table hockey. Happy hours are between 4:00 and 6:00 pm, and the bar's speciality is pizza (several sizes, moderately priced).

## Services

*Medical:* The 'Mountain Surgery' is on Kirk Street in National Park: 0–7–892 2999.

*Police:* The police station is on Buddo Street, National Park: 0–7–892 2869. In emergencies, phone 111.

*Post Office:* The general store on Carroll Street, National Park, acts as the local post office.

# Information

The Whakapapa Visitor Centre on the ski road, just past the Château, is the best source of information in the National Park–Whakapapa Village region. It contains a fine display on the history of skiing on Mount Ruapehu that shouldn't be missed. Any ski shop or hotel/hostel reception should also be able to help you out with local information.

# Getting around

It's no trouble getting around either National Park or Whakapapa Village. The problem is covering the 15 kilometres between the two. If you don't have a car, and can't borrow one, and really want to get from one place to the other, try hitching. You may be very lucky. There are no taxis or regular buses.

There's no real need to travel from one to the other (both places have a small general store), other than to check out a specific restaurant or bar. Mountain bikes can be hired from the Chalet on the Rocks in National Park (0–7–892 2938), and it can be a nice cycle from there up to the Village and back.

# Travelling on

*Train*
Trains from National Park go north to Auckland or south to Wellington (via Ohakune). The railway station is on Ruapehu Drive. For bookings or enquiries, contact the Ski Haus on Carroll Street or call New Zealand Rail Central Reservations Centre on 0800–802 802 (toll free).

*Bus*
Intercity/Ritchies runs services to destinations throughout the North Island. Contact Howards Lodge (0–7–892 2827) or Ski Haus (0–7–892 2854).

# OHAKUNE

The village of Ohakune began as just a small natural clearing on the banks of the Mangawhero River. In 1890 a surveyor, John Rochfort, built a small hut there and made it his headquarters while he carried out explorations into finding the most suitable route for the North Island's main trunk railway line.

While the village's origins are largely a result of Rochfort's efforts (he decided the best route for the railway would pass through the Ohakune area), the vast amounts of native bush in the region also directly contributed to Ohakune's subsequent growth. Felling occurred on a small scale initially, but once the railway was put in, logging for timber became a major industry. The potential the bush held as a source of timber was a persuading factor in the Government's decision to direct the railway through the region.

Settlers started arriving in the region in 1892 and, in 1894, the first permanent building – a general store and post office – was constructed. During the late 1890s, the Government sent 600 men to Ohakune to carry out preparatory work for the railway line. Following this influx, a number of businesses began appearing – grocers, butchers, bakers, tobacconists, billiard saloons, boarding houses and livery stables – not only at the Ohakune village, but also two kilometres to the east, where it was planned to build the railway station. When the main trunk line was completed in 1908, this new settlement became known as Ohakune Junction, from where a separate railroad was constructed which connected the main trunk line to Raetihi in the west. This line has since been removed, but the name 'the Junction' remains.

By the 1930s, most of the region's forests had been milled and much of the land, which had been cleared by the felling, became farm land. It was Chinese immigrants who first noted that the region's soil was ideal for growing vegetables, and began market gardening. Vegetables from Ohakune quickly gained a reputation throughout the central North Island, and then New Zealand. During the Second World War, vegetables from the region were supplied to the entire New Zealand armed forces, as well as the American bases in the Pacific. Vegetables are still grown there, and the huge carrot at the southern end of the town reminds visitors that they're entering 'carrot country'.

In 1978, Ohakune took on a new role as the accompanying village to Turoa ski area. From the railway, to timber, to vegetables, to skiing, the village has had a colourful past. Today, it is rivalled only by Queenstown as the liveliest of New Zealand's ski towns. In the evenings during the ski season the Junction's Thames Street, lined with bars and restaurants, has a constant hum of people.

A great time to visit Ohakune is during its Spring Festival, held annually in the last week of September. It's a week in which fun events, displays and presentations take place on and off the mountain; and the place is at its liveliest.

## ARRIVAL

*By train*
The train station is in Ohakune Junction so, if you're staying at the Junction, it may be only a short walk to your hotel or hostel. On the other hand, if you're staying in the Ohakune township, you can either make the four-kilometre walk or call a taxi: 0–6–385 8573.

*By bus*
The only bus company making regular trips to Ohakune is Intercity/Ritchies. Its depot is the Ruapehu Visitors Centre at 54 Clyde Street in the Ohakune township.

*By shuttle*
Shuttle operators will take you wherever you want to go in Ohakune or the Junction.

*By car*
Ohakune's main road is actually Highway 49, so the town is hard to miss. A signed turn-off in the centre of Ohakune will take you east toward the mountain and Ohakune Junction.

## SKI AND SNOWBOARD SHOPS

There are nine ski/snowboard shops – five in Ohakune and four at the Junction. Those marked with an asterisk are in Ohakune.

**Bootworks**\*(0–6–385 8267; after hours 0–6–385 9079) on Ayr Street is the country's only boots-only shop (although a few skis are available). There is a good range of boots and an excellent boot-fitting service. The shop motto is 'The competition will be sore'.

*Boot fitting charges:*
Initial service: $10 to $30; any work required is extra.
It is best to make an appointment.

**Downtown Ski and Sport**\* (0–6–385 8433) is on Clyde Street (the main road). The shop has a good range of second-hand and new ski equipment, and a few second-hand snowboards.

*Hire charges:*
Full ski set:  Adult  $25 (one day); $20 each additional day.
            Child  $12 (one day); $10 each additional day.
If you hire for five days, you get the sixth day free.
The shop also offers a Family Special (for four or more people) and a Group Special (for five or more) – a 20 per cent discount, provided gear is hired for two or more days.

*Repair charges:*
Hot wax: $5.
Edge and wax: $8.

The **Junction Ski Shop** (0–6–385 8361) is on Thames Street, opposite the railway station. Along with the Powderhorn Ski

Shop, this shop has one of the best ranges of skis, snowboards and clothing in Ohakune.

*Hire charges:*
Full ski set for one day: $25 (Adult); $20 (Youth); $15 (Child).
Snowboard hire: $30 per day.
Discounts (up to 30 per cent on weekly concessions) are available for long-term hire.
Budget hire equipment: $15 per day.
Executive hire (full set): $40 per day.
Also for hire are chains, roof racks, sledges and clothing.

*Repair charges:*
Crystal glide: $45.
Snowboard grind: $45.
Edge and wax (skis or snowboard): $25.
Wax: $7 (skis); $10 (snowboards).
Serious repair work: $40 per hour.

**Off Piste Mountain Hire** (0–6–385 8623) at 27 Thames Street is strictly a hire outfit.

*Hire charges:*
Full ski set per day: $17 (Adult); $13 (Child).
Snowboards (with boots): $40 per day.
The shop also hires out chains ($18 per day), toboggans and clothing.
Discounts are available for long-term hire.

*Repair charges:*
Hot wax: $6 (skis/snowboards).
Edge and wax: $15 (skis/snowboards).

The **Powderhorn Ski Shop** (0–6–385 8888) is half of what is known as the 'Powderzone', the renowned Powderkeg bar/restaurant making up the other half. The Powderzone is at the bottom of the Turoa access road, on the corner of Mangawhero Terrace and Thames Street. The shop has an excellent range of ski and snowboard equipment, clothing and every imaginable accessory. There are three standards of hire equipment – budget, economy and executive.

*Hire charges:*
Full ski set per day: $15, $25, $35 (Adult); $10 (Child).
Budget snowboard per day: $20, $30, $40.
Special rates apply if equipment is hired for four or more days. If gear is hired for seven days, you get an extra three days free.
Also hired out are monoboards, toboggans, chains, roofracks and clothing.
With every ski hire over $15 you get a free beer at the Powderkeg.

*Ski repair charges:*
Full tune (with crystal glide): $40 and $50.
Tune (with crystal glide) without base repair: $35.
Edge and wax: $20.
Wax: $5.

*Snowboard repair charges:*
Full tune: $45.
Side edge and wax: $30.
Wax $10.

The **Ski Rack** (0–6–385 8173) at 2 Thames Street is primarily a hire shop, with a few accessories.

*Hire charges:*
Budget ski equipment: $13 a day (the cheapest in Ohakune).
Standard equipment: $19 a day.
Discounts are available for longer-term hire.

The **Ski Shed**° (0–6–385 9173) on the corner of Goldfinch and Ayr Streets stocks a good range of ski equipment and accessories but no snowboard gear.

*Hire charges:*
Full ski set: first day $25 (Adult); $16 (Junior).

$20; $13 per day (two or more days midweek).
$18; $11 per day (five or more days).
Also hired are clothing, roof racks, sledges and chains.

*Repair charges:*
Crystal glide: $35.
Edge and wax: $25.
Wax: $4.

**Sports Country Ski Hire**\* (0–6–385 8656) is on Clyde Street, Ohakune's main road, opposite the petrol station. The shop stocks second-hand ski and snowboard equipment only, and has an excellent range of both.

*Hire charges:*
Full ski set (day): $25 (Adult); $20 (Youth); $15 (Child).
Snowboard and boots (day): $35; $28; $25.
Discounts are available for longer-term hire.
The shop also hires out big feet, clothing, toboggans and chains.
No ski or snowboard repairs are done in the shop, but they will do a hot wax for $7.

To hire or buy telemark equipment, see the people at **Ossie's Luxury Ski Apartments** (0–6–385 8088), 59 Tainui Street. They're the local specialists. A full set of telemark gear can be hired for $25 per day.

**BOA**, or **Board of Authority**\* (0–6–385 9024) is the only 'snowboard-only' shop in Ohakune. It's on Ayr Street, in the same building as Bootworks. There's a huge selection of boards for sale and hire.

*Hire charges:*
Board and boots: $40 (day).
Board: $35 (day).
Boots: $10 (day).
Discounts are available for longer-term hire.

## PLACES TO STAY

Most accommodation in Ohakune has two rates – a standard mid-week rate and a slightly more expensive weekend (Friday and Saturday nights) rate. It's considerably harder to find a place to stay on Friday and Saturday nights, particularly in August and September. Book ahead in all cases.

Another point worth bearing in mind is that Ohakune consists of two distinct parts – the lively 'Junction' (often referred to as the 'party side of town') and the more sedate 'Village' (the 'family side of town'). If it's your intention to make the most of the Junction's salubrious *après-ski* nightlife, it would pay to stay in that part of town. It will save you a small fortune in taxi fares, and save your legs for the daily work-outs they'll get on the slopes.

**Rimu Park Lodge and Chalets** (0–6–385 9023) are at 27 Rimu Street, a five-minute walk from the Junction. The lodge is a renovated 1914 villa, with share, twin and double rooms available. It has an excellent kitchen with a great coal-range stove. There's a large open fire in the living/TV room, and complimentary tea- and coffee-making facilities. If you stay midweek, your fifth night is free. The chalets (one 10-berth; two 2–4 berth), all fully equipped, are across the road from the villa. If there's a group of you, these places are ideal. The charge for staying in the lodge, including a large cooked breakfast, is moderate. The chalets cost between $80 and $180 a night.

Nowhere is the pulse of Ohakune Junction felt more strongly than at the **Powderkeg** (0–6–385 8888) on the corner of Thames Street and Turoa Mountain Road. Until very recently, the Powderkeg was just a bar and restaurant; probably the most popular in town. Now it offers accommodation as well. It has rooms that can sleep two, three and four people, all done out in the timber-log style of the building itself. Each room has an en suite, TV, tea- and coffee-making facilities, and a fridge. There is a drying room, laundry, and an enormous hot pool (non-residents welcome for a small charge). Rooms go for $145 a night ($23 per extra person).

**Alpine Motel** (0–6–385 8758) in the Ohakune Village on 7 Miro Street consists of motel units, some chalets and a separate backpackers' lodge. The units (sleep four) and chalets (sleep eight) are modern and fully self-contained (en suite, TV, telephone, fridge, kitchenette, tea- and coffee-making facilities and electric blankets). The lodge consists of four-bed dormitory-style rooms. Some linen is provided and facilities are shared. It has a kitchen/TV room/dining area and has been known to get quite lively following the nightly exodus from the Junction. For the use of all guests are a laundry, drying room and spa pool. There is a guest house bar in Sassi's Bistro (see Places to eat). A night in the lodge is in the low price range (slightly higher on Friday and Saturday), a unit is $80 per night ($100 on Friday and Saturday), and a chalet is $95 per night ($130 on Friday and Saturday).

The **Ohakune Motorcamp** (0–6–385 8561), as well as having plenty of sites for campervans and tents, has a number of cabins and caravans that can be hired on a nightly basis. The cabins are quaint little timber buildings that can sleep two to three people. They are heated but linen or a sleeping bag is required. There are communal kitchen, laundry and facilities blocks, as well as a cosy TV lounge/dining building. The caravans sleep two to three people, and come with a fridge and cooking facilities (linen required). Also in the motorcamp is an 18-hole minigolf course with floodlights, which can be quite enjoyable following a day's skiing. Both the cabins and the caravans are in the low price range. A tent site is $7 a night; a caravan site $25. The motorcamp is at 5 Moore Street, a two-minute walk from the village centre.

The **Hobbit Motel Lodge** (0–6–385 8248) was named, as you

might expect, by a Tolkein fan, and pictures of the book's characters and scenes abound on the lodge walls. Situated on the corner of Goldfinch and Wye Streets (one kilometre from the village; two kilometres from the Junction), the lodge consists of studio units, two-bedroom units, and a number of bunkrooms. The studios (sleep up to four people) and the two-bedroom units (sleep up to seven) are fully self-contained with an en suite, TV, telephone, tea- and coffee-making facilities and a fridge. The bunkrooms sleep two to six people (electric blankets and linen supplied), and share a TV/common room and facilities. There is a laundry, drying room, spa pool (non-residents $5), and its own bar and restaurant (see Places to eat). Studio units go for $95 a night ($15 for each extra person), two-bedroom units go for $165 a night. A bed in a bunkroom is in the low price range.

**Beechers Motor Lodge** (0–6–385 8771) is at the southern end of the village, past the big carrot, at 3 Karo Street. It's a modern place with eight units that sleep up to five people. All units have en suites, a TV, and tea- and coffee-making facilities. It has a laundry, drying room, spa pool and a sauna. A short walk away are tennis courts and a nine-hole golf course. There is a fantastic guest lounge and bar, with large sofas surrounding a huge open fire (which has the obligatory hickory skis hanging above it). Adjoining the lounge is the Beechers Restaurant (see Places to eat) which also serves breakfasts. A room costs between $95 and $115 a night, plus $15 for each extra person.

The **Mountain View Lodge** (0–6–385 8675) at 2 Moore Street is a two-minute walk from the village centre. It has a wide variety of rooms – a bunkhouse (low price), cabins (low price), studio rooms ($75 a night), standard units ($130 a night) and luxury units ($150 a night). The bunkhouse and cabin accommodation is fairly basic, with a communal kitchen/TV lounge and shared facilities. The others (studio, standard, and luxury) are fully equipped with en suite, TV, kitchenettes and tea- and coffee-making facilities. There is also a drying room, a laundry and a spa pool.

**Ossie's Luxury Ski Apartments** (0–6–385 8088) are on the corner of Tainui and Shannon Streets, a 10- to 15-minute walk from either the village centre or the Junction. The apartments are modern one- or two-bedroom chalets, capable of sleeping up to six people. All are fully equipped with full kitchen facilities, TV, drying room and central heating. There is also a laundry and large sauna. The apartments are ideal for families or groups. It's a fair way out of town and tends to be a little more peaceful than some of the places in the village and Junction. Ossie, the manager, is a Norwegian who is very keen on telemark skiing, and is able to offer plenty of advice on local skiing conditions. The units go for between $120 (one bedroom) and $150 (two bedroom) a night.

## PLACES TO EAT

The **Powderkeg à la Carte Restaurant** (0–6–385 8888) is upstairs in the Powderkeg complex. It's a huge place, done out in the same timber style as the rest of the complex, and both the meals and the atmosphere are exceptional. Of all the restaurants in town, this would have to be regarded as the liveliest. Mains are in the moderate price range. It's licensed, and open from 4:00 pm until late. Book ahead.

**Sassi's Bistro** (0–6–385 8758) in the Alpine Motel on Miro Street is a popular dining spot. It's a small place with a relaxed atmosphere, and serves great food. There's a real variety of dishes available (with a separate children's menu), and a wide selection of wines and ales. It's licensed and BYO. A moderately priced restaurant, it is open from 6:00 pm. Book ahead if possible.

The **Hobbit Restaurant** (0–6–385 8248) is in the Hobbit Motel, on the corner of Goldfinch and Wye Streets, and as in the rest of the motel, the walls are adorned with pictures of scenes from Tolkein's book. The menu is written in a style that Tolkein himself would have been proud of. The dishes, fortunately, are not from the book. It's quite a large restaurant, with a huge open fire, an old piano and a good wine list (no BYO). Moderately priced, it's open from 4:30 pm until late.

**Beechers Restaurant** (0–6–385 8771) in Beechers Motor Lodge (3 Karo Street) is a very small restaurant, with a relaxed and friendly atmosphere. Adjoining the restaurant is the motel bar, with a large open fire surrounded by a group of settees. For laid-back dining and a few quiet drinks, Beechers is hard to beat. It's licensed. It is moderately priced and open from 6:30 pm until late.

**Clichés Café**, on the village's main road, is a bar/restaurant popular with locals and skiers alike. It serves good-sized dinners and breakfasts at moderate prices. The roasts are great and the coffee here is the best in town. It has a great old wood burner, and what must be the only pool table in the country surrounded by Van Gogh portraits.

**Bee Dees** coffee shop/takeaways on the main road serves good, low-priced cooked breakfasts and light meals. The takeaways aren't bad, either. It's open for breakfast from 8:00 am.

## HAPPENING PLACES

**Hot Lava**, once the old town cinema, is these days the town night club. It's the size of a hay barn, with a mezzanine-type floor for viewing the dance floor and stage. There's often live music and, when there isn't, the sound is usually loud enough to make you think there is. Hot Lava is where a large percentage of town seem to congregate after spending the early part of the night elsewhere (it tends to open for longer than most other places). It's on Thames Street, in the Junction, and with its flashing neon sign it's impossible to miss.

The hugely popular **Powderkeg**, like the Hot Lava, is also difficult to miss. In the Junction, on the corner of Thames Street and the Ohakune Mountain Road, it's basically where everyone gathers early in the night. Some go; some stay. It's a fantastic log-wood bar with a huge solid table capable of supporting the teems of bodies that usually end up dancing on it. Split in two, half the bar has the big table and a large open fire, half has dining tables and a raised fireplace in the centre. The half with dining tables is marginally less lively, and it's possible to get a good, moderately priced, bar snack here.

**Margueritas** is just along Rimu Street from Hot Lava. If you're cold, head to this place. There's an excellent raised fireplace with surrounding tables. Its name seems to be the only real sign of any Mexican theme (the menu is German), although it is renowned for its jugs of Marguerita. It's also renowned for its pool table and table hockey, the latter being taken pretty seriously in these parts. The food is good and moderately priced. Happy hours are from 4:00 to 6:00 pm and 9:00 to 10:00 pm.

**Turoa Lodge** on Thames Street is one of the oldest establishments in Ohakune, enjoying what could be termed a 'renaissance' since Turoa was developed. It's a regular venue for live music, and the whole place virtually becomes a dance floor on Friday and Saturday nights.

The **Summit Bar**, on the village's main road, is often referred to as the 'local's bar'. It's frequented largely by the Turoa staff, and is by far the liveliest bar in the village end of town. There's a large open fire, a well-used dart board, and the place is usually packed.

## Services

*Medical:* There is no medical centre, but there is a doctor at 28 Goldfinch Street: 0–6–385 8356.

*Police:* The station is on the corner of Rata and Tay Streets: 0–6–385 8551. In emergencies, phone 111.

*Post Office:* In the village at 23 Clyde Street: 0–6–385 8300.

## Information

The Ruapehu Visitor Centre is at 54 Clyde Street, in Ohakune: phone/fax 0–6–385 8427. Ohakune's hotels, hostels and ski shops are also good sources of local information.

## Getting around

Both Ohakune Village and Ohakune Junction are small places and easy to get around. The only logistical problem is that of getting the three kilometres between the two centres.

If you don't feel like walking or hitching, there are taxis (0–6–385 8573). The Junction is where it all happens at night so, if you're staying in the Village, taxis are the way to go.

Alternatively, you could hire a mountain bike from Sunbeam Lodge (0–6–385 8470) at 178 Mangawhero Terrace (near the Junction).

## Travelling on

*Train*
Trains from Ohakune go north to Auckland (via National Park) or south to Wellington. The railway station is at the Junction. For bookings or enquiries, contact either the Ruapehu Visitors Centre or call New Zealand Rail Central Reservations Centre on 0800–802 802 (toll-free).

*Shuttle and bus*
Intercity/Ritchies (0–6–385 8427) runs services to destinations throughout the North Island.

Kiwi Safaris (0–6–385 8427 or 0800–800 616, toll-free) runs services to Wellington.

# TARANAKI

## SKI AREA
Manganui 75

## RESORT
New Plymouth 82

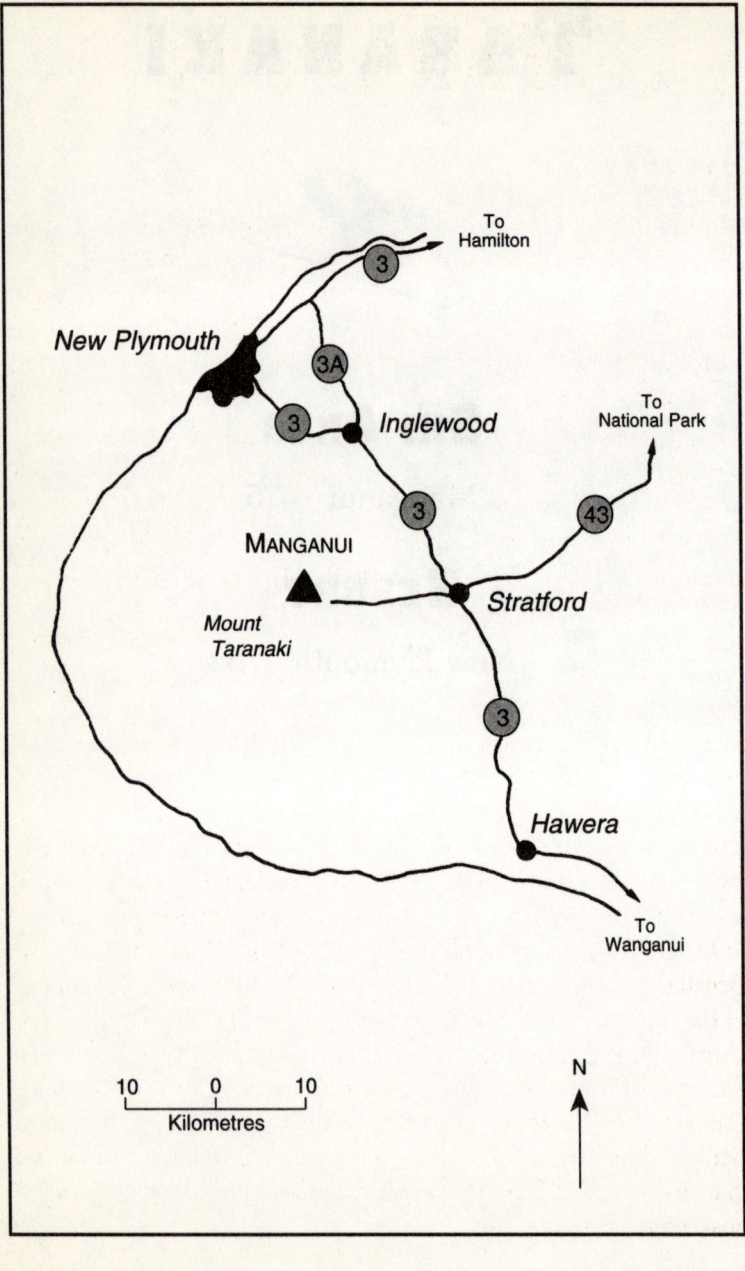

# MANGANUI

## HISTORY

Mount Taranaki is a nearly perfect symmetrical volcanic cone, the result of eruptions over 16,000 years ago. The Maori made it a God, Taranaki. Captain Cook, the first European to see it, named it Egmont in 1770, in honour of Earl Egmont, First Lord of the Admiralty. The name was changed to Mount Taranaki in 1992.

There is debate as to whether the volcano is still active. While the last eruption occurred in 1755, evidence indicates that it had been dormant for periods of up to thousands of years prior to that. In 1900, the mountain and surroundings became the country's second National Park. These days it is regarded as the most-climbed summit in the country.

In the late 1800s, a group of keen local trampers and climbers began cutting tracks and building huts on the mountain. A club was formed in 1910 and, in February 1914, the original Stratford Mountain Club was formed. It disbanded soon after because of World War One, and wasn't revived until 1928.

Initially, the club revolved entirely around tramping and climbing. The first skiing on Taranaki occurred in 1917, when a local man, R. Tyrer, took a pair of home-made skis up to the snow. It's likely that this sort of skiing continued sporadically until 1929 when two club members, Vic Williams and Alf Brustad (a Norwegian, who also played a role in the formation of the Tasman Ski Club on Fox Peak) cleared a 'ski track' on the Curtis Ridge not far from the Plateau (site of the present lodge).

Later in the 1929 season, members Frank Addis, John Carryer, Neville Johnson and Ron Moss skied in the Ngarara Gully. Addis, when reflecting on his home-made skis, remarked that 'they lacked stability (in all directions). In fact, they were possessed of the devil!'

In the 1930 season, most skiers used Ngarara Gully, which was considered a more exciting slope. On 3 August, a climbing accident occurred in the vicinity of the ski slopes, and a club member, Lance Gibson, died of hypothermia during rescue operations. Consequently, the club met with the Park Board and it was decided that some sort of shelter was required on that part of the mountain. Work on the new hut began in 1931. The club's first 'working bee' was on 26 April and the 'Manganui

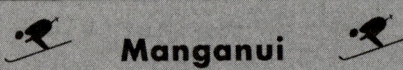

## Manganui

*Location:* 20 km from Stratford.
54 km from New Plymouth.
240 km from Ohakune.

*Season:* Usually open by mid–late June and closed by early–mid October.

*Elevation:* The Top Tow runs between 1420 and 1680 metres.
The T-bar runs from the lodge at 1260 metres to 1380 metres.
The peak of Mount Taranaki is at 2518 metres.

*Vertical drop:* 420 metres.

*Terrain:* Beginner 5%, Intermediate 30%, Advanced 65%.

*Snowmaking:* None.

*Groomers:* One.

*Road toll:* None.

*Lifts:* One T-bar and three rope tows.
Low charge, with special student, children and learner rates.

*Ski hire:* Available from the Mountain House, three kilometres down the access road from the car park.

Hut' was completed by June. At that time, the road went only as far as the Mountain House, an hour's walk to Ngarara Gully, so a start was also made on extending the road to the Plateau.

That same year, with more people trying the new sport, the club purchased and hired some skis for members. However, there weren't enough and, in 1932, Brian McMillan and John Carryer began importing ash and hickory, and manufacturing skis in McMillan's father's engineering shop (native woods

## Manganui

Full set: $25 per day; $15 for half a day.
They have very little children's equipment and no snowboards.

*Specials:* If you phone the club you may be able to negotiate a multi-day rate or a group discount.

*Ski school:* Instruction available. To guarantee a lesson, phone Peter Quinn on 0–6–758 7251 and make a booking.

*Accomm:* As a rule the lodge is used by members and guests only, and it's generally not possible to stay on a casual basis. However, if the lodge is not full, it may be possible to spend a night there. To find out, phone the club secretary on 0–6–758 0928.

The Mountain House, a short way down the access road, provides high-cost accommodation. It has a sauna, a fantastic silver-service restaurant, and a great bar (The T-bar), making it an excellent place to stop on your way down the mountain.

*Address:* Stratford Mountain Club, PO Box 3271, New Plymouth. Telephone: 0–6–758 0928.

*Snow reports:* Phone 0–6–765 7669, or listen for updates on the 93.2 Energy FM radio station.

couldn't be bent into shape as easily and tended to warp). With these new skis and the road completed, making it only a 20-minute walk, skiing at Manganui really took off. The first club champs were held in August 1932.

By 1935, skiing on the Policeman slopes above Ngarara Gully was becoming more common as members' skills improved. On 13 October, Carryer, McMillan and two others made the first full ski descent from Taranaki's summit, down the eastern face.

With the outbreak of World War Two in 1939, a large number of members went abroad on duty. At one stage, the club was reduced to 16 members. Very little skiing occurred, but the remaining members made sure those overseas received club newsletters. Rumours got back in 1942 that John Carryer was in the Lebanon teaching troops to ski.

In 1946, things started picking up again and, in 1947, the club installed a rope tow, one of the first in the country. The New Zealand Championships were held at Manganui the same year.

While tramping and climbing continued to be the club's main activities, skiing was fast gaining in popularity. In 1952, another rope tow, 'Top Tow', was installed on the Policeman slopes. The flying fox over Manganui Gorge was also put in that year. In 1958, increasing use of the ski area by day-trippers led to the construction of a public shelter near the hut. A learners' tow was installed in 1964, and construction of Manganui Lodge (which began in 1961) was finished in June 1968, replacing the old hut. The lower rope tow was replaced with a T-bar in 1974.

These days, Manganui attracts skiers from throughout the North Island. Naturally, its strongest followers are the residents of Taranaki, who, with this solitary mountain towering above them, must feel constantly drawn to its slopes.

## THE SKI AREA

The access road is a sealed, 18-kilometre road which passes through thick native forest on its way up Mount Taranaki, before reaching a car park on the bush-line. At the end of the

## GETTING THERE

**From New Plymouth**
*By car*
Head south on Highway 3 to Stratford. About one kilometre out of Stratford you'll see a turn-off on your right with a signpost to 'The Plateau'. This takes you past the Mountain House Lodge (after 15 kilometres), with the car park a further three kilometres up the road.

*Hitching*
If you're hitching, call the club before you intend going to see if a club member can take you up. If that's not possible, try to be on Highway 3 by 8:00 am. It shouldn't be too difficult getting to the turn-off outside Stratford, but from there it may take a while.

*By shuttle*
There are no scheduled shuttle services to Manganui.

The two New Plymouth-based shuttle companies — Tubbys (0–6–753 6306) and C Tours (0–6–758 1777) — may run a trip, depending on demand. There is a minimum fare of $60.

From Stratford the B.J.'s Mountain Shuttle will run a trip to the Plateau on demand. It makes pick-ups from the Stratford Holiday Park and the Stratford Information Centre at 8:00 am. One-way costs $8.50; return is $14. Booking is essential. You can book at the Holiday Park or the Information Centre, or by phoning 0–6–764 6738.

---

car park, there's a locked gate with an opening for walkers. From the gate it's a 10-minute walk along a dirt road to the ski area's goods lift, the 'flying fox'.

Because Manganui seems to open on an erratic basis, it pays

to phone the club on the morning before you go. If weather conditions permit, it will be open every weekend, but opening on weekdays depends on the weather and the eagerness of club members on the day. Surf is another factor in the equation. The surf on the Taranaki coast is some of the best in the country, and many club members are avid surfers. So, if the swell is good, interest in skiing may be lacking. 'The swell' is a common topic of conversation on the mountain, and often the people you are skiing with will be surfing later in the day. This being the case, snowboarding has really taken off here, and it's not unusual to have more snowboarders than skiers on the mountain.

Anyway, make sure the ski area is going to be open. If it is, you can put your gear in the flying fox, knowing that it will eventually make its way up to the lodge. From the flying fox it's a further 10-minute walk to the lodge. The track sidles the Manganui gorge before descending into it and up the other side. Try spending as little time as possible in the base of the gorge as it's in the path of the 'Manganui Monster' avalanche, which can be huge.

When you arrive at the ski area the first building you reach is the public shelter and ticket office. The shelter is the place to base yourself (you're not allowed in the club's lodge unless accompanied by a member). The people in the ticket office will be able to organise the running of the flying fox for you, and once you've got a ticket and your skis on, the slopes await.

The Learners' Tow is excellent for those who have never skied before. The T-bar runs are not a lot steeper and are within most novice skier's ability. In fact, due to the terrain, the lack of crowds, and the friendly club atmosphere, these T-bar runs rate as some of the best learning grounds in the North Island. What's more, the slopes are on tussock, so there's not a rock in sight. Early or late in the season, when there's little snow at the lower altitudes, the T-bar can still operate as club members mow the tussocks in summer and mowed tussocks are a good enough base for skiing on. Some club members have mastered the sport of tussock-skiing.

Top Tow is a rope tow and you'll find tow belts for it in the small room beneath its bottom station. There are also a few tables and chairs in this room, with tea- and coffee-making facilities. To get here you make a short traverse from the top of the T-bar to the Access Tow, a rope tow that can be used without a tow belt.

There is quite a large difference between skiing the slopes of the T-bar and those accessed by the Top Tow. All runs from the top of Top Tow are steep, and it really is no place for the less confident skier. In icy conditions, these upper slopes require extreme caution and are best left to the more experienced skiers.

Most of the time, however, the skiing up there is fantastic. The top part of the ski area consists of gullies and ridges running down the mountain, and you're never quite sure of what's going to be over the next rise. The opportunities for getting 'big air', intentionally or unintentionally, are plentiful. On your first day here, don't ski over any rise unless you're absolutely sure about what's on the other side. If visibility is poor, it's an idea to ask to ski with a club member for a while. The runs to the right of Top Tow are down wider gullies and this is the place for long, cruising turns.

A great run from the top of the area is to make the traverse out to Drop In (probably the steepest run) into Walters Slalom and down the Big Schuss to Ngarara Gully and the T-bar. There's something indescribably eerie about skiing beneath the Ngarara Ridge.

It's possible to ski-tour to the summit of Mount Taranaki, but before going check on the route with a club member and make sure someone knows you've gone. If there's bad weather anywhere around the North Island, the mountain usually gets it, and this can occur incredibly quickly. Be prepared.

No ski area in New Zealand has quite the same type of terrain as found on Manganui's Top Tow, and skiers who come here on a good day are often heard talking about it for years afterwards.

# NEW PLYMOUTH

In pre-European days, the coast of Taranaki was quite densely populated by two rival Maori tribes – the Ngati Awa and the Taranaki. In 1836, tribes from the Waikato invaded the coast and most of the Ngati Awa and Taranaki fled south to Wellington. By the time the Europeans arrived in 1841 there was just a handful of Maori left in the region.

New Plymouth was settled almost entirely by people from Devon and Cornwall in England, the name coming from the Devon seaport of Plymouth. Disputes between land-hungry settlers, and the Ngati Awa and Taranaki tribes, who were returning to their ancestral lands, led to war in 1860. New Plymouth became a military settlement, and it wasn't until 1880 that peace was restored.

The city became the main servicing centre and port for the Taranaki province, a largely agricultural part of the country. Today, the city is also the base for workers from the Maui natural gas and oil field, located off Taranaki's southern coast.

The city has a population of approximately 68,000, many of whom appear to surf, wind-surf or snowboard. It's the site of some of the best surf conditions in the country and, under any given conditions, an hour's drive up or down the coast will virtually guarantee a good wave. The city itself has a relaxed, hospitable charm to it, perhaps not unusual for a place in such a beautiful location. The Tasman Sea stretches out of sight to the west, while the view to the east is dominated by Mount Taranaki, which looks spectacular with the sunrise behind it.

There are plenty of good places to stay in the town. In the budget category, sharing rooms, check out:

❏ **Shoestring Budget Lodge**, 48 Lemon Street: 0–6–758 0404.

- Backpackers Hostel 69, 69 Mill Road: 0–6–758 7153.
- The Rotary Lodge, 12 Clawton Street: 0–6–753 5720.

The **Carrington Guest House** (0–6–758 2375) at 32 Carrington Street offers good bed and breakfast accommodation, close to the city centre, in an old colonial house for a moderate price.

At the upper end of the pricing scale are the **Quality Hotel** (0–6–755 0379) and the **Plymouth Hotel** (0–6–758 0589). The Quality is on the corner of Devon and Henwood Streets, close to the airport. The Plymouth is on the corner of Courtenay and Leach Streets, close to the centre of town. Both have a good in-house bar and restaurant, and a spa pool.

For more information on where to stay, contact the Information Centre, on the corner of Leach and Liardet Street: 0–6–758 6086.

As far as 'happening places' go, nowhere is more happening than **The Mill**, an old flour mill converted into a bar and nightclub, on Courtenay Street. It would appear that a vast proportion of New Plymouth and environs end up in the Mill on Thursday, Friday and Saturday nights. It's a huge place, with loud music and an enormous dance floor. You can also get a good, low-priced meal.

Another spot worth checking out is **Peggy Gordons**, a thoroughly Irish bar, with live music (Irish, of course) on Thursday, Friday and Saturday nights that can make the floor feel like a trampoline. It's on the corner of Egmont Street and Devon Street West.

For a more refined atmosphere, try **L'escargot Restaurant and Wine Bar** (0–6–758 4812) on Brougham Street. It's a sophisticated little French place, with a small bar offering a fine choice of wines, and a licensed restaurant serving very good, moderately priced meals. Bookings are essential. It's open from 11:00 am until late. The **Portofino Italian Restaurant** (0–6–757 8686) on Gill Street is another good dining spot. It's BYO or licensed, and moderately priced. It is advisable to book.

For a good, old-fashioned meal with no frills, try **Piccadillys** on Devon Street West. It's a great place to dine if you're famished (meals are huge) and not too particular about your dining decor. It's BYO, open between 4:00 and 10:00 pm, and has daily 'Blackboard Specials'.

For all your snowboarding and skiing requirements, see the people at **Del Free n'Easy** (0–6–758 8480), 34 Devon Street East. It's the only real ski/snowboard shop in town. It has a good selection of equipment for sale and a complete repair workshop.

*Repair charges:*
Full tune, with crystal glide: $50 (snowboard); $45 (skis).

*Hire charges:*
Snowboard and soft boots: $45 a day.
The shop doesn't hire out ski equipment, nor does anyone else in town. The only place in the region that does is the Mountain House, on the road up to the Manganui ski area.

Del Free n'Easy is also the best place to find out about the on-mountain conditions, and the staff are usually more than happy to tell you about what's happening in town, too. They tend to be quite fervent snowboarders, and rumours abound that people have walked into the shop with skis and come out with a new snowboard.

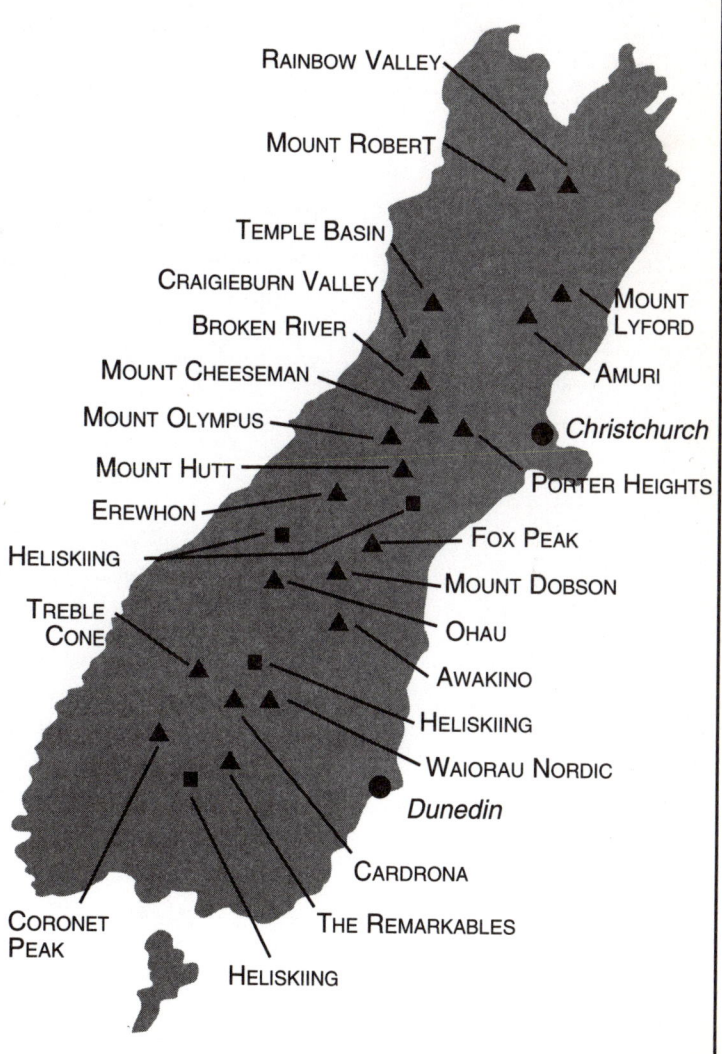

# Nelson/ Marlborough

## Ski Areas

Mount Robert 89
Rainbow Valley 96

## Resorts

Saint Arnaud 104

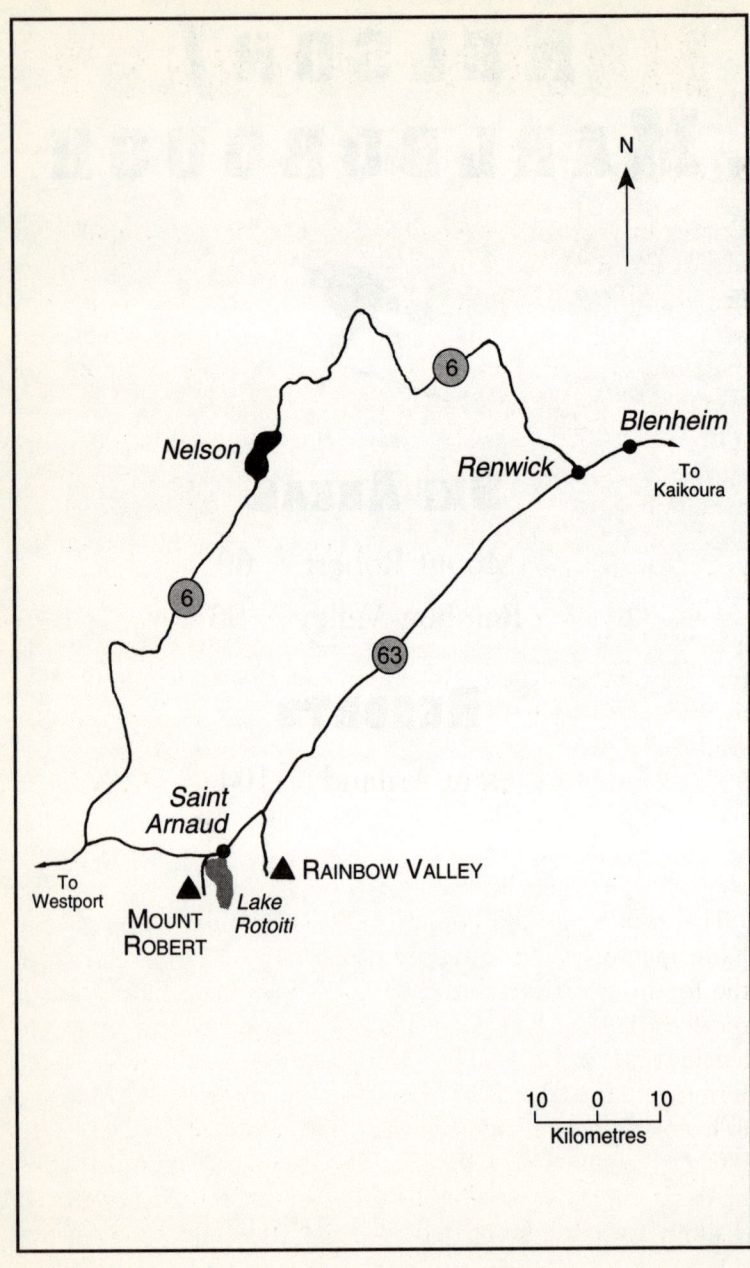

# Mount Robert

## History

European geologist and explorer, Sir Julius Von Haast, after whom Haast Pass is named, climbed the 1433-metre Mount Robert in 1860, and named it after his 12-year-old son, Robert, whom he had never actually seen. He wrote: 'The summits form meadows of short smooth snowgrass, the whole reminding me greatly of the wild alpine scenery of Switzerland'.

In August 1929, Eric Chittendon, Harry Kidson and Les Tiller stayed in a cottage at Saint Arnaud and made three trips to Mount Robert. There they skied the slopes on which the ski area now lies. Kidson and Tiller had bought skis; Chittendon had made his own pair.

This trio made other ski trips to the Mount Arthur Tableland, a large mountainous region to the northwest of Nelson during the following two years. They were keen to establish a hut close to a ski area and, although they enjoyed the skiing on the Tablelands, they decided to build it on Mount Robert.

Skiers wanting to get to Mount Robert in those days had to row a boat across Lake Rotoiti. The men considered this an advantage, as anyone crossing the lake would be observed and, consequently, vandalism would be less likely.

The row across the lake was necessary until 1947, when a footbridge was built across the Buller River. Eight years later, the footbridge was replaced with a road bridge. Early records recall the trip across the lake in an overloaded 12-foot dinghy on a cold windy night, with the oars making tinkling sounds on ice forming on the lake. The Nelson Ski Club must be the only one in history to list among its assets a boat and boat shed!

Over the summer of 1933–34, the group of enthusiasts, now up to six, set about building Kea Hut on the bush line of the old 'Paddys' track to Mount Robert. Skiing throughout the country at that time was a sport taken on by the hardy and enthusiastic. In Mount Robert's case, most of these enthusiasts came from Nelson. They would drive to Saint Arnaud on a Friday night, row across the lake, and carry their gear up to Kea Hut. On Saturday and Sunday, depending on snow cover, they would walk up to Second Basin, where the ski area now lies, for a day's skiing. Shelter in Second Basin was a japara tent. On Sunday afternoon, they would make their way back down the mountain, row across the lake, and drive back to Nelson.

In August 1944, the Nelson Ski Club was formed, with Eric Chittendon its first president. That summer, the club built

## Mount Robert

*Location:* To the car park: 7 km from Saint Arnaud; 113 km from Nelson.

*Season:* Usually from early July until late September/early October.
Weekends only; every day during the August school holidays.

*Elevation:* The top of Flagtop Lift is about 1700 metres.
The base of Downhill is at about 1400 metres.

*Vertical drop:* Approximately 300 metres.

*Terrain:* Beginner 10%, Intermediate 70%, Advanced 20%.

*Snowmaking:* None.

*Groomers:* None.

*Road toll:* None.

*Lifts:* Five rope tows. Charges are low.

*Ski hire:* A limited selection of equipment on the mountain, but check first with the club. Price is negotiable.

Bushline Hut, 60 metres below Kea Hut. With two huts, the club could now accommodate 30 people. About 120 people used these huts in the 1945 season.

By then, it had become apparent that the best ski slopes were in Second Basin, and that a shelter there would be a great advantage. In 1948, the 'Berghof', a five by two-and-a-half metre shelter, built largely of corrugated iron and flattened biscuit tins, was erected in the basin. This was the first step in developing the site of the present ski area. Also in 1948, the first ski tow operated on the mountain.

Two years later, the club decided to build a new

## Mount Robert

*Specials:* Not necessary, as the cost of a night's accommodation is also low. Take food for the night's cook-up and breakfast and lunch.

*Ski school:* Two instructors.

*Ski weeks:* During the August holidays only. Last from Sunday evening to Saturday morning, and include all meals, accommodation, lift passes and two hours' instruction each day: $270 (Adult); $170 (Child). To book, phone the club at the number given below.

*Accomm:* There are two lodges on the mountain. Both are modern and well equipped with a total of 50 bunks available between them. They are located on a flat area at the base of the main slope and have superb views across the Travers Valley to the Saint Arnaud Range, home of the Rainbow ski area, and of peaks in the immediate region.

*Address:* Nelson Ski Club, PO Box 344, Nelson: 0-3-548 8336.

*Snow reports:* Phone the club on 0-3-548 8336.

accommodation hut in Second Basin and, in April 1953, Mount Robert Lodge was completed and first used. The Berghof was moved alongside this lodge. Since then, the lodge has evolved into the modern facility that it is today. Much of the building equipment was dropped in by aircraft of the nearby Marlborough and Nelson Aero Clubs.

With membership at 205 in 1962, it became clear that more

## GETTING THERE

**From Saint Arnaud**
*By car*
Drive west toward Murchison on Highway 63, the main road through Saint Arnaud, for two kilometres. A signposted turn-off to the left then takes you down an unsealed road for five kilometres. The car park is at the end of this road. From here, you either start a two-hour walk, or, if it's a weekend and before 9:00 am, you can get a ride on the helicopter.

*Hitching*
Bearing in mind that it's only seven kilometres to the car park from Saint Arnaud, you're best to start walking to the turn-off. If the area's open and you're on the road before 9:00 am, it shouldn't be difficult getting a lift to the car park from there.

**From Nelson**
See the Rainbow Valley ski area for details on how to get to Saint Arnaud. Both shuttle companies mentioned in the Rainbow Valley section – JJs Ski Transport and Nelson Lakes Transport – will make trips from Nelson to the Mount Robert car park, subject to demand. Fares are the same as between Nelson and Rainbow Valley.

accommodation was needed. From January to August 1964, the Christie Lodge was built in Second Basin, a short distance from Mount Robert Lodge. Air drops by helicopter had been made since 1962 but over half of the building materials were carried up by volunteers. In 1971, a helicopter started transporting people from the car park to the lodges for ski weeks.

Over the last 30 years, the club has continued to develop its huts and install further rope tows. Kea and Bushline Huts have since been given to the Nelson Lakes National Park. Road access and purchasing a groomer are two matters that have arisen over the years. The road debate has seemingly been put to rest, but the grooming debate continues, many members preferring the natural, ungroomed snow. (Mount Robert is not the only club area where grooming is an issue.)

Club membership peaked at 700 in 1977, but these days varies between 200 and 300 a year. One of the main reasons for this fall must be the development of the nearby Rainbow Valley ski area. Of the two areas, Rainbow Valley is by far the easier to get to.

## The Ski Area

Mount Robert is the most isolated ski area in the country. Although it's less than 10 kilometres from Saint Arnaud, a two-hour walk is required to get there. Fit club members lay claim to having done the walk in an hour and ten minutes. For the rest of us, the first hour to hour and half takes us up the steep and winding Pinchgut Track to the Bush Edge Shelter. From there it's an excellent walk along a broad ridge to the Prospect Ridge Shelter, and a short descent to the ski area. This stretch takes between 30 and 60 minutes, depending on snow cover. The ridge is very exposed, so warm, waterproof clothing is essential.

If you don't fancy the walk, it is possible to go in by helicopter during the weekends. Flights go on demand from about 8:30 to 10:00 am. For a charge of $35, you and your gear – skis, boots, poles and pack – can be on the snow in four to five minutes. If you want to walk in unhindered, it is possible to have your gear flown in for a small price. On a fine day, it really is worth getting there early and making the walk.

The 'isolation factor' is an inherent part of the whole Mount Robert experience. During a night in one of the lodges, enjoying the food, a quiet drink and conversation, the world can seem light years away. The weekend meals are usually a stew of some sort, for which everyone is expected to bring something to contribute. Call the club to find out what ingredients you will need.

The ski area is on a very wide eastern-facing basin below the ridge leading to the summit of Mount Robert. From the ridge there is a long slope down to a flat area where the lodges are. Most skiing is done on this slope, so it has three of the five lifts – Main Tow, South Tow and Christie Tow. Further out to the left is Flagtop Tow. Because this is higher than the others, it is used mainly in poor snow seasons or if there are enough skiers to warrant it being started; and if it's not buried! The other tow, Downhill, runs from the bottom of Main Tow to about 100 metres below it. All lifts are rope tows and you can hire a tow belt from the hut at the bottom of Main Tow. Lift passes are usually sold by a club member standing at the base of Main Tow.

The main run seems to be to the left of Main Tow. Because there is no groomer, skiers preferring the groomed type of snow are best to keep to this part of the mountain, as it gradually develops into a semi-groomed type of run. This 'grooming' also occurs on the Christie run, which is a shorter, beginner/intermediate run. The Christie is quite steep toward the top, but nearly flat at the bottom – a good spot for 'never-evers'.

Those skiers who enjoy wide and varied terrain covered in untouched snow (although it's only a matter of time before it becomes 'touched') should head out to the left, or right, of the main ski area. While it has a reasonable vertical drop (300 metres), the beauty of Mount Robert is its easy, rolling terrain. Out to the right of South Tow, in the Flagtop Tow area, there are a number of large mounds and dips with short, steep pitches. It's actually a large area out there, and seemingly more so due to the small number of skiers who venture out that way. That could also be said for the whole ski area – it's a big place, with usually only a few skiers on it.

Fresh tracks are almost guaranteed on Mount Robert. They are, however, more difficult to find as the day progresses. One of the first areas to go, after the left of Main Tow, is the face further out to your left leading to the bottom of Downhill Tow. To get there, go up Main Tow and traverse way out to your left. The further you go out, the steeper it gets. It's a great run with a steep section, then a flatter bit, and another steep section as you reach the bottom. To the right of Downhill Tow is a steepish slope, excellent for intermediate to advanced skiers. If the snow is right, a fantastic lip, from which good 'air time' is always available, forms down this slope.

Touring potential in and around the basin is huge. Even going out past Flagtop Tow to the top of the ridge is a good trip. If you intend to go touring from the ski area, make sure you've checked the avalanche hazard with the Department of Conservation people in Saint Arnaud.

When leaving the ski area, the best idea is to ask someone who is staying to follow you to the top of Main Tow. Once there, give them your tow belt to return and make the traverse out to your left, toward the small hut (Prospect Ridge Shelter) on the ridge. From there, it's an easy ski down to the Bush Edge Shelter, provided there's enough snow. The whole trip from Mount Robert to the car park takes about an hour and a quarter.

# Rainbow Valley

## History

In the mid-1970s the New Zealand Forest Service, which in 1987 merged with the Department of Lands and Surveys to become the Department of Conservation, conducted various studies in the Rainbow State Forest Park, east of the Nelson Lakes National Park. Investigations concluded that an area of the park, Six Mile Basin, was suitable for a ski area.

Why the Forest Service decided to investigate the feasibility of a ski area in the park is a bit of a mystery. During the early 1970s, the service had carried out large forest-clearing operations in the park, cutting down native trees and replacing them with pine plantations that would eventually be milled and sold. This destruction of native forest had attracted bad publicity, particularly from the locals, and speculation has it that the 'ski area idea' was a public relations exercise to try to appease the locals.

The Forest Service approached the Nelson Ski Club operating on Mount Robert in the Nelson Lakes National Park, and enquired if the club would consider moving its ski area to Six Mile Basin. A member of the club, Philip Coutts, and Forest Service staff spent a day skiing the basin in July 1976. Coutts recognised the area's potential and the following weekend he took members of the club's committee up for a ski. They too were impressed, and over the winters of 1977 and '78 the club and Forest Service staff carried out further investigations, using satellite photographs and having parties stay in the basin to monitor snow depths and conditions. The service even prepared an Environmental Impact Assessment for the proposed road.

Early in 1979 the Nelson Ski Club's committee decided against shifting from Mount Robert. Aside from the enormous cost involved with moving lifts and lodges, the committee was also of the opinion that putting an access road into Six Mile Basin would be too difficult and expensive; and that the basin's terrain was not as good as Mount Robert's, although members did acknowledge that it was an excellent area for beginner and intermediate skiers.

A lawyer from Blenheim, Don Holden, then formed a group with 21 other local businessmen and farmers, and wrote to the Forest Service expressing interest in developing the ski area. The group formed a public company – Rainbow Ski-Field Developments Ltd – and commissioned an Environmental Impact Assessment for the proposed ski area. A hearing of the proposal was held in December 1980. Few submissions were made, and most of these were supportive. A commercial ski area was seen by many living in the Nelson Lakes region as an added attraction for tourists who already visited the region for its great fishing, tramping and wine trails.

In April of the following year, the company was granted permission to begin developing the area. The New Zealand Electricity Department had a road running up the Wairau Valley from Highway 63, and the company had permission to use this as far as the Six Mile Basin, from where an access road could be cut up to the ski area. Doug Hood, who had constructed Mount Hutt's access road the previous decade, put Rainbow's road in during May and June of 1981.

Over that winter, the group sought advice from Reinholdt Zauner, an Austrian ski area engineer, and bought two rope tows from the Mount Cook Group. These, and an A-frame shelter building were installed in early 1982, and the Rainbow Ski Area was officially opened on 17 July 1982. An adult day pass was $8. A groomer was purchased and went into action during the ski season.

The ensuing years saw developments slowly occur as people in the Nelson–Marlborough region (population 120,000) discovered skiing, a sport that had previously involved either a two-hour walk up Mount Robert, or a five- to eight-hour drive south to Canterbury. In 1986, Rainbow Valley attracted 18,500 skier visits, and in early 1988 another rope tow was installed.

When snow making began in 1990, Rainbow Valley became a bit of an oddity, having both the latest and the oldest ski area

## Rainbow Valley

*Location:* 24 km from Saint Arnaud.
144 km from Nelson.
130 km from Blenheim.

*Season:* Usually open by mid June and closes by early/mid October.

*Elevation:* The top of the ASB Bank Double Chairlift is at 1758 metres. The base buildings are at 1540 metres.
The bottom of the lowest lift (the Overton Ford T-bar) is at 1438 metres.

*Vertical drop:* 320 metres.

*Terrain:* Beginner 25%, Intermediate 55%, Advanced 20%.

*Snowmaking:* Snow is made down the chairlift's slopes, on both learners' areas, and down the T-bar's runs.

*Groomers:* Two.

*Road toll:* $8 per day.

*Lifts:* One double chairlift, one T-bar, two learners' handle tows.
Moderate charge, with reduced rates for learners and over 65s. Under fives are free.

*Ski hire:* Full set (per day): $26 (Adult); $20 (Student); $16 (Child).

technology. It was a commercial ski area with snow-making equipment, yet had only rope tows for lifts. The company recognised the need for a modern lift and, in the summer of 1991, purchased the defunct Tekapo ski area's double chairlift and installed it in the main basin, replacing the rope tows. (Tekapo ran from 1972 to 1990.)

## Rainbow Valley

Snowboards will be available from the 1995 season.

*Specials:* A Learners' Package (a learners' lift pass, full ski hire and a 90-minute group lesson) is $48 (Adult); $38 (Student); $32 (Child).

*Ski school:* The Snow Bizz ski school runs a number of clinics and programmes for racers, children, women only, etc. To find out about these, write to Snow Bizz Ski School, Private Bag, Saint Arnaud.

Group lessons (two hours):
10:30 am, 1:30 pm: $28 (Adult); $15 (Youth/Child).
A minimum of three students required.

Private lessons (one hour): $45 ($15 each extra person).
At 9:30 am: $45 for one or two people.
A half-day (3 hours): $140 for one to four people.

*Address:* Rainbow Valley Ski Area Ltd, Private Bag, Saint Arnaud. Telephone: 0–3–521 1861.

*Snow reports:* Listen to Radio Fifeshire 93FM Nelson, Radio Nelson, Radio Marlborough, 93FM Marlborough, Radio Scenicland, Radio 2ZB, The Breeze, or More FM. The report can also be heard by phoning the Rainbow Snowphone on 0900–34444 (costs 99c per minute).

Since 1991, a handle tow has replaced the original learners' rope tow, the base buildings have been expanded and improved, and the Overton Ford T-bar has been installed. Major shareholders have changed from time to time over the years. These days Rainbow Valley is run as a private company.

## GETTING THERE

**From Saint Arnaud**
*By car*
Head east on Highway 63 toward Blenheim. About ten kilometres along this road you come to the Rainbow Valley signpost and an unsealed road on your right. Take this turn-off. The first eight kilometres of this road takes you up the Wairau River valley and fords five small streams before arriving at the toll gate. From here the road leaves the valley and begins the steep climb to the ski area. Chains can be hired at the toll gate for $25, a cost that includes fitting. If you'd rather leave your car at the toll gate, you can catch a shuttle from here at 9:30 am (and 10:30 am subject to demand) which costs $10 return for adults; $5 for children.

*Hitching*
You really need to be on Highway 63 by 8:00 am. Any car with skis on it will most likely be going to Rainbow, and catching a ride isn't usually too difficult.

*By shuttle*
JJs Ski Transport makes pick-ups from outside the Saint Arnaud Ski Services shop at 8:15 am every day. The return fare is $10. To book a seat, phone 0–3–5447081 or 0800–502 002 (toll-free).

Nelson Lakes Transport also picks up from outside the

# The Ski Areas

Rainbow is about 24 kilometres from Saint Arnaud. The access road is about 14 kilometres long and fords five streams along the Wairau River valley before making the climb up to the ski area.

ski shop. They charge $15 return and leave at 8:30 am every day. To book a seat, phone 0–3–548 6858.

**From Nelson**
*By car*
Head south on Highway 6 towards Murchison. After 93 kilometres, you'll arrive at Howard Junction. Turn left here on to Highway 63. After a further 26 kilometres, you'll arrive at Saint Arnaud, from where the ski area is sign-posted. It's 24 kilometres from Saint Arnaud.

*Hitching*
Be on Highway 6, heading south of Nelson, by 7:00 am. Any car with skis on will be going to either the Rainbow or Mount Robert ski areas. A car going to Mount Robert will take you close enough to Saint Arnaud to make catching another lift to Rainbow Valley fairly easy.

*By shuttle*
JJ's Ski Transport starts making pick-ups in the Nelson city area from 7:00 am. A return trip is $25 for adults; $15 for children. Phone 0–3–544 7081 or 0800–502 002 (toll-free) to make a booking.

Nelson Lakes Transport departs from the Nelson Visitor Information Centre daily at 7:30 am. A return trip is $30 for adults; $15 for children. Phone 0–3–548 6858 to make a booking.

Because much of the road remains in the shade during the day, it can get icy and requires caution at all times. You can hire chains from the toll gate if need be.

The ski area is in a wide basin, with a long, gentle central slope surrounded by steep faces. The steepest parts of the ski area are the faces and chutes to the left of the chairlift. Advanced skiers will enjoy the runs on this side of the basin and the runs in the West Bowl area. Some of the more exciting runs are the routes down to the base of the T-bar from the traverse between the top of the chairlift and West Bowl. It's a great run, full of short steep sections and numerous small chutes.

With Alan's Way and the other runs on that side of the basin, and those out toward West Bowl, there is plenty of terrain for the advanced skier. What's more, because Rainbow seems to largely attract beginner and intermediate skiers, these runs see relatively few skiers. For 'never-ever' skiers, beginner, and intermediate skiers, Rainbow is superb. The learners' area, between the top of the T-bar and the base of the chairlift, is a wide and very gentle slope, a fantastic place to learn the basics. The step up from there is the other learners' area, to the left of the chairlift, in front of the cafeteria. This slope is a little steeper and longer. Both learners' areas are well located and have few faster, advanced skiers crossing them.

Perhaps the greatest aspect of Rainbow for the novice skier is that so much of the terrain is suited to a beginner's standard. The run from the top of the chairlift to the base area is well within the means of a confident beginner, with just a short steep section on the last stretch of the run, which is easily avoided by taking the Easy Way Home cat-track. The fact that all this terrain is accessed by one chairlift is another aspect many skiers appreciate. East Face is the steepest of the groomed runs and could get a bit tricky for the less-confident beginner.

The Overton Ford T-bar services good intermediate/advanced groomed slopes. It's a great slope for those fast, wide turns that are not always possible on the gentler slopes beneath the chairlift.

It is almost certain that the faces to the left of the chairlift will prove irresistible to the adventurous. The best way to get the most out of these slopes is to make a short walk from the top of the chairlift to the peak above East Face. From there it's possible to make a few turns before traversing to the col above Alan's Way. From the col you can make a few more turns and traverse again, and so on until you come out on Easy Way Home. Alternatively, you can traverse straight to the top of Alan's Way and make one run down the long, steep face. If it starts getting tracked-out on this side of the basin then head to West Bowl where fresh tracks are as good as guaranteed.

From the ridge above the chairlift you get a good view of the Mount Robert ski area, and Lake Rotoiti below.

Some of the best chutes on the mountain are on the peak to the right of the top of the chairlift. A short walk is required, but once you've skied a chute you can still make the traverse toward West Bowl and find a few more en route to the T-bar.

There is excellent touring terrain around Rainbow. Powder Valley, over the col above Alan's Way, offers some great skiing, and it's possible to follow the valley down to the access road. There are also some great slopes out past West Bowl that often have enough snow to make a run down to the access road possible. Remember to check on the avalanche hazard with ski patrol before heading out.

# SAINT ARNAUD

Following the European settlers in the Nelson area came the early European explorers, who headed south in search of more flat land. In 1843, John Silvanus Cotterell became the first European to sight Lake Rotoiti, where he was faced with mountain ranges to the south, east and west. Further explorers followed, but found the same barriers. Charles Heaphy, William Fox and Thomas Brunner all searched for the 'large interior valley of level or undulating lands extending, with perhaps slight occasional interruption, throughout the whole extent of the island', so optimistically described by Heaphy. It was, of course, never found. In fact they found the complete opposite – the Southern Alps. The rugged land around Saint Arnaud was the stopping point for the settlers' hopes of finding more flat land.

In 1847, Scotsman George McRae became the first settler in the Saint Arnaud region, bringing 400 sheep into the area and establishing a 'Right of Occupation' over land that later was to be called Lake Station.

A rough track was cut between Nelson and Saint Arnaud in 1846 and, with the discovery of gold on the West Coast in the 1860s, a track was cut through the Buller Gorge from Lake Rotoiti to Westport on the coast. The village of Saint Arnaud started as a place where gold diggers heading westward could stock up with supplies. The name of Saint Arnaud was given by a Nelson solicitor and explorer, William Travers, after a French commander in the Crimean War.

In the 1930s, Saint Arnaud and the two lakes, Rotoiti and Rotoroa, became popular holiday spots for people living in the Nelson and Marlborough regions. Fishermen, boaties, trampers, climbers and skiers made their way to the lakes, hills, mountains and snowfields of the Nelson Lakes park.

Once only busy during summer, Saint Arnaud is today

becoming increasingly popular over the ski season, acting as a base for skiers visiting the two nearby ski areas, Rainbow Valley and Mount Robert, although most people skiing on Mount Robert choose to stay on the mountain. Beside a large lake and with the snow-capped mountains of the Saint Arnaud and Travers Ranges nearby, it would be difficult to pick a more idyllic setting for a ski town.

The centre of town is the **Lake Rotoiti Alpine Lodge** (0–3–521 1869), a modern place with all the trimmings. Each room has a private bathroom, tea- and coffee-making facilities, a TV, a telephone and a refrigerator. There's a large restaurant, and the hotel bar is the only one in town, which consequently means this is where it all happens in Saint Arnaud. In the bar there's a huge open fire and a pleasant view through wall-sized windows over a small stream to native bush. Accommodation costs are in the high price range. Bookings are essential.

Adjacent to the lodge is the **Alpine Chalet** (0–3–521 1869). Also run by the lodge, the chalet offers backpacker-style accommodation ranging from budget to moderately priced. Sleeping bags are required. It has a large kitchen and common-room area in the upstairs section. Bookings are essential.

**Yellow House** (0–3–521 1887) at the eastern end of town offers backpackers' accommodation as well as log chalets. The hostel – with a laundry, TV/living room and full kitchen facilities – is in the budget price range. The chalets sleep up to six, are fully self-contained and cost $75 a night, plus $12 for each extra adult; $8 for each extra child. At the back of Yellow House is an outdoor spa pool that offers great views of the Saint Arnaud Range. The cost is $4 an hour for residents and non-residents alike. Bookings for the chalets should be made well in advance. If possible, book ahead for the hostel, too.

About nine kilometres east of the township is the historic

**Tophouse Hotel** (0–3–521 1848) is a recently restored cob (mud) hotel dating from the 1880s. As a place to return to following a day's skiing at Rainbow, it is unsurpassed. It has a very comfortable living room/dining area with a huge open fire, over which your toast is cooked in the morning. The whole place is furnished and fitted out as it would have been in days gone by, only now with the benefit of inside bathrooms. Situated on a hill in the centre of a 300-hectare farm, it's also graced with spectacular views. It's possible just to call in for a tea or coffee and a homemade bun, so even if you're not staying, you can still visit. It's the closest accommodation to Rainbow (a 35-minute drive). Dinner, bed and breakfast is moderately priced, with a sliding scale (based on age) for children. Bookings are essential. The hosts are Melody and Mike Nicholls, and the address is Tophouse, RD 2, Nelson.

For places to dine in Saint Arnaud you have a choice of the restaurant in the Lake Rotoiti Lodge, with its cordon bleu menu in the high price range, or the take-away at the garage. Also at the garage is the town's supermarket. The small café in the Alpine Chalet is probably the best place in town for a coffee or snack.

Beside the garage is the small **Saint Arnaud Ski Services** (0–3–521 1850) building. It's open seven days between 7:30 and 10:30 am, and 4:00 and 6:00 pm.

*Hire charges:*
Full ski set for a day: $25 (Adult); $18 (Student); $10 (Child).
Snowboard: $35 a day.
Snowboard with boots: $40 a day.

# North Canterbury

## Ski Areas

Amuri    109
Mount Lyford    115

## Resorts

Hanmer Springs    122

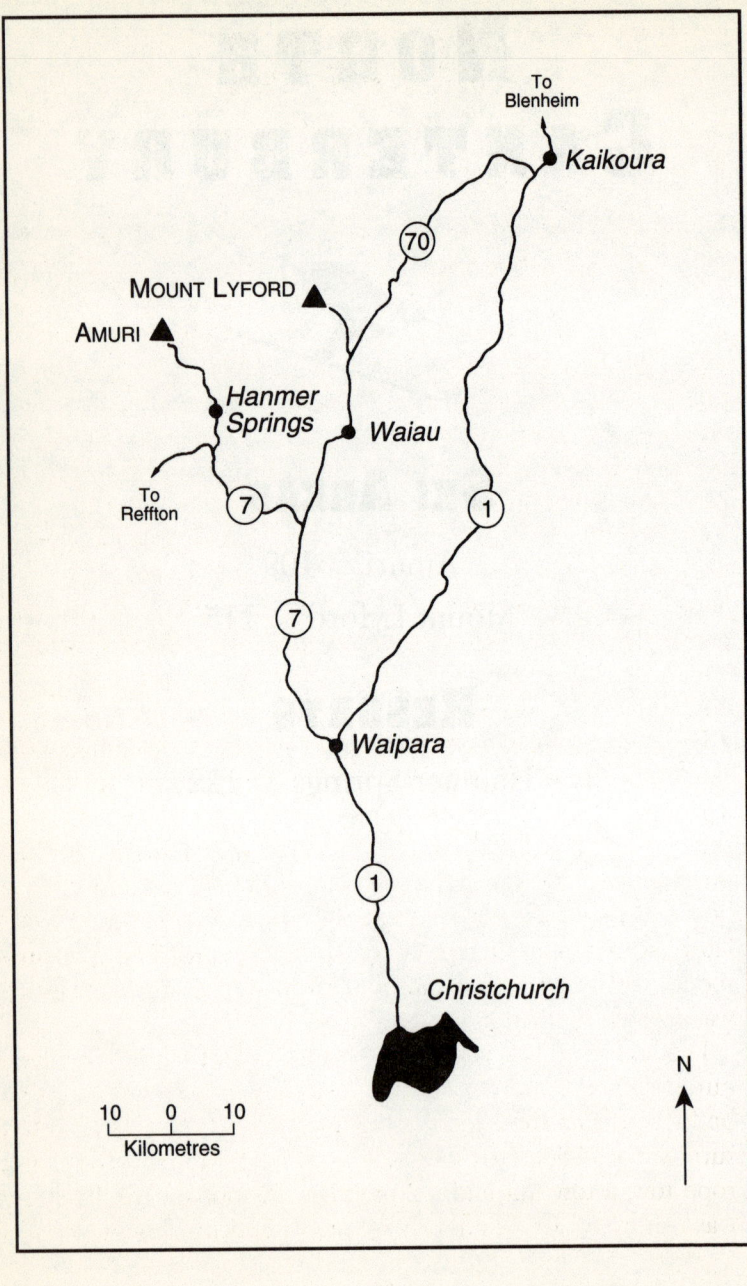

# AMURI

## History

Situated on Mount Saint Patrick in the Saint James Range, the Amuri ski area lies about 15 kilometres northwest of Hanmer.

The inception of this ski area was due as much to Hugh Grigg as it was to the New Zealand Electricity Department who, in 1956, put in a road from Hanmer to Saint Arnaud to service a power line. Without this road the area was inaccessible, and without Grigg's enthusiasm, local residents may not have been interested. (Grigg had moved from Hororata, where he was president of the Windwhistle Ski Club on Mount Olympus.)

In October 1956, Grigg, Hawdon Davison and Dick Hiatt walked into the area in search of a suitable location for a ski area. Grigg knew about snow conditions; the others represented people in the distcrict keen to develop a ski area. The basin in which the ski area presently lies, with its reasonable gradient and ability to retain snow, was deemed the best location.

In September 1957, John Chaffey became the first person to ski Amuri Basin. He was followed into the basin in October by a group of 20 local residents. Eager to see a ski area established, they tramped in to form their own views. It was this group who, on reaching the top of Mount Saint Patrick, cracked open a bottle of Bordeaux Blanc which, unknown to them then, would later give its name to one of the ski area's runs. The following month, the Amuri Ski Club held its inaugural meeting. Grigg was elected the club's first president.

The club's initial finance came from its 200 founder members purchasing 1800 £1 debentures, enabling an access road to be bulldozed from the Electricity Board's road to the basin in the summer of 1958. That autumn, work began on constructing a rope tow, a tow hut and a 20-foot by 18-foot shelter. The tow was run by a four-cylinder diesel motor and winching gear.

Ready to go for the 1958 season, members' hopes were dashed when a very lean snow season meant no skiing was possible. The following season, there was too much snow and access was very difficult. Nevertheless, it was in the winter of 1959 that skiing began on Amuri.

Development over the years has been steady. In 1960, a bunk hut was constructed alongside the shelter. In 1962, a top rope tow was installed, running from the top of the main tow along a ridge to just below Mount Saint Patrick's summit (this tow has since been removed). In 1967, the main tow motor was replaced

## Amuri

*Location:* 15 km from Hanmer.
149 km from Christchurch.
155 km from Kaikoura.

*Season:* Usually from early/mid July through to mid/late September.

*Elevation:* Mount Saint Patrick is 1772 metres high.
The Bordeaux platter takes you to 1769 metres.
The base buildings are at 1432 metres.

*Vertical drop:* 337 metres.

*Terrain:* Beginner 10%, Intermediate 60%, Advanced 30%.

*Snowmaking:* None.

*Groomers:* One.

*Road toll:* None.

*Lifts:* One platter and two rope tows. Low charge, with reductions for students and learners. Under 5s are free.

*Ski hire:* 120 pairs of skis.
A full set (day): $18 (Adult); $15 (Youth, 14 and under); $8 (Child, 11 and under).

by a 112-horsepower converted tractor engine, giving the lift a capacity of 500 people per hour. In 1970, a beginners' tow was installed at the bottom of the basin and a new access road constructed since the old one, carved through soft earth, frequently became a 'muddy mess'. In 1976, the club built what has since been termed its 'pride and joy', a 168-square-metre day lodge constructed of natural timber.

Perhaps the biggest development for the club occurred in July 1981 with the opening of its kilometre-long Poma platter lift running up the Bordeaux Basin. The lift had been purchased

## Amuri

Snowboards: $29 a day; $16 half-day; $8 an hour.

*Specials:* A family of two adults and two children can ski for $70.

*Ski school:* Three instructors and flexible times.
Group lessons: $15 (Adult); $10 (Child).
Private lessons: $25, with $10 each extra person.
Snowboard lesson: $30 (includes board hire).

*Ski weeks:* From Sundays to Saturdays (accommodation in the mountain lodge, tow fees, one lesson per day, and dinners and breakfasts): $310 (Adult); $270 (Student); $250 (Child). For enquiries or bookings, write to the address below or phone 025–341 806.

*Accomm:* All on-mountain accommodation is in the lower, modern lodge. It has family rooms and bunk rooms and can sleep up to 55 people. Dinner, bed and breakfast is moderately priced.

*Address:* Amuri Ski Area, PO Box 129, Hanmer Springs.
Telephone: 025–341 806.

*Snow reports:* Phone the Press Inpho line 0–3–366 6644, then 1101.

second-hand from the Whakapapa ski area, and transported down and installed almost entirely by voluntary workers. A design engineer from the Pomagalski Lift Company in France visited Amuri in 1982 and is quoted as saying, 'What an amazing job a pack of amateurs have done.'

Amateurs they may be, but if you visit Amuri you may, at the end of the day, perhaps while bathing in Hanmer's hot pools, find yourself agreeing with that engineer.

## The Ski Area

The road from Hanmer to the base of Amuri's access road is generally kept in good shape. It's a pleasant drive through pine forest, then alongside the Clarence River. About 10 kilometres

### Getting there

**From Christchurch**

*By car*
Follow the instructions for Mount Lyford, only stay on Highway 7 instead of taking the turn-off to Waiau after Culverden. Follow the signs to Hanmer. Once in Hanmer, turn left at the Old Post Office Restaurant and follow the signs to Jacks Pass or Amuri Ski Area. The ski area is about 15 kilometres north of Hanmer.

*Hitching*
Follow the instructions for Mount Lyford. If your lift is going to Kaikoura, take it as far as Waipara. If your lift is going to Mount Lyford, take it as far as the turn-off from Highway 7 to Waiau (this is called Red Post Corner). If you're very lucky, you'll get a lift from here to Amuri. Chances are you'll get a lift to the Hanmer turn-off or to Hanmer itself. When you reach Hanmer, walk through

down this road you come to a farmer's house and a sign pointing left to Amuri Ski Field. From here it's another five kilometres to the ski area. The road climbs slowly through a barren, tussock- and matagouri-covered valley. It can be tricky in places, with a few sharp corners towards the top.

The ticket office is in the higher of the two lodges. Tow belts for the Shirt Front Tow can be hired from the ticket office. You can actually ski most of the slopes from the top of the Poma, but for the extra $2 (plus $10 deposit) it's worth picking up a tow belt for the added variety. The cafeteria is also in this lodge. It's a standard ski-club café, with a cooking area, a wood-burner and walls covered with photos chronicling the area's growth over the years. The ski-hire department is in the small building below the Shirt Front engine shed.

---

town to the Jacks Pass road and try your luck from there.

Hitching to Amuri is not easy and, if you don't have a car but want to ski there, the best idea is to spend a night in Hanmer and go up the following day. Failing that, call the club (025–341 806) and see if someone can organise you a ride from Christchurch.

*By shuttle*
No regular service. If there are enough of you, about eight, one of the companies may take you. For a list of Christchurch shuttle companies, see Mount Hutt.

**From Hanmer**
*By shuttle*
The Amuri Ski Shuttle runs on demand, requiring at least three passengers before it will operate. It leaves from outside the Stagepost Shop on Hanmer's main road at 9:30 am and returns there at 5:00 pm. A return fare is $15. To book a seat, phone: 0–3–315 7201.

Amuri is not a large ski area. The variety of terrain, though, is excellent. There are basically three gullies, the largest being the Bordeaux Basin with the Poma lift. The other, shallower gullies, are the SG and GS Race Track and the Shirt Front runs. A big advantage is Amuri's northerly aspect, ensuring that, as long as the sun's out, the area will get it.

Advanced skiers are likely to most enjoy the runs from the top of the Poma. The Bordeaux Basin Run is the steepest slope of the area. A lip that runs down this slope can itself provide hours of fun. Slopes to the right of the Poma are also quite steep. The run called Snowboarders Best is a long natural half-pipe and is popular with skiers as well.

It's worth taking a bit of time to savour the views from the top of Mount Saint Patrick. To the south you can see the Hanmer Range and the plains beyond. To the north you can see up the Clarence River Valley, and to the northeast is the Kaikoura Range. There is a slope off the back of Mount Saint Patrick that looks particularly enticing and is ideal for ski touring, or just plain skiing, if the walk back up doesn't bother you. To the left of the top of the Poma you can go along the Backside Run, which takes you down a gentle gradient with great views to the SG & GS Race Track.

Shirt Front is really the main run. It's a wide, groomed slope with a gradient ideal for beginner and intermediate skiers. Table Top is much the same, although requiring shorter turns. The Honey Mooners Run off the side of the mountain may look like an afterthought on the part of the trail-map artist. It is, however, quite legitimate and a good challenging run for advanced skiers. With good snow cover, it's possible to traverse from the bottom of the run back to the base area.

Spring Favourite is the longest run, finishing about 300 metres down the road from the car park. It runs down a slight gully that collects and holds snow well. There's no better way to finish your day at Amuri than to ski Spring Favourite, particularly if you can organise someone with a vehicle to meet you at the bottom.

# Mount Lyford

## History

The newest ski area in New Zealand, Mount Lyford is unique in that it has a private 'wilderness village' at the base of its access road. In fact, it was the village that came first; the ski area being almost an after-thought.

In 1978, Doug and Jenny Simpson bought the Snowden sheep station north of Waiau. Four years later, they sold 4000 acres of the station, retaining 3000 and naming it Mount Lyford station. The station covers part of the Amuri Mountain Range with the highest point in this range, Mount Terako, lying within the station's land. From 1981 to 1984, a private heli-ski operation, based in Kaikoura, made trips to Mount Terako's slopes.

The Simpsons had been planning the wilderness retreat for several years and, in 1988, with the assistance of a large Auckland-based construction group, work began on developing house sites. During that summer, the Simpsons had a road cut up to the Stella Lake Basin. Snow cover was good on the south-facing slopes above the lake and it was decided that it was worth trying a ski venture there. By the start of the 1989 ski season they had installed a rope tow (purchased 'second-hand' from Amuri Ski Club for $100) and arranged the lease of a groomer.

Along with a portable toilet and a portable shed for an office, Mount Lyford ski area opened in the first week of June 1989. During this first season, the field attracted up to 400 people on some days. The rope tow was well used by beginners, while the more advanced skiers could get a lift on the groomer up to Stella Basin's steeper slopes.

The following summer, another rope tow was installed in Stella Basin and a more permanent base building constructed in place of the portable one. Wilderness Village was proving to be a success, with more and more sites being sold and chalets going up. The Auckland-based construction group went into receivership late in 1989 and their shares in the venture were bought by the Simpsons.

The 1990 ski season was a good one for Mount Lyford and over the summer of '90–'91, further development took place. A ski-hire department was added to the base building and a road

 **Mount Lyford**

*Location:* 26 km from Waiau.
78 km from Hanmer.
146 km from Christchurch.
67 km from Kaikoura.

*Season:* Early June to mid/late October.

*Elevation:* At Lake Stella, the top rope tow takes you to 1554 metres and the base lodge is at 1249 metres.
In Terako Basin, Deer Valley platter takes you to 1555 metres; the base lodge is at 1510 metres.
A new rope tow will take you up to 1750 metres.

*Vertical drop:* At Lake Stella, 305 metres.
At Terako Basin, 85 metres. (240 with new rope tow.)

*Terrain:* Beginner 45%, Intermediate 40%, Advanced 15%.

*Snowmaking:* None.

*Groomers:* One.

*Road toll:* $5.

*Lifts:* Three platters and three rope tows. Moderate charge. Student and child rates apply.

*Ski hire:* 280 pairs of skis: $15–$25 full set, depending on model.
5 snowboards: $10 (hour); $20 (half a day); $30 (day).

*Specials:* A Learners' Package (lift pass, ski hire and lesson): $45.

was cut from Lake Stella up to Terako Basin. During the 1991 season, the groomer carried skiers up the slopes of Terako Basin.

Terako Basin is a natural ski-bowl with huge development potential. This was a point not missed by the Simpsons, and construction of the Paradise Valley platter lift in the basin began

##  Mount Lyford

*Ski school:* Four or five instructors.

Group lesson (two hours): $25.

Private lesson (one hour): $40 for one or two people.

$30 for one or two between 9:00 and 10:00 am, or $50 for three or four.

Snowboard lessons are the same prices.

*Accomm:* In lodges in Wilderness Village. Charges worked on a per-night basis (as opposed to the ski weeks available at club fields).

One night and a lift pass: Moderate charge, with lower youth and child rates.

A private chalet and a lift pass (minimum of two people): Low charge.

Food for breakfast, lunch (prepared on the field for you) and dinner costs $20.

To find out more or to book, phone 0-3-366 1220. It's a popular place, so the earlier you book, the better.

*Address:* Mount Lyford Ski Area, Private Bag, Waiau, North Canterbury. Telephone: 0-3-315 6178.

*Snow reports:* Phone the Press Inpho Ski Line 0-3-366 6644, then 1101.

in late 1991. Work was stalled because of an early start to the 1992 season, but the lift was completed and carrying skiers by the end of the season. Over the following summer, another platter and rope tow were installed in Terako Basin and a two-storey lodge was built, effectively moving the area's headquarters from Lake Stella to Terako Basin.

Today, as the country's youngest ski area, Mount Lyford continues to maintain the friendly, 'down-to-earth' atmosphere with which the area began.

## GETTING THERE

### From Christchurch
*By car*
Take Highway 1 north out of Christchurch. About 60 kilometres toward Kaikoura you come to Waipara, where you turn left (west) on Highway 7. Follow the signs to Hanmer Springs. Thirty kilometres past Waipara, you'll pass the historic Hurunui Hotel, which was established in 1868. This is a place worth stopping at for a pie and a game of pool on the way home. Fifteen kilometres on from Hurunui, after you've been through Culverden, take the turn-off to Waiau along Highway 70. Waiau is the largest settlement in the immediate region and has a food store, a petrol station and a pub. From Waiau, continue on Highway 70 for another 20 kilometres before arriving at the Mount Lyford Village and Ski Area turn-off. Drive up through the village to get to the access road toll gate. Chains may be required.

*Hitching*
It's not that easy catching a lift to Mount Lyford, and it's often worth the $25 to get the shuttle. But, if you've got

# The Ski Area

Mount Lyford actually consists of two ski areas – Stella Bowl and Terako Basin. They are connected by the access road. Stella Bowl is the first you come to and has a southerly aspect, while Terako Basin is about a kilometre further along the road and has a westerly aspect.

The access road from Highway 70 is unsealed and 10 kilometres long, and passes through the Wilderness Village on its way to the ski area. The toll gate is located at the end of the village, before the road starts its steep climb to Stella Bowl. Just

your mind set on doing it 'by thumb', try to be on the Main North Road by 7:00 am. Bus Numbers 1 or 4 will get you there. The earliest bus leaves the Square at 7:05 am and gets you on the Main North Road by 7:25 am. If you're lucky, you'll get a lift with a skier going to either Mount Lyford or Amuri. Otherwise, just stick to the directions above and be dropped off at any of the intersections.

*Shuttles and buses*
The Mount Lyford Shuttle operates on demand from the Information Centre on Worcester Street in the central city. It seems to operate regularly at weekends and during holidays, departing at 7:30 am and arriving at the mountain by 9:20 am. It will have you back in Christchurch by 6:30 pm. A return fare is $25; one-way is $15. To book a seat, contact the Information Centre: 0–3–379 9629.

**From the Wilderness Village**
A shuttle runs to the field daily and costs $7 return.

past the toll gate the road enters a thick forest, in which it remains until Stella Bowl. The road is kept in good repair, but can be a bit bumpy on the section just before Stella Bowl.

Stella Bowl, which was where skiing started at Mount Lyford, is now the secondary area, and is used as required by demand, weather (Stella is more protected from the nor'west wind common in Canterbury), and snow cover on the stretch of road between it and Terako Basin. There are two rope tows in the bowl, one servicing good learners' and 'never-evers' terrain; the other, a steep slope, good for advanced skiers. Tow belts can be borrowed at no charge from the café/shelter at the base of the slope. There is also a frozen lake, Lake Stella, good for ice-skating if you feel like a rest from skiing (or if you just feel like a skate). Ice-skates can be hired from the café/shelter.

Terako Basin, with its large base building (café, hire shop, ski school and ski-patrol offices), is really Mount Lyford's centre. Terako at present is a novice skier's bliss. The lifts are easy to use, the slopes are mostly on gentle gradients, and it is never crowded.

For the advanced skier, there is not much to hold the attention for very long. Surrounding the basin are large, wide, steep faces that, unfortunately, must be climbed in order to ski. This, however, is all about to change. Over the summer of 1994–1995, a platter lift will be installed, running from the slope on the right of the basin up to the ridge of Mount Terako. The northern slopes of the mountain offer superb skiing; several powder-eight competitions have been held there. It is also planned to put a rope tow on these slopes over the summer. Once these developments are complete, the advanced skiing on Mount Lyford will be excellent.

At present, the Terako Basin has two platters. One runs from the base building down to the road, offering the most advanced lift-accessed runs. The other is unique in New Zealand in that it runs up two slopes, with its get-on points in the middle of the lift, at the base of a small valley. This makes it possible to get on the lift to go up either of the facing slopes. The runs down both slopes can be reasonably challenging, but are really best suited to intermediate or beginner skiers. The fixed grip lift is located on a large, broad, gentle slope which is absolutely perfect for beginner and 'never-ever' skiers. It is, arguably, the best learners' slope in the Canterbury region.

There is great ski-touring potential in the region, and it's worth taking touring gear up just to make the trip between the two ski areas, skiing some of the bowls and faces in between. There, you'll see some tempting slopes leading down to the access road. There is also some excellent skiing on the eastern slopes of Mount Terako. It's wise to check on the avalanche hazard with ski patrol before heading out of Terako Basin.

# Hanmer Springs

At 372 metres above sea-level, with its natural hot springs, and surrounded by forested mountains, the tourism potential of Hanmer was noted very early. The hot pools were discovered by Pakeha settlers in 1859, and word soon got out of the therapeutic benefits of bathing in them. The first accommodation house was built there in 1860, and the site was gradually developed by the Tourist and Health Resorts Department until 1922, when the Health Department took charge of administering the resort.

The Queen Mary Hospital for Sick and Wounded Soldiers was opened on 3 June 1916. During, and after both world wars, the hospital was used for rehabilitating returned troops. These days, it is called Queen Mary Hospital and is used for alcoholic rehabilitation. It is no longer the town's major draw card, having been superseded by tourism.

Hanmer is not so much a 'resort', as a 'retreat', and most visitors are there to relax, not to party. As a place to recoup, New Zealand has few equivalents.

## Ski Shops

The **Amuri Ski and Hire Shop** (0–3–315 7125) is in the Greenacres Motel on Conical Hill Road. The shop has a small range of new and second-hand ski gear, often for good prices.

*Hire charges:*
Skis, boots and poles for a day: $18 (Adult); $15 (Youth, 14 and under); $8 (Child, 10 and under).
Snowboards: $29 (day); $16 (half day); $8 (hour).

*Repair charges:*
Vary according to requirements and are not written in stone.

## PLACES TO STAY

There's very little in the way of budget accommodation in Hanmer. The first place to check is **Amuri Backpackers** (0–3–315 7196) run by the Amuri Ski Club. At 41 Conical Hill Road, it's basically a house that has been converted into a lodge. There's a dormitory-style room upstairs and a private double room downstairs. It's a clean, modern place with a good kitchen and living-room area. Use of the washing machine and dryer is free. There's also a TV and a log burner. A night in the dormitory is in the budget price range; in the double room, low.

If there's no room there, try the **Pines Motor Camp** (0–3–315 7152; PO Box 193, Hanmer Springs). It has a budget-priced backpackers' bunkroom. Missing are the frills of the Amuri, but it does have a laundry and good communal kitchen facilities. If there are two or more of you, you can still get budget-priced accommodation in a cabin at the Pines. Cabins don't have toilets or cooking facilities (these are in the main building), but they are cosy. The Pines is on Jacks Pass Road, across the road from the Amuri Ski Areas access road.

If you have still had no luck, try the **Mountain View Holiday Park** (0–3–315 7113) on the main road as you come into town. It has cabins that for two or more give budget accommodation for $31 a night. Failing that, you may have to splash out a little more.

**Hanmer Lodge Hotel** (0–3–315 7022) is a large, Spanish-style villa in the heart of town, at 35 Conical Hill Road. It is surrounded by a large park that includes a tennis court and croquet course. Built in 1932, the lodge is very authentic, with plenty of archways, a couple of towers, a huge ballroom, and a restaurant/bar that looks like it's been taken straight from the set of 'Casablanca' (with a mezzanine dining area, and a staircase that Humphrey and Ingrid would look right at home on). Each room has its own bathroom, tea- and coffee-making facilities, and TV. Prices are in the high range.

The **Glenalvon Bed and Breakfast** (0–3–315 7475) is a fine-looking colonial house at 29 Amuri Avenue. It offers good-quality bedrooms, free tea- and coffee-making facilities, and a guest lounge with a TV and log burner. Prices are in the moderate range. For a small extra charge, you can get a cooked breakfast. Bookings are essential.

## Places to eat

**Keiths Café** (0–3–315 7274) on Conical Hill Road is open between 8:30 am and 9:00 pm. It serves good meals in generous servings for a moderate price. The walls are covered in old farming and forestry tools, and dining is by candlelight. Keith is a keen skier and able to give you a good run-down on local conditions. Low-priced breakfasts are served all day. The café is not licensed and you can't BYO. The cappuccino, though, is excellent. It's a good idea to book ahead.

A couple of doors down from Keiths is the **Jaywalk Café** (0–3–315 7214). The menu includes some tasty dishes (lobster, crayfish, and so on) and the restaurant is done out in the style of a French wine bar. Prices are at the higher end of the moderate range. It's fully licensed (no BYO), open from 6 pm.

The **Alpine Village Inn** (0–3–315 7005) on Jacks Pass Road is a large restaurant often frequented by families, many of whom have spent the day skiing at Amuri. The atmosphere is good and prices are moderate, with small meals in the low price range.

For a sumptuous night out, try the **Old Post Office Restaurant**

(0–3–315 7461) on Jacks Pass Road. The dining is fine and the surroundings lavish. Accordingly, it is highly priced. It's licensed but you can BYO by arrangement.

Also worth checking out is the restaurant in **Hanmer Lodge Hotel** (0–3–315 7021). It has a fine menu and is moderately priced. The Set Menu Option is a very good deal – three courses with tea or coffee for $25. The smoked Amuri Salmon is superb! It is best to book.

## Happening places

Hanmer doesn't have a lot in the way of 'places to party'. About the nearest is the **Lodge Hotel's Sportsmans Public Bar**, a bastion of the proverbial Kiwi pub culture. The 'Sportsman' is a melting pot for Amuri skiers, local farmers and tourists. The wood-burner is huge, quite capable of turning the bar into a sauna. There's also a pool table, and live music some Saturdays.

Hanmer does have a number of places such as **Keiths**, the **Jaywalk Café** and the **Alpine Village Inn** with relaxed surroundings in which a quiet drink or cup of coffee can be thoroughly enjoyed after a hard day skiing.

## Services

*Medical:* The Queen Mary Hospital is on Amuri Avenue, south of the hot pools: 0–3–315 7016.
*Police:* The police station is on Conical Hill Road, next to the Amuri Backpackers: 0–3–315 7117. In emergencies, phone 111.
*Post Office:* There is no post office as such. Stamps can be bought from the Hanmer Book and Gift Shop in the main shopping centre, and there is a post box nearby.

## Information

Hanmer is not short of information centres. Any of the following will help you with any queries you may have.

- ❏ Hurunui Visitor Information Centre on Amuri Avenue, beside the hot pools: 0–3–315 7128.
- ❏ Stage Post Information Bureau on Amuri Avenue, across the road from the hot pools: 0–3–315 7401.
- ❏ Amuri Jet Visitor Centre on Conical Hill Road: 0–3–315 7323.

## Getting around

Hanmer is a small place and walking is really the best way to get around. There are some excellent walking tracks just a short walk from the town centre, and some great mountain-bike tracks, too. Mountain bikes can be hired from Mountain Bikes Dust'n'Dirt (0–3–315 7096) beside the petrol station on Conical Hill Road. A day's hire costs $25; half a day $15; an hour $7.

## Travelling on

There's only one way out of Hanmer, and that's the way you came in. The road takes you south to Highway 7, from where you can go west, toward Lewis Pass, or east toward Christchurch. If you're hitching, it's usually easy to catch a ride back to the highway (and further).

The Hanmer Shuttle makes a daily trip to Christchurch at 2:30 pm. You can book a seat through one of the information centres, or phone 0–3–315 7575 or 025–332 088.

Two companies run services past the Hanmer turn-off on Highway 7, and will make pick-ups from there by arrangement – East West Daily Coach Service (0800–500 251, toll-free) and Mount Cook Land Line (0800–800 287, toll-free).

# Central Canterbury

## Ski Areas

Broken River     129
Craigieburn Valley     135
Erewhon     142
Mount Cheeseman     149
Mount Hutt     156
Mount Olympus     165
Porter Heights     172
Temple Basin     179

## Resorts

Arthurs Pass     186
Christchurch     188
Methven     212
Springfield     220

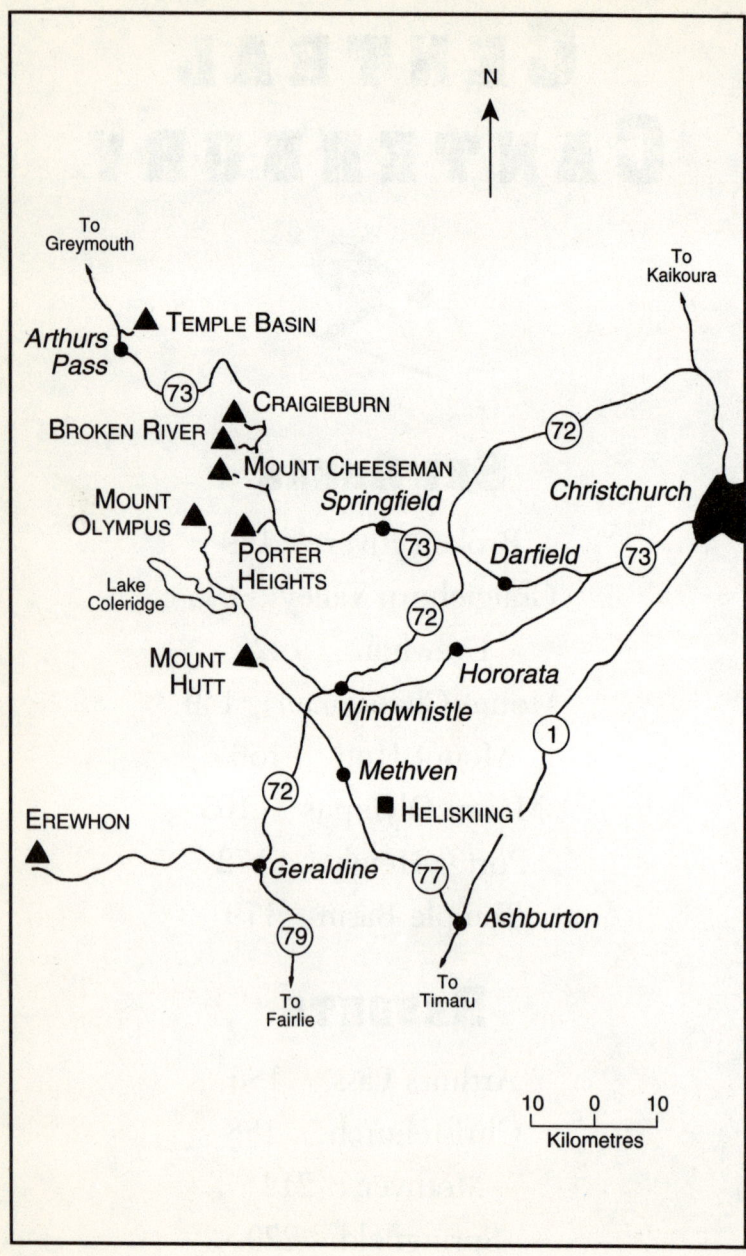

# TUKINO

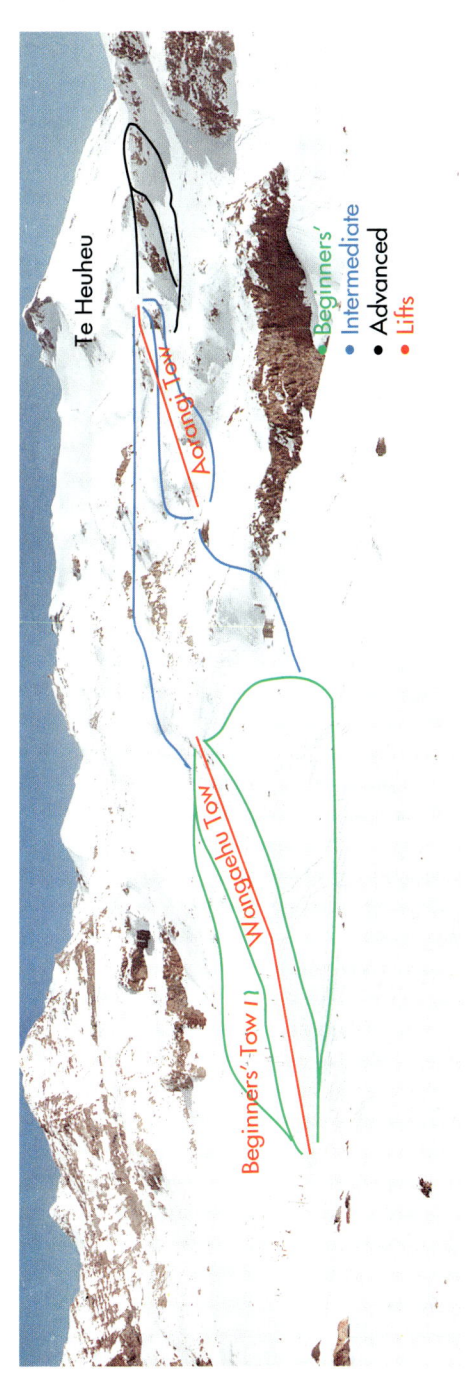

# WHAKAPAPA

| Toilets | Information |
|---|---|
| Food | Ski School |
| Overnight Parking | Snowmaking |

### TRAILS MERGE
When approaching a junction of trails, reduce speed and beware of other skiers.

### TRAIL INFORMATION
These signs are at the start of many runs. The emblem indicates the trail's degree of difficulty. This sign indicates whether the trail is open or closed.

### DANGER
An area marked with this sign is NOT skiable. Marks cliffs, holes, etc.

### CAUTION
An area marked with this sign is skiable but requires caution to negotiate. Marks ice, rocks, etc.

### BLACK MAGIC AREA
This area is outside the ski area boundary. There is no signage, fencing or active avalanche control undertaken in the area. Hazards are not marked. Please respect the back country and ski with care!

### AVALANCHE DANGER
Do not go past this sign. The run is closed due to avalanche danger.

### RUN CLOSED
Do not go past this sign. The run is closed.

### SKI AREA BOUNDARY
There is no Ski Patrol or avalanche control work beyond these signs.

Whakapapa Ski Area wants your skiing experience to be pleasant and safe. Please observe all signs and ski with care. Our staff watch for reckless skiers and if necessary will revoke skiing privileges for the protection of other skiers. Reckless skiing is defined as jumping in blind areas, skiing fast in crowded areas, or skiing fast and out of control.

The sacred mountain peaks Ruapehu, Tongariro and Ngauruhoe burned in the nucleus of New Zealand's first national park. The peaks were gifted to the people of New Zealand by the Paramount Chief of the Ngati Tuwharetoa, Horonuku Te Heu Heu Tukino, in September 1887, thus ensuring their protection for all people for all time. Whakapapa, New Zealand's largest ski field, is part of Tongariro National Park, New Zealand's oldest national park, and a world heritage area.

# MANGANUI

# MOUNT ROBERT

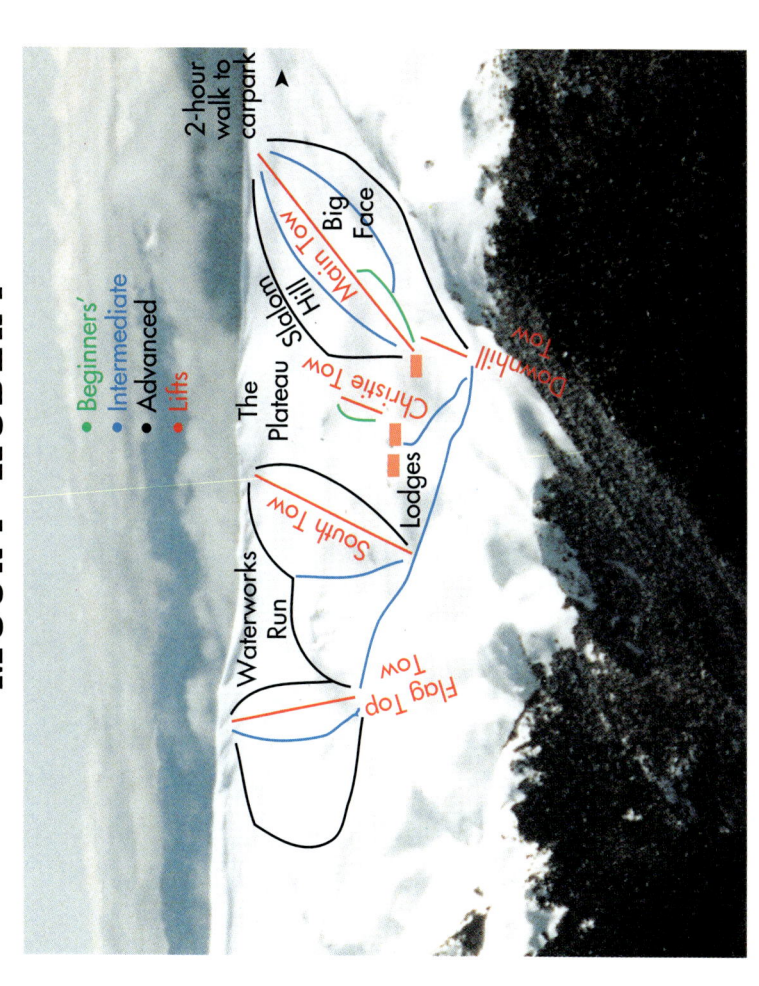

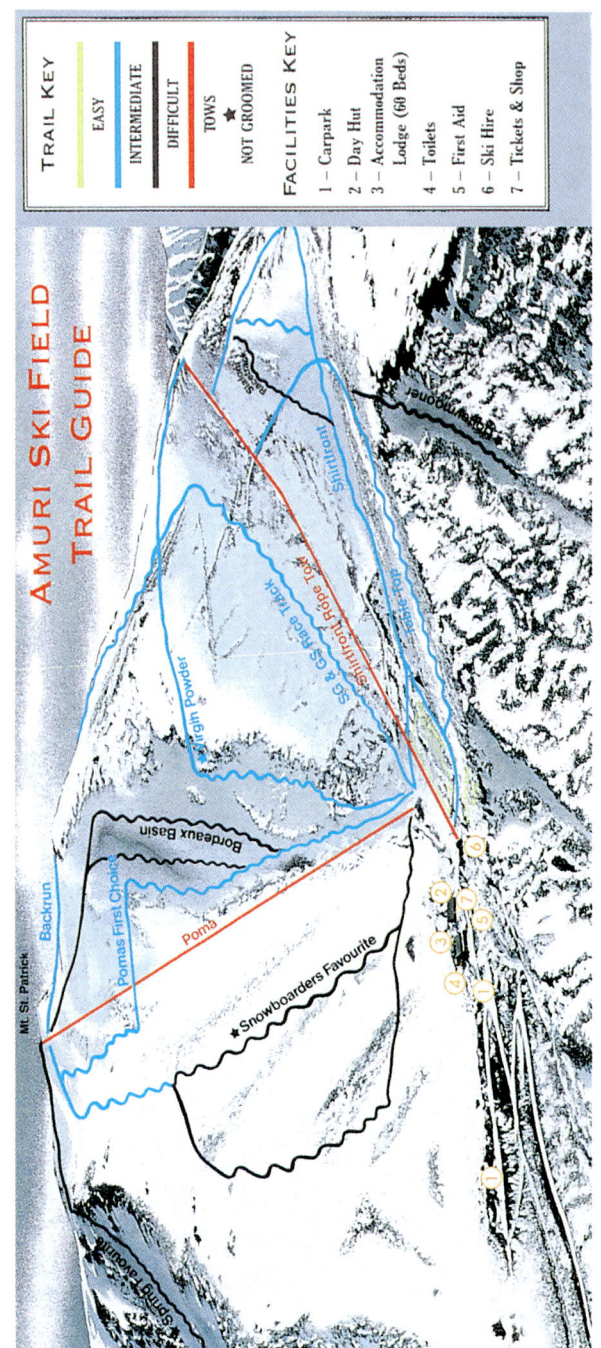

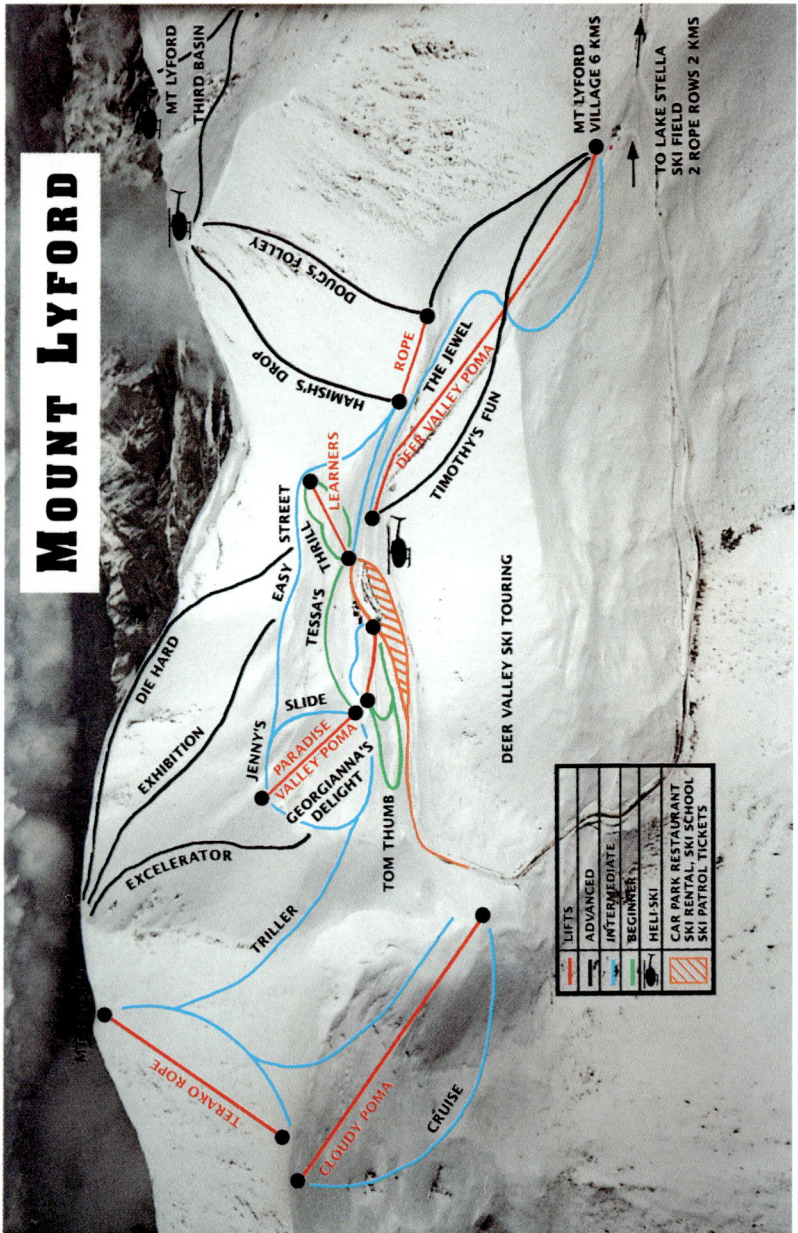

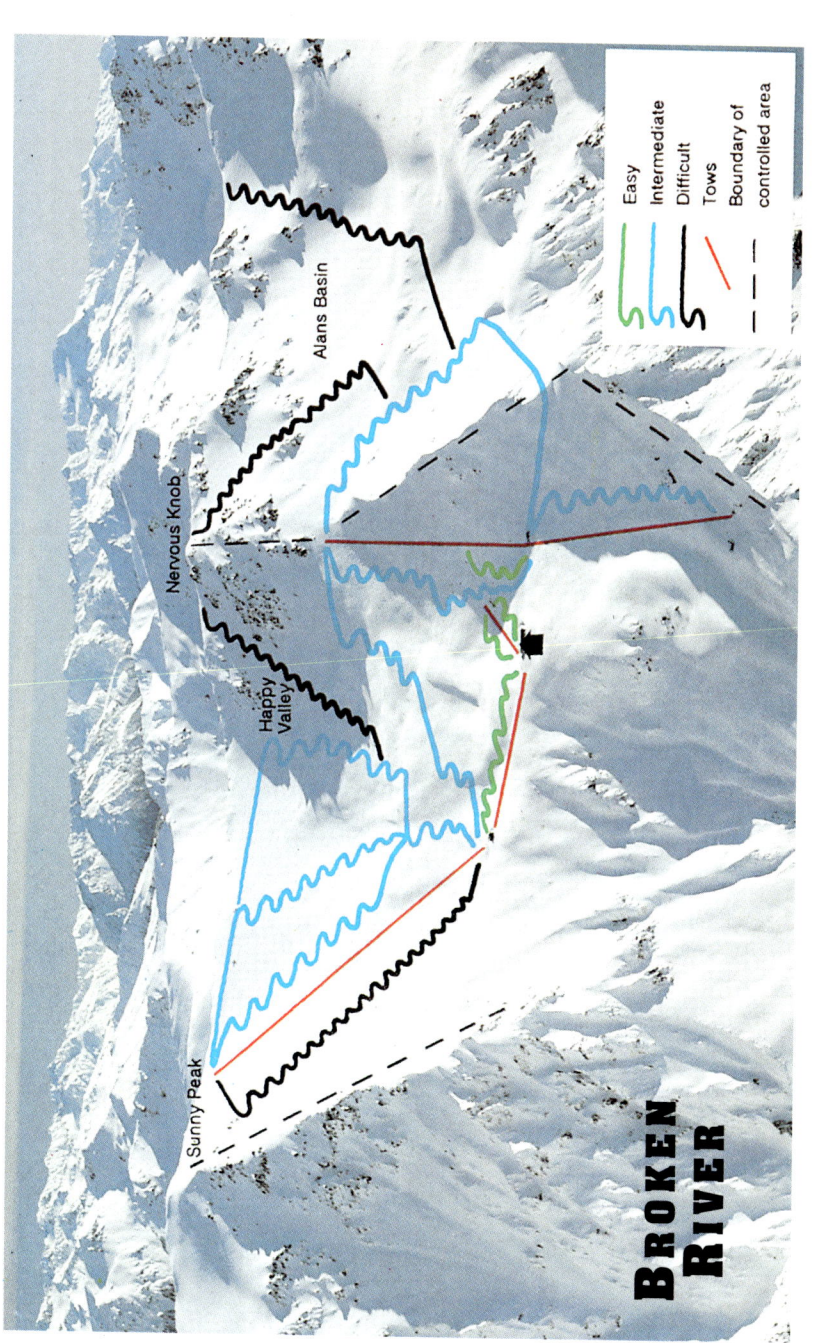

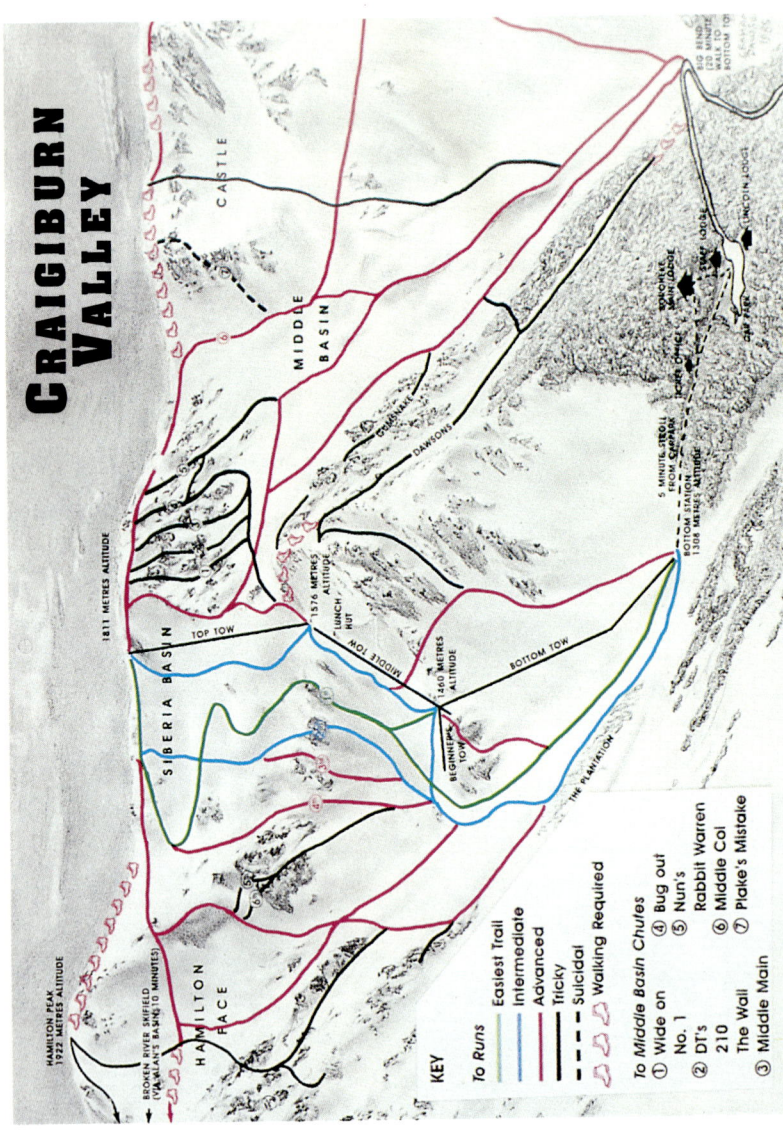

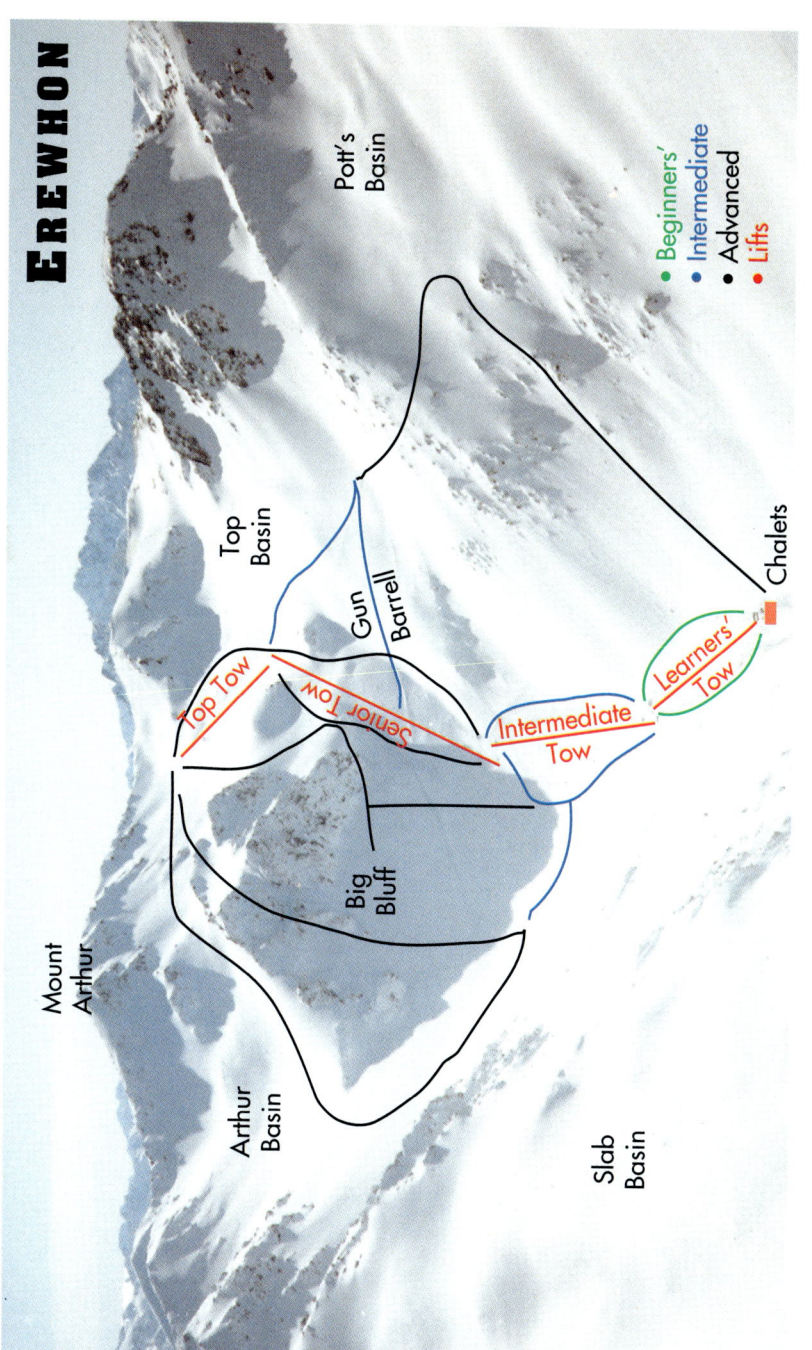

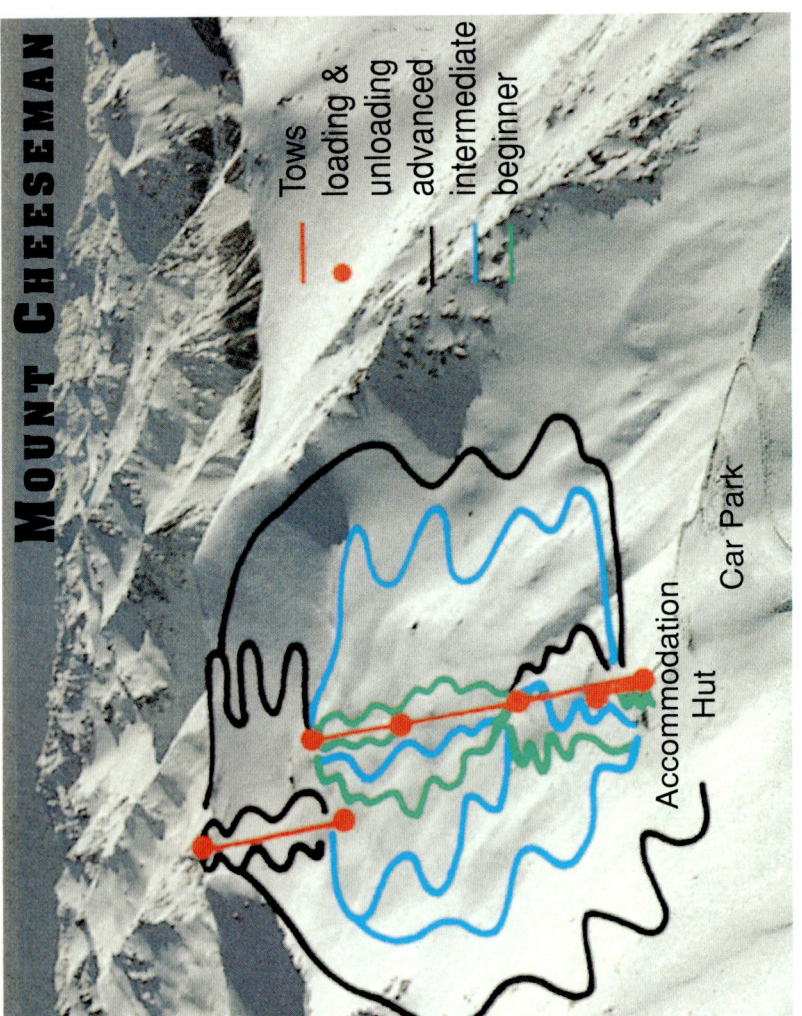

Snowboarding above Crater Lake, Mount Ruapehu.

Happy Valley learners' area, Whakapapa.

Manganui ski area, Mount Taranaki.

Lodge, Mount Robert.

Looking from Hamilton Face toward Middle Basin, Craigieburn Valley.

Raft race during the annual Christchurch Winter Festival at Mount Cheeseman.

T2 T-bar, with Big Mama on the left and Bluff Face on the right, Porter Heights.

Temple Tow, Temple Basin.

South Basin, Fox Peak.

Top of the T-bar at Ohau ski area, with Lake Ohau in the background.

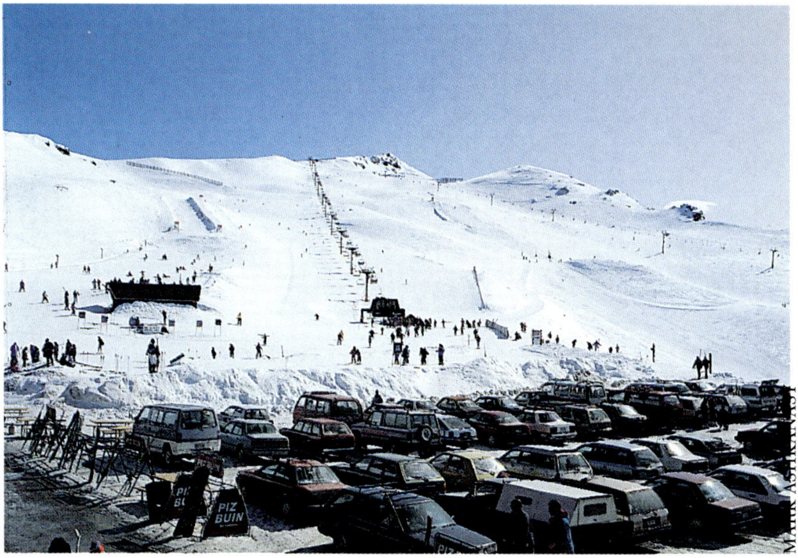

MacDougall's Quad, Cardrona.

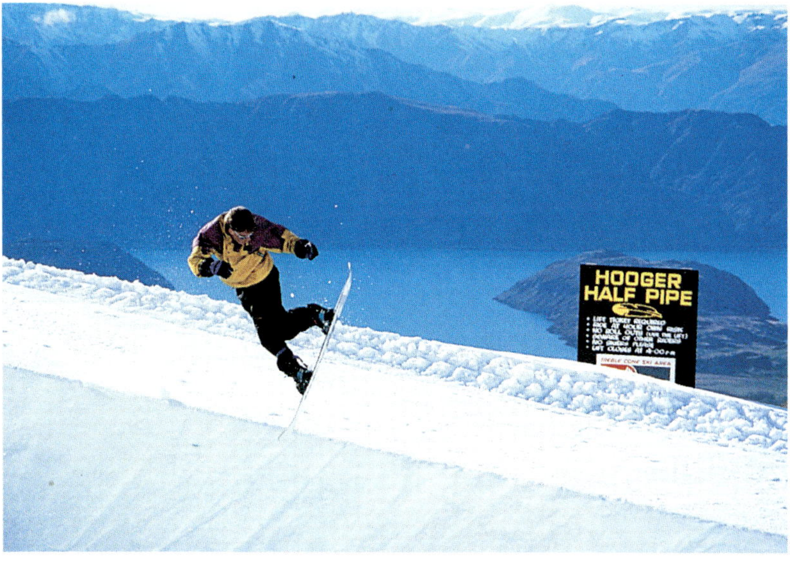

Snowboarders half-pipe at Treble Cone, with Lake Wanaka in background.

Cross-country skiing at Waiorau Nordic.

Heliskiing in the Southern Alps.

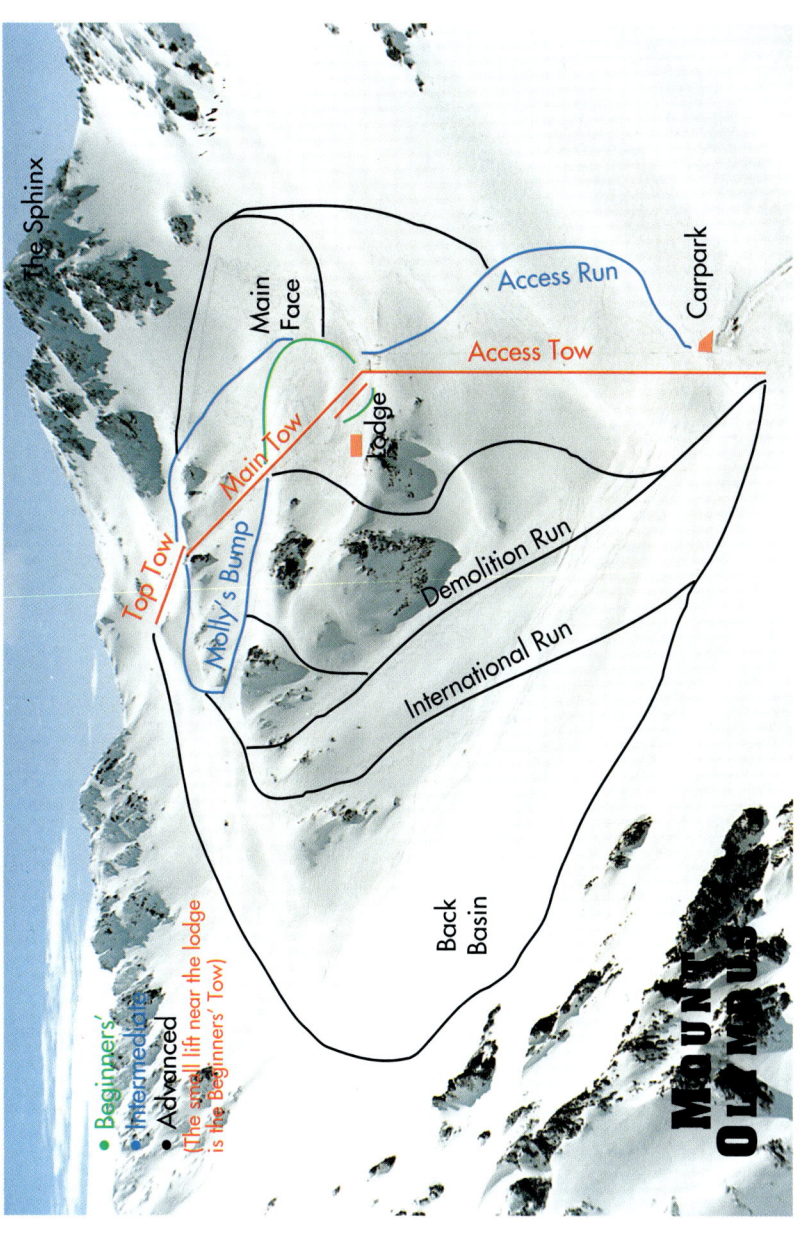

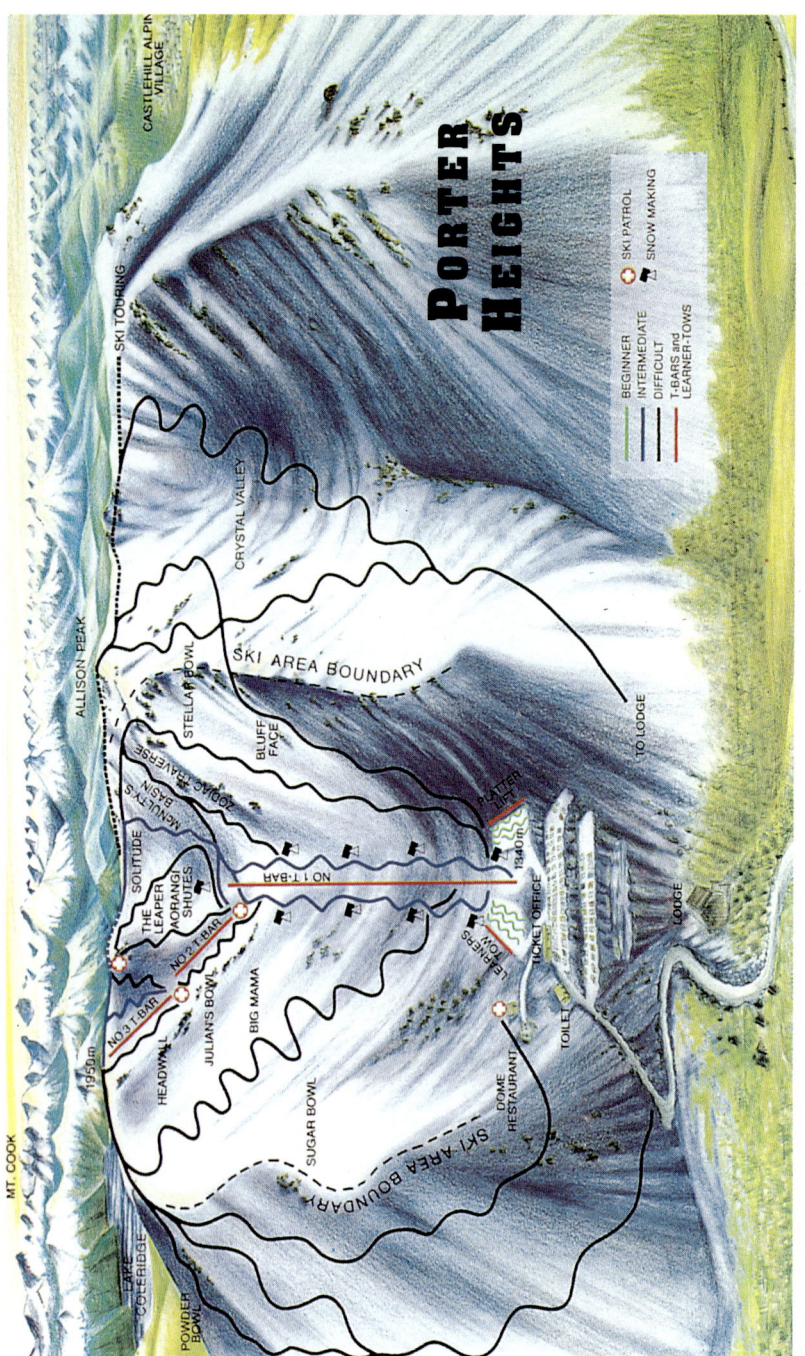

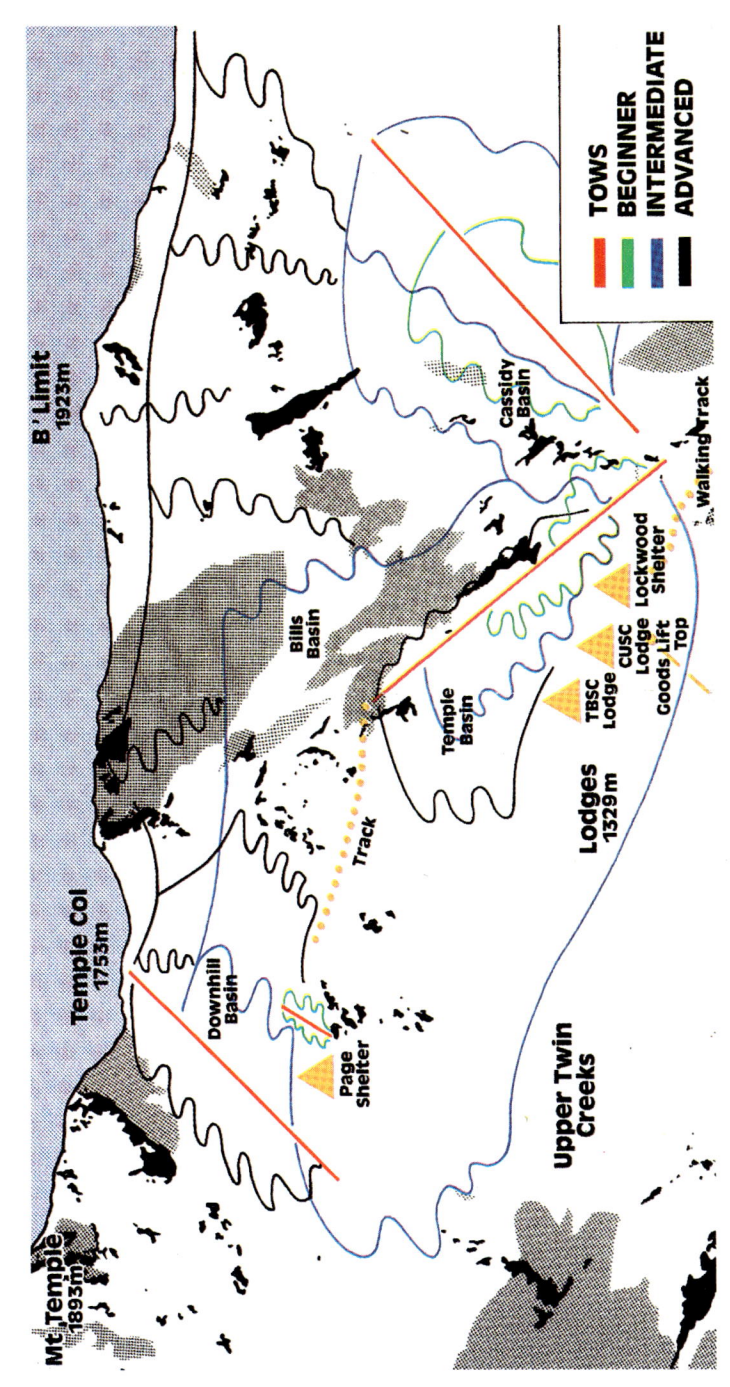

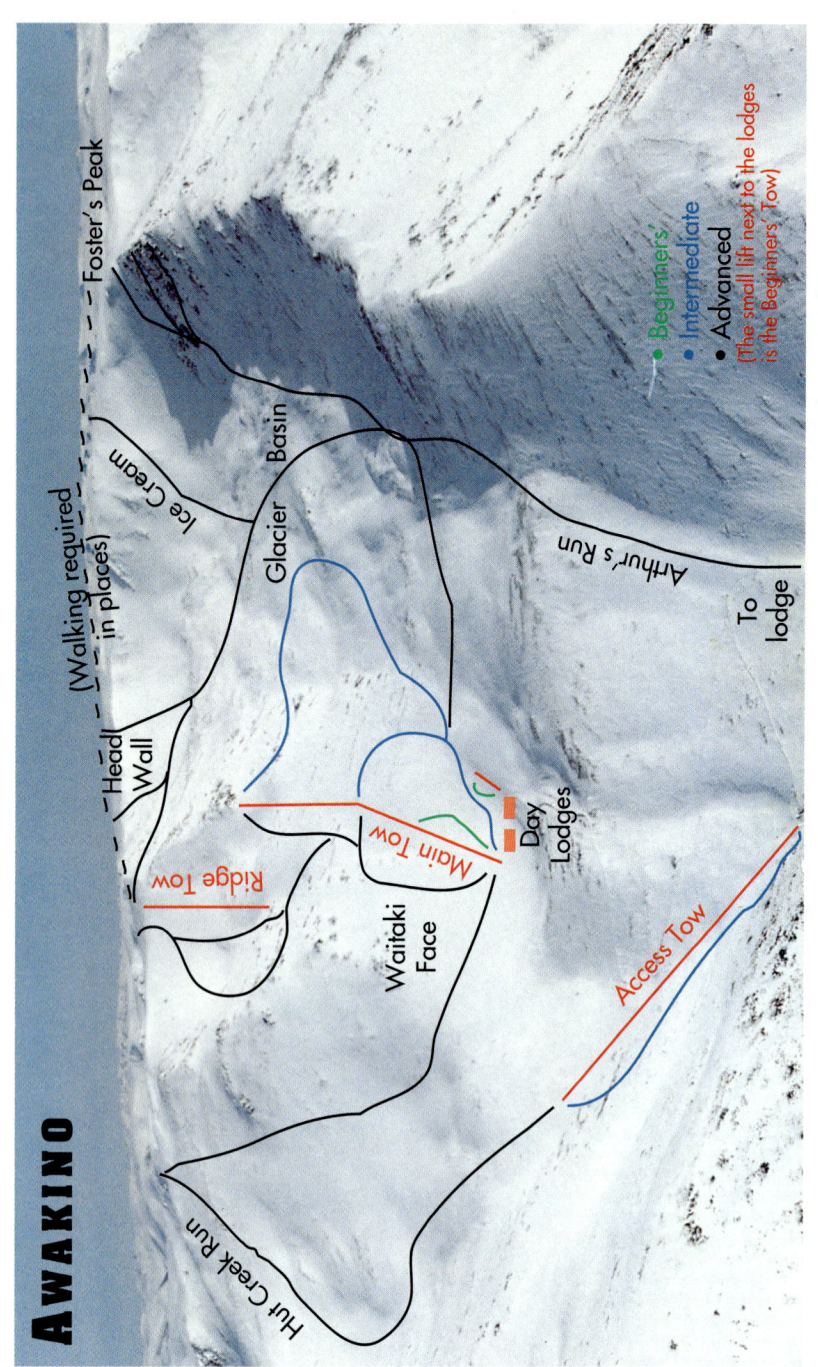

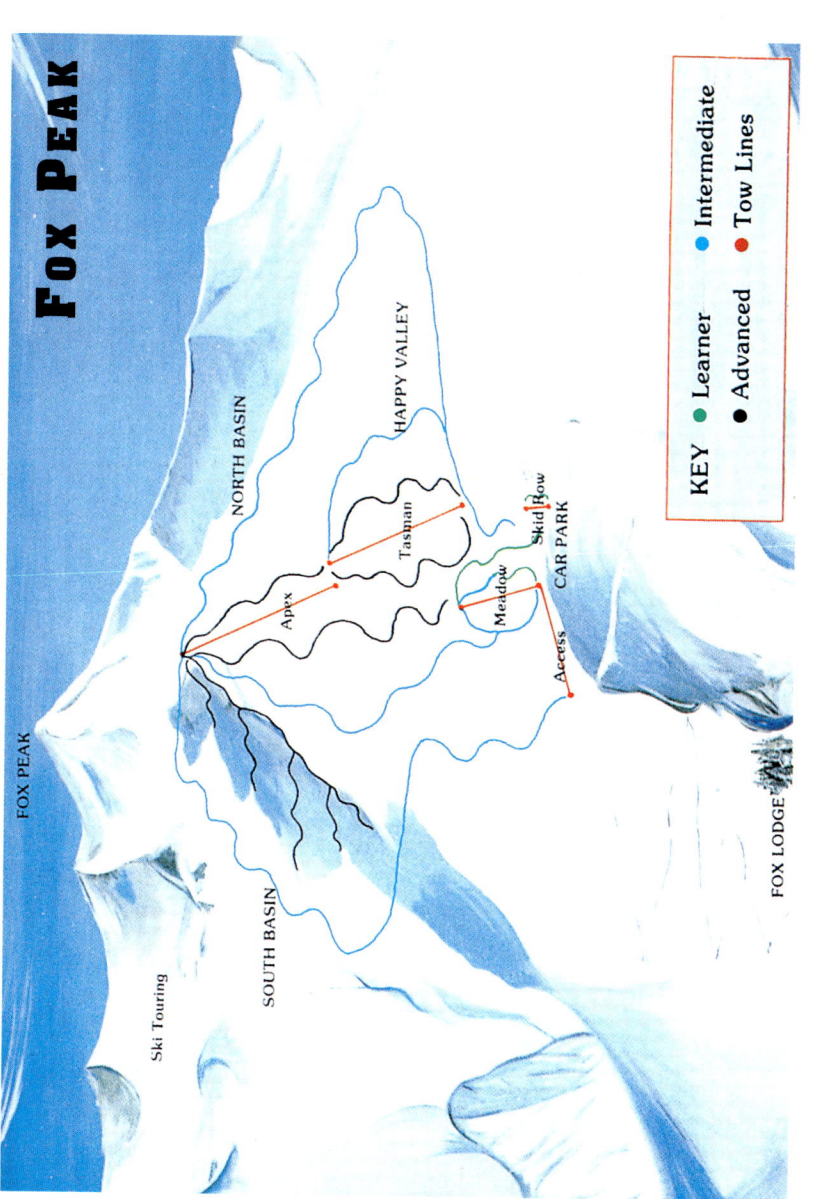

# MOUNT DOBSON

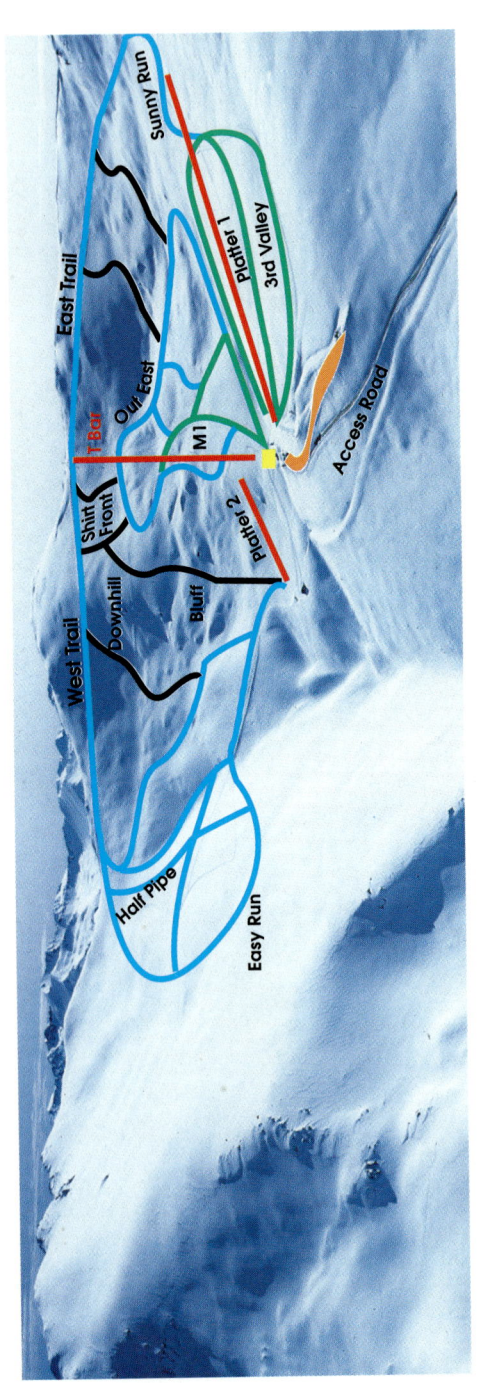

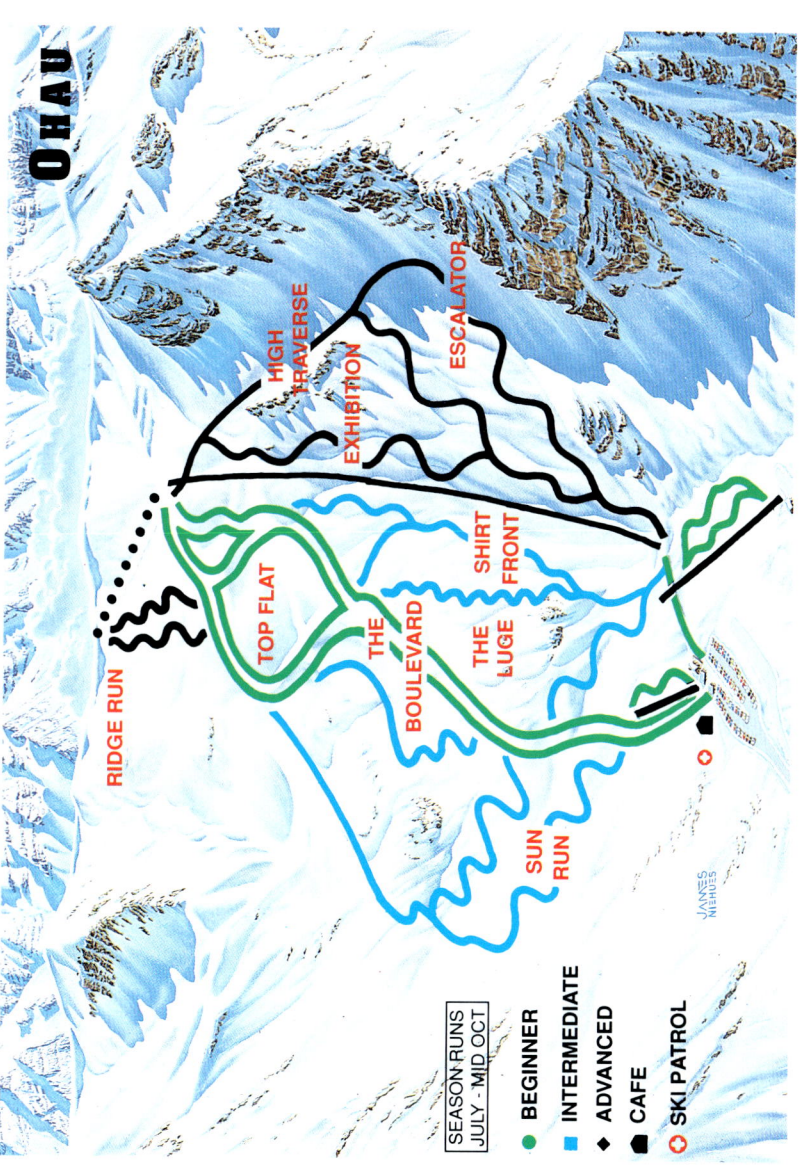

# CARDRONA

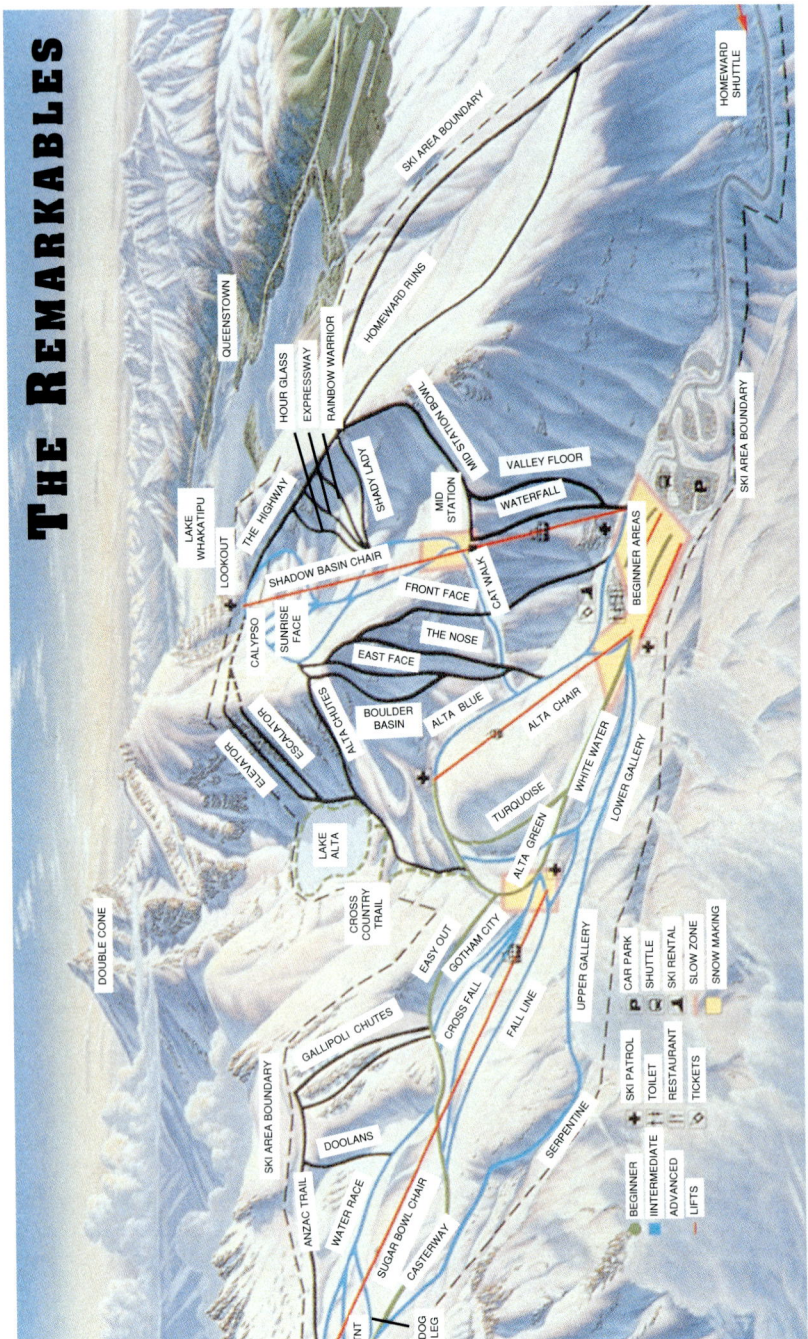

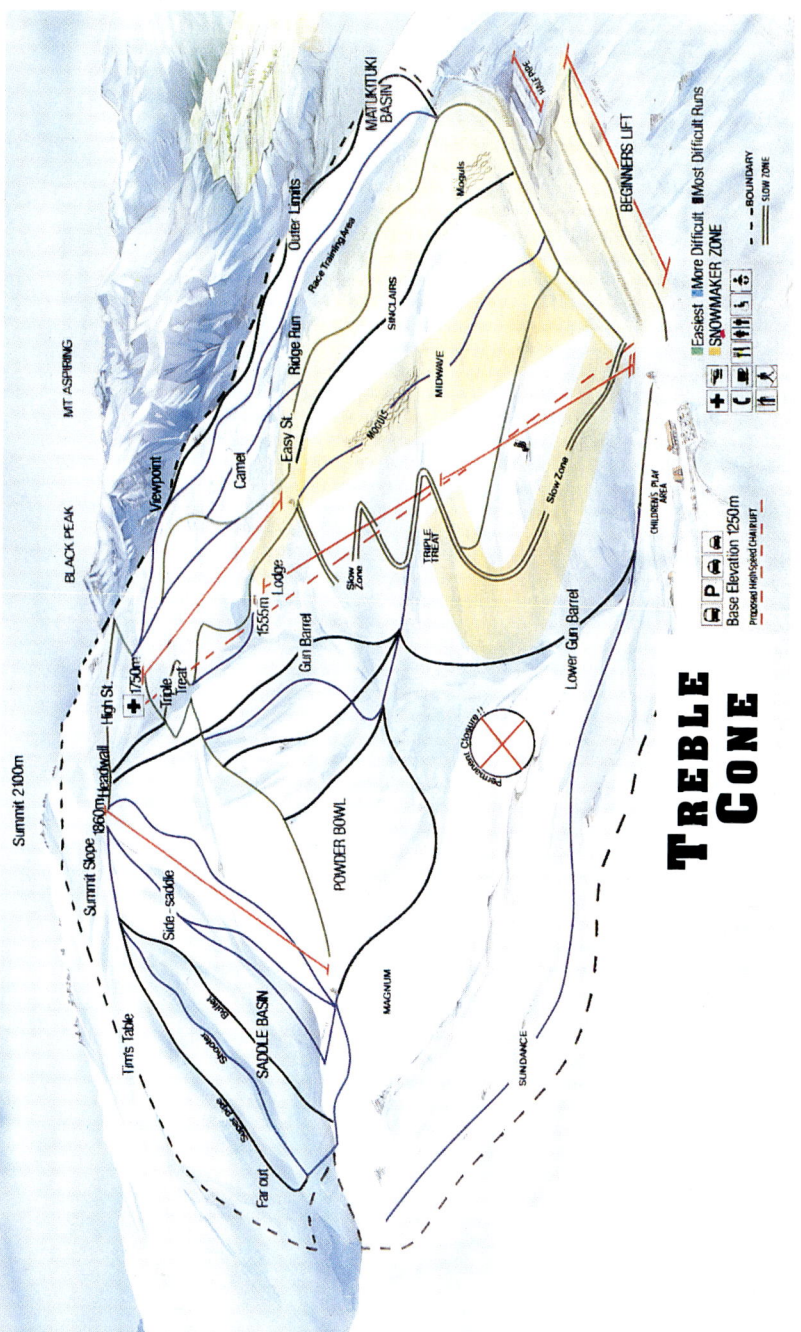

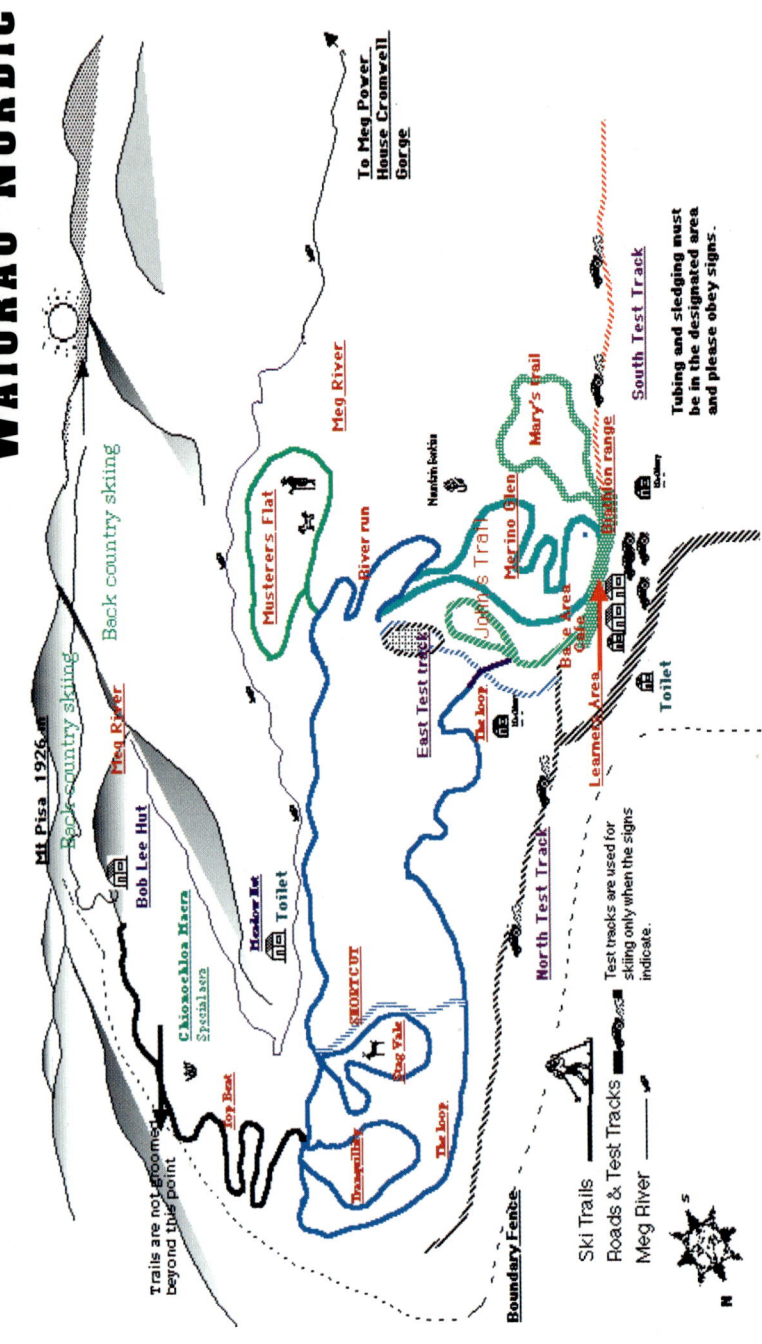

# BROKEN RIVER

## HISTORY

The Broken River Ski Club's roots lie in the Rangiora Youth Recreational Club. Formed in Rangiora after World War Two, 64 members set up a 'Winter Sports Section' and spent time every winter at Lake Lyndon, just west of Porters Pass, where they'd ice-skate, tramp, climb and occasionally ski. In pursuit of further activities, they made a ten-day skiing visit to Coronet Peak, Queenstown, in 1950. After that, members found that Porters Pass, where they did most of their skiing, left something to be desired. In 1952, club president Jack Newell wrote: '. . . rocks and tussocks were rather rough on our skis and bodies'.

Members of the group made a few visits to the Canterbury Mountaineering Club's Craigieburn ski area, and it was there that some Canterbury members offered to show the visitors a nearby basin that might be suitable for developing into a ski area. On 7 October 1950, six of the group and five Canterbury members tramped to the head of the Broken River forks. On viewing the large open basin with its southeasterly aspect, the group can't have needed much convincing that the area had great potential.

During Easter weekend 1951, Rangiora club members began clearing a track from Cave Stream (on Highway 73) up to the bushline. Almost every weekend from then on was a 'working bee', with members starting to cut a road with picks and shovels in May. A crawler tractor with a bulldozer blade was obtained for the cause and, during the Christmas period of 1951–52, with a permanent camp established at Cave Stream, progress on the track picked up. The North Canterbury Ski Club, revolving primarily around nine enthusiasts, was formed in February 1952. Thereafter, there was no longer any formal association with the Youth Recreational Club.

In May of the same year, the club prepared a site for a hut on the bushline. Work on the access road was still under way, but there was a rough foot track up to the hut site. With the help of 28 visitors, mostly Canterbury Mountaineering Club members and some Canterbury Winter Sports Club and Craigieburn Ski Club members, building materials were deposited at Cave Stream and the unenviable task of packing them up to the hut site began. Timber for the hut came from the trees cleared for

##  Broken River

- *Location:* 123 km from Christchurch.
  53 km from Springfield.
- *Season:* Usually open mid to late June, closing mid to late October.
- *Elevation:* The highest lift takes you to 1783 metres on Sunny Peak. The day lodge is at 1500 metres.
- *Vertical drop:* 470 metres from the top of the top lift to the base of the access tow.
- *Terrain:* Beginner 20%, Intermediate 50%, Advanced 30%.
- *Snowmaking:* None.
- *Groomers:* One.
- *Road toll:* None.
- *Lifts:* Four rope tows. Low charge, with student, junior and over 60s reductions. Under 10s are free.
- *Ski hire:* None.
- *Ski school:* Two instructors.
  Group lesson (at least four): $10 per hour.
  Private lesson: $25 per hour.

the road and milled in Rangiora. Weekends throughout the rest of 1952 and early 1953 were spent packing these materials to the site and constructing the White Star Hut.

Over the winter of 1952, a rope tow was constructed in Christchurch and transported to the base of the access road. This tow, which was powered by an old 'Rugby' car engine (hence the name of the lift) was mounted on a sled and dragged up the track to its final position. By the start of the 1953 season,

## Broken River

*Ski weeks:* These include accommodation from 10:00 am Sunday to 10:00 am the following Saturday, lift fees from Sunday to Saturday, three vouchers for instruction, one evening's skiing under lights, and dinners and breakfasts. Non-peak prices are $280 (Adult); $210 (Junior); $130 (Under 10s). A ski week during peak season (6 August–2 September) is $350 (Adult); $275 (Junior; $165 (Under 10s). For enquiries, phone 0–3-318 8713, or write to the address below.

*Accomm:* There are three lodges – Lyndon and Broken River with 24 bunks each, and White Star with 14. With the three huts nestled amongst the beech trees and their lights reflecting on the snow, the place at night has a real Swiss mountain village appearance. If you're up there for a night, the sauna (below White Star) is not to be missed. Ask a club member for details and treat yourself to the ultimate muscle-soothing experience. Dinner, bed and breakfast is $30 for adults, $25 for anyone else.

*Address:* Broken River Ski Club, PO Box 2718, Christchurch. Telephone: 0–3-318 8713.

*Snow reports:* Phone The Press Inpho Ski Line 0–3-366 6644, then 1101.

the club had grown to 32 financial members, and skiing began in the Broken River Basin.

Since then, the club has gradually developed its own niche in the New Zealand ski industry. It is a unique field and certainly

---

### GETTING THERE

**From Christchurch**
*By car*
Follow the instructions for Porter Heights, carrying on a further ten kilometres along Highway 73 to get to the Broken River turn-off on your left.

*Hitching*
Follow the instructions for Porter Heights. Fewer people will be going to Broken River so it would be an idea to be on the road earlier, say by 7:30 am. In fact, your chances of getting a lift to Broken River are not great, so try calling the club (0–3–318 8713) a few days before heading up. They may put you on to someone taking a car. The Snow and Surf Ski Shop has the Broken River booking list and, if you leave your name there, someone going up will contact you.

*Shuttles and buses*
There are no regular shuttle or bus services, although one of the ski shuttle companies may run a trip provided there are enough of you. Snowman Shuttles, for example, will run a trip for four or more people. See the Mount Hutt section for contact details.

Otherwise, you can catch the Coast To Coast shuttle and get dropped off at the access road, from where it's quite easy hitching. The Coast To Coast shuttle makes pick-ups around Christchurch from 7:30 am. A one-way fare is $25. Book on 0800–800 847 (toll-free).

one of the more progressive of the country's ski clubs. This is perhaps best exemplified by the club's funicular goods lift – 'The Inclinator' (constructed in 1984–85). The club's name was changed to the Broken River Ski Club in May 1979.

## THE SKI AREA

The access road takes you on a winding trip through a beautiful beech forest before arriving at the base of the 'Inclinator', a goods tramway that carries your gear up to the lodges. The Inclinator runs daily from 9:00 to 10:00 am and from 4:30 to 5:30 pm. Once you've loaded the lift, start walking up the road. After a ten-minute walk, you'll see a sign and a track on the left-hand side. The track zigzags through the forest and, after ten or 15 minutes, brings you to Lyndon Lodge on the bushline. The Inclinator's top station is here and, all going well, your gear will be there too. From Lyndon Lodge it's a further five-minute walk up past the other lodges to the base of the access tow, where there's a small hut with a cache of tow belts for use on the lifts. There's no charge for these.

The first thing you'll probably want to do is drop off your lunch at the day lodge. As you go up the access tow, the lodge will come into view on your left. Once high enough on the tow, it's a short traverse to the lodge.

In front of the lodge, there's a small beginners' area that has a gentle gradient and is suitable for first-timers. The step up from this is either the run alongside Traverse Tow, or from half-way between the mid-station and the top of the access tow down to the lodge.

Broken River is ideally suited to intermediate and advanced skiers, especially those who enjoy untracked powder. The groomer cuts trails in the centre of the basin but leaves much of it, and all of Alan's Basin, untouched. Main Tow must be the fastest nut-cracker tow in the country and wastes no time in getting you back to the top. From the top of the tow you can traverse to the left and pick your route down into the bowl, or head to the right on to the steeper Sunny Peak face. Appropriately named, Sunny Peak is in the sun from 9:00 am every day of the season – provided the sun is out, of course.

If you want to ski the chutes on Nervous Knob (which is named for a reason) or the slopes of Alan's Basin, traverse as far along the ridge to the left of Main Tow as you can. After the traverse it's about a ten-minute walk to the top of Nervous Knob. Happy Valley is a great constant gradient slope down to the centre of the bowl. The clearly visible chute on Nervous Knob (just inside the ski area boundary) is called Margot's Gut. It's relatively easy to get into and is a steep, not too narrow, run down to the top of the access tow, from where you can ski over the ridge into Alan's Basin for a few turns before returning to the main bowl.

If you love powder and wide open spaces, and don't mind the short walk up Nervous Knob, you'll be tempted to spend the whole day making the circuit between Main Tow, Nervous Knob and Alan's Basin. From the top of Nervous Knob looking north you can see the top of Hamilton Peak, over the other side of which is the Craigieburn Valley ski area. It's possible to traverse to this point (you'll have to walk for short distances) and ski into Craigieburn Valley, where Broken River day passes are accepted on lifts. This also applies to skiers coming to Broken River from Craigieburn.

If you hear club members joking about their snowmaking, they're not referring to the conventional method of artificially making snow, but Broken River's own natural snowmaking machine. The field is in an east-facing basin with ridges to its west and south. The predominant winds, nor'westers and southerlies, blow snow over these ridges and dump it into the basin. It's actually possible to stand at the top of Main Tow on a windy nor'west day and see this natural snowmaking machine in action. Members have just to find a way to switch the machine on and off at will!

# CRAIGIEBURN VALLEY

## HISTORY

In July 1947, a group of members from the Canterbury Mountaineering Club – John Sampson, Geoff Harrow, Ed Cotter and his sister Judith – decided to look into the possibility of skiing in the Craigieburn Valley. The idea of skiing in the winter to keep fit for climbing in the summer was the motivating factor.

The group visited the upper reaches of the valley, and presented a report and photographs to the club committee. The club approved the idea and obtained permission from the Forest Service to cut a walking track up to the slopes. The eight-kilometre track was cut by volunteers using hand tools during the summer weekends of 1947–48. A club member, Fred Hulston, spent time over that summer building a pre-fabricated hut in Christchurch. This was later carried up to a prepared site and constructed by club members between January and March 1948. Also that year, a number of small private huts were built on the mountain by club members. While many of these have been removed, some remain in use today.

Organised skiing began in the 1948 season. After one season of carrying their gear for an hour and a half to the hut and then climbing a further half hour for a good run, members saw the need for some sort of ski tow. The following summer, John Sampson and helpers constructed the 'Jonsam Allbits Ski Tow', a rope tow that served the club faithfully for the next 12 years.

In 1954, the skiing fraternity of the mountaineering club decided to split away and form the Craigieburn Valley Ski Club. The committee of the newly formed club wasted no time in

# Craigieburn Valley

*Location:* 120 km from Christchurch.
50 km from Springfield.

*Season:* Usually late June/early July through to mid/late October.

*Elevation:* Hamilton Peak, rising above the field and between it and Broken River, is 1917 metres.
Craigieburn's 'top tow' takes you to 1811 metres.
The bottom station of Bottom Tow is at 1308 metres.
The 'lunch hut' is at 1570 metres.

*Vertical drop:* 609 metres.

*Terrain:* Beginner 0%, Intermediate 60%, Advanced 40%.

*Snowmaking:* None.

*Groomers:* None.

*Road toll:* None.

*Lifts:* Four rope tows.
Moderate charge. Student and youth rates apply.
Tow-belt hire is $2 day or $10 week, with $10 deposit.

*Ski hire:* None.

*Specials:* For $50 you get a day pass, instruction, accommodation in the Koroheke Lodge and three meals. This may change for the 1995 season – phone the club to check on the current deals. Bookings are essential.
For any enquiries or bookings, write to the address below or phone the Craigieburn Infoline 0-3-365 2514.

*Ski school:* Three instructors.

Group (at least four people):

$25 per hour (Adult); $10 per hour (Under 18).

Private: $25 (Adult) per hour; $15 per hour (Under 18).

#  Craigieburn Valley

*Ski weeks:* A ski week starts on Sunday night and finishes Saturday morning. The price, depending on the week, varies from $295–$395 (Adult). An under-18 rate ($240–$315) applies on some weeks only. This price covers accommodation, all meals from Sunday night to Saturday morning, seven days' skiing and five lessons of 90 minutes.

Discounts are offered to groups of six or more on some weeks and any bookings made before the end of May get a $20 discount.

For any enquiries or bookings, write to the address below or phone the Craigieburn Infoline 0–3–365 2514.

*Accomm:* The Koroheke Lodge is a short ski from the bottom of Bottom Tow. The lodge has room for 48 in six-person bunk rooms, as well as five double rooms. There's a large living area and kitchen, a large drying room and a ski-tuning workshop. The lodge also has a small store from which you can buy anything you may have forgotten. You can get dinner, bed and breakfast in the lodge for a moderate charge, with a special rate for under 18s. For enquiries or to book, contact the address below.

*Address:* Craigieburn Valley Ski Club, PO Box 2152, Christchurch. Telephone: 0–3–365 2514.

*Snow reports:* The C93FM Snowphone 0–3–366 6782; or the Press Inpho Ski line 0–3–366 6644, then 1101.

developing the area. Following the 1954 season, members began installing New Zealand's first T-bar. It would be 18 years before another ski area in the Canterbury region installed a T-bar.

An operation that could well be called the New Zealand ski industry's most ambitious, it involved an air drop of four and a half tons of ski tow equipment from a New Zealand Air Force Bristol Freighter. On 24 December 1954, the aircraft made 20 runs above the ski area, flying about 50 feet above the ground while three crew members bundled the parts, attached to static line parachutes, out the door. The entire operation took less than an hour.

After all that, the T-bar proved to be unsatisfactory, fell into

## Getting there

**From Christchurch**

*By car*
Follow the instructions for Porter Heights and just carry on a further 11 kilometres along Highway 73 to get to the Craigieburn turn-off. The field is a further six kilometres.

*Hitching*
Follow the instructions for Porter Heights, only there will probably be fewer people going to Craigieburn so it would be an idea to be on the road by 7:30 am.

*Shuttles and buses*
The Snowman Shuttle makes a daily trip to Craigieburn on demand, though requires at least four people to run. It starts making pick-ups from 7:15 am, arriving on the mountain at 9:15 am. A return fare is $25 for adults or students. There is no one-way fare. A weekend or week return fare is $40. To book, phone 0–3–364 7223.

disrepair, and was eventually dismantled. It used to run from where the base of Middle Tow is now, up through the 2nd Gut and on to the flat area in Siberia Basin.

Over the summer of 1960–61, contractors, club members and the Forest Service began constructing a road up to the ski slopes, a much-welcomed development for club members. Celebrations on 9 April 1961, when the road was officially opened, involved bagpipers perched on the front of utility vehicles travelling in convoy. Members, most likely reminiscing about their walks up to the lodge in days gone by, partied into the early hours; a pastime that has been continued by successive members to this very day.

Over the summer of 1965, the club purchased a tractor motor which it installed at the junction of its three rope tows – the Bottom, Beginners' and Middle Tows. Using one motor to run three rope tows was thought to be a world first.

During the summer of 1986 the club took on another major project. A Poma lift was purchased from the Whakapapa ski area and installed on the north face of Hamilton Peak. Due entirely to its location and the weather conditions it was subject to, the lift proved to be of no use and never actually carried a customer. It was purchased by Mount Lyford in 1994.

In recent years, the club's claim to fame has been the fact that the American extreme skier-guru, Glen Plake, is a member of the club and makes regular visits to the field, calling it, 'Simply the best skifield terrain in the Southern Hemisphere'.

## THE SKI AREA

First, it must be noted that Craigieburn does live up to its reputation – it's big, it's steep and it's challenging. For advanced skiers it can be heaven; for intermediates, it's a great learning ground; for beginners, it can be sheer hell! Rest assured, though, that no field in New Zealand will pose you a problem if you can master Craigieburn.

The six-kilometre access road winds through beech forest

and, although requiring caution, is generally a pleasant drive. You eventually come to the car park and a few huts. Once the car is parked and the paraphernalia donned you can start walking the track leading uphill into the forest. A short way along the track is the ticket office, definitely the most picturesque in the country, where you can also hire tow belts. From the ticket office it's a five-minute walk to the base of Bottom Tow.

Bottom Tow is a rope tow and not the best for the uninitiated. About a third of the way up it does a 40-degree turn, which can be quite tricky for even the most experienced rope tow users. A good warm-up run is from the top of Bottom Tow to the base via the gully on the right. Chances are, though, that once you're at the top of Bottom Tow and can see the extent of Siberia Basin and Hamilton Face, you'll want to go straight to the top. This isn't a bad idea either as Siberia Basin down to the base of Top Tow is amongst the easiest skiing of the area.

When skiing Siberia Basin there's a small roll before you arrive at the Guts. The Guts are numbered from 1st to 6th and, as coincidence would have it, get trickier the higher the number. In fact, they couldn't have been designed better as a training ground for building up to the chutes in Middle Basin. If you start in 1st Gut and progress to 5th and 6th confidently by lunchtime, you can spend the afternoon attempting the chutes. Be warned: if you can't ski the 5th and 6th Guts well, stay away from the chutes. They can firmly place the fear of God in anyone!

From the top of Top Tow, it's an easy traverse to Hamilton Face. If you have the time, make the 15-minute climb to the top of Hamilton Peak. The 360-degree vista is magnificent, as is the skiing down the upper Hamilton Face. It's possible to cross the ridge and ski into Alan's Basin and over to the Broken River ski area from Hamilton Face. Craigieburn passes are accepted at Broken River. The traverse back from Broken River requires a little more climbing.

Middle Basin is accessed by a traverse from Top Tow. If you

don't fancy going down the chutes, carry on to the col. The basin is huge and it's really just a matter of choosing your route down. It's about as close as you'll get to heliskiing without getting in a chopper. Plake's Mistake speaks for itself, more so if you've seen his movies. The walk to Castle is worth it for advanced skiers. First tracks are basically guaranteed.

The whole Middle Basin and beyond is great ski-touring country. Before heading into Middle Basin it would be advisable to ask Ski Patrol about conditions.

It's not necessary to ski all the way down Middle Basin to Big Bend. There is a walking track through the forest that takes you to Koroheke Lodge. You'll find the track about half-way up the forest from Big Bend.

Other runs advanced skiers should try are Dawsons, a long run of short turns through the forest, and the runs to the right of Hamilton Face. It's a long, steep run to the base of Bottom Tow.

The lunch hut close to the top of Middle Tow is a fairly basic affair, but full of character. There's no running water, but if you're thirsty there's a hose with fresh mountain water just above the base of Middle Tow. It tastes like no other water, and were it bottled and sold could be quite a source of revenue for the club.

# EREWHON

## HISTORY

The sheep station Erewhon was originally called Stronechrubie by its first European settler, George McRae, a Scotsman who named it after his home town in the Scottish Highlands. English author Samuel Butler travelled to New Zealand in 1859 and spent four and a half years sheep farming at the Mesopotamia Station, across the Rangitata River and ten kilometres south of Stronechrubie. Years later, when Butler was back in England and his acclaimed book *Erewhon* had been published (1872), Stronechrubie's name was changed to Erewhon.

In 1943, runholder Arthur Urquhart took over the 35,300-acre station, later adding to it the 27,000-acre Mount Possession station. Initially, Urquhart's interests lay solely in sheep farming, particularly merinos. Starting with a flock of 2000, he built it up to 9000 by 1964, the year he decided to make use of the area as a tourist attraction. The region was able to offer the visitor a range of activities – ice-skating, horse-riding, mountaineering, fishing, tramping, hunting, jet boating and skiing.

Over the summer of 1964–65, a road was put in to a basin on Mount Potts above the Erewhon homestead, and a rope tow installed and operational for the '65 season. Urquhart named the ski area Powder Snow Valley and became the first person to wholly own a private ski area in New Zealand. It was Canterbury's first privately owned commercial ski area. All the other ski areas in the province were operated by clubs.

Urquhart had great foresight and grand plans. In 1966, he constructed an airstrip big enough for a DC-3 aircraft; converted the old Erewhon homestead to provide accommodation for 30 skiers; and turned a woolshed into a community hall and dance floor for visitors. Until these developments, only a few hundred cars would travel the road to

Erewhon each year. In 1967, 4000 visitors stayed in the homestead, and several thousand others made day trips.

The real advantage of Powder Snow Valley was that it made Erewhon a year-round resort. The ski area was established in an extremely good location – high in elevation (1500–1800 metres) and just east of the Main Divide, ensuring a regular snowfall from the dominant nor'west weather pattern. It was quickly regarded by Canterbury skiers as an area well worth visiting. As well as the good snow conditions, the area had the advantage of being commercially run at a time when club-operated ski areas were catering more for their members than for visitors.

One of the area's disadvantages was that it was 159 kilometres from Christchurch, the nearest population base. This wasn't too much of a problem in the area's early years, when there were only six club ski areas within a 190-kilometre radius of the city. However, by the mid-1970s, two larger commercial areas – Porter Heights (opened 1968) and Mount Hutt (opened 1974) – were both operational, and both were within 105 kilometres of Christchurch. These areas certainly affected Erewhon's patronage.

With the advent of Porter Heights and Mount Hutt, all Canterbury ski areas noted a decline in their number of visitors. While the clubs could keep their areas running with voluntary labour, the Urquharts could not. Arthur, his wife, Freda, and two sons, Alisdaire and Colin, were running the large sheep station, as well as the new tourist ventures. It was not easy to run the two, and at the same time keep them both economically viable. Farming commitments always came first and, consequently, the ski area was often closed when others weren't.

Arthur Urquhart died in 1981, and his wife and sons, wishing to keep the ski area going, but unable to spend time doing so, put it up for sale. There were no buyers, and the ski area remained closed for the 1983 and 1984 seasons.

But the ski area had built up a strong following in its short existence, and it was largely because of these people that it had kept operating throughout the 1970s. In 1985, this group formed the Erewhon Ski Club. They leased the land and homestead from the Urquharts, and began running the operation as a club ski area. The club has slowly made developments, and to this day continues to successfully run the Erewhon ski area. The name was changed from Powder Snow Valley to Erewhon in 1986.

Perhaps the last words on Erewhon should be those of an American visitor who once stayed in the lodge and noted of the

 **Erewhon**

*Location:* 159 km from Christchurch.
87 km from Methven.

*Season:* Late June/early July through to late September.

*Elevation:* The mountain above the ski area, Mount Potts, is 2194 metres high.
The top rope tow takes you to 1941 metres.
The bottom tow starts at 1392 metres.

*Vertical drop:* 549 metres.

*Terrain:* Beginner 20%, Intermediate 40%, Advanced 40%.

*Snowmaking:* None.

*Groomers:* One.

*Road toll:* None.

*Lifts:* Four rope tows.
Low charge. Junior and child reductions.
Tow belts for lifts are provided with day passes at no extra cost.

*Ski hire:* 120 pairs of skis.
Full set: $15 (Adult); $10 (Child).

*Specials:* Dinner, bed and breakfast in the restaurant's bunkhouse sheep station that, 'it would be bigger than Texas if it was flattened out'.

## THE SKI AREA

Erewhon is set in a long, thin basin and is quite possibly the 'narrowest' ski area in New Zealand. The area has four rope tows – Learners', Intermediate, Senior and Top.

 **Erewhon**

costs $30 (Adult); $15 (Under 12s). For these prices you must supply your own linen and pillows. For made-up beds the costs are $35 (Adult); $23 (Under 12s).

*Ski school:* Three instructors.
Group (one hour): $10 per person.
Private (one hour): $15 (Adult); $5 (Child).

*Ski weeks:* Three ski weeks only during the August school holidays: $270 per person. This covers six nights' accommodation (Sunday–Saturday), five days' skiing, instruction, all meals, and ski hire if necessary.
For more information, phone 0-3-351 8196 or 0-3-303 9883, or write to the address below.

*Accomm:* The Erewhon Lodge, at the base of the access road, has room for 50. In addition to two large bunkrooms, the lodge has four double units (with two single beds in each) and various miscellaneous accommodation to cater for overflow. Charges are moderate.

*Address:* Erewhon Ski Club, c/o 20 Morley Street, Christchurch.
Telephone: 0-3-351 8196

*Snow reports:* Phone the Press Inpho Ski Line 0-3-366 6644, then 1101.

Learners' Tow services an excellent broad, and long (approximately 150 x 50 metres) beginners' area. The slope's gradient is ideal and, with the chalet at the bottom of the run, it's the perfect site for families with children learning to ski (you needn't be in a family though – it's a great slope for anyone learning to ski).

For advanced skiers, Erewhon can be absolute bliss. A busy day means 90 skiers on the area, so there's rarely any semblance of a queue, the basin is well situated to receive good snow, and Erewhon has some of the steepest terrain in the country. Add all these factors up, and it's apparent that, on the right day, Erewhon rates amongst New Zealand's best.

Senior Tow opens up the majority of the area's advanced

## GETTING THERE

### From Christchurch

*By car*

Follow the instructions for getting to Mount Hutt, only carry on along Highway 72. About 25 kilometres past the Mount Hutt turn-off you'll come to a turn-off on the right that takes you to the tiny township of Mount Somers. Go through Mount Somers and carry on heading west. It's about a 40-kilometre road to Erewhon station, the last half of which is unsealed. About four kilometres from the lodge you come over a rise and the huge expanse of the upper Rangitata unfolds before you. The views of the river and the Southern Alps from here are spectacular. Four-wheel drive vehicles are usually essential from the lodge up to the ski area. The club has a couple of vehicles it uses to take skiers up (free of charge), and most people choose to leave their cars at the lodge and go up in one of these.

skiing. From its top you can traverse to the left and descend down the narrow gully called Gun Barrel to the base of the tow. This is probably the most popular run on the area. Alternatively, you can traverse further on to the southern face of Mount Potts, from where it's a steep, and often very tricky, run down to the chalet. If you're unable to kick-turn on your skis, think long and hard before heading out this way.

From the top of Senior Tow, you can ski a short steep face on the right of the lift, and then traverse beneath the huge bluff that dominates the ski area. The slopes beneath the bluff are also very steep, and can be a bit bumpy thanks to some large boulders beneath the snow. The more adventurous – or crazy – skiers will have a keen eye on the chutes in the bluff. These can

---

*Hitching*

Realistically, the only place you'll get a lift to the ski area from is Mount Somers. If you can get there somehow, catching a ride shouldn't be a problem. The best way of organising a lift to Erewhon is by phoning the club secretary in Christchurch (0–3–351 8196 or 0–3–303-9736), who may be able to put you in touch with a club member who's going up and has a spare seat. You may have to help out with petrol costs, and this can be negotiated. Bear in mind that, if you're going all the way out there, it may be worth spending a night in the lodge.

*Shuttles and buses*

No companies run a regular service to Erewhon. If there are enough people interested in going, usually a minimum of eight, one of the Christchurch shuttle companies may run a trip. See the Mount Hutt section for details about the Christchurch shuttle operators.

in fact be skied, though it's usually only the most adventurous of the crazy skiers who do so.

Top Tow is usually used only in poor snow seasons when there is not enough snow around the lower tows. The terrain opened up by this tow is excellent and, even if the tow is not running, it's well worth making the climb anyway. From the top of Senior Tow it's about a 15-minute walk up to the large basin behind the bluff. It's from this point that the chutes on the bluff can be accessed. Ideally, these should be skied with someone who knows where they're going. If you don't fancy the chutes, ski around behind the bluff and into the huge Arthur's Basin. This area is renowned for collecting snow and, after a fresh fall, the run from the bluff through the basin and down to the chalet can be absolutely incredible. Good enough, even, to make the walk up Top Tow again.

With excellent beginner and advanced skiing terrain, it's only the intermediate skiers who may find this area a little restrictive. The only truly intermediate terrain is that which, funnily enough, is accessed by Intermediate Tow. A strong intermediate skier would manage a run from the top of Senior Tow, provided, that is, that they could get up it. The tow climbs some of the area's steepest terrain and, for those not proficient with a 'nutcracker', it can be very difficult.

The chalet at the base of Learners' Tow contains the ticket sales counter, as well as the ski rental and repair room, the first-aid quarters, and a food counter with seating and tables for skiers. It's not a huge complex, but it's very cosy.

Ski-touring in and around Erewhon is fantastic. The basin is surrounded by peaks, most of which can be climbed with touring gear. The skiing from the tops of these is matched only by the views they give of the Southern Alps. Ask a staff member about the current avalanche hazard before setting out.

# Mount Cheeseman

## History

The beginnings of the Mount Cheeseman Ski Club go back to a New Zealand teenager attending a Swiss college before World War One. Sent to Switzerland at the age of 15, Allan Giles of Christchurch became 'hooked' by the sport and the school's other winter activities – ice-skating and bob-sleighing.

Returning to New Zealand after World War One, Giles was keen to continue skiing. He visited the Mount Cook region a few times in the early 1920s but found it a little expensive. By 1928, he had become determined to set up some sort of club that could cater for his winter passions. In later years, the club's first vice-president, T. T. (Nui) Robins would recall Giles' search for a suitable location: 'Back country runholders looked with disfavour at "crackpots" whose idea of recreation was to get cold, wet and exhausted amongst snow and ice.'

Eventually, Giles and companion Bill Day found a friendly runholder in Rob Blackley of Castle Hill Station. Following a look around the area and finding a suitable location for the three winter sports, Giles and Day contacted the Canterbury Mountaineering Club (CMC) in order to find out about setting up a club. It was through the CMC that they met Nui Robins.

A meeting was held at the Christs College Old Boys' rooms in August 1929. Attending the meeting were Giles, his sister Marion, Day, Robins, and some other CMC members. The Canterbury Winters Sports Club (CWSC) was formed at this meeting, with Mr (later Sir) Arthur Dudley Dobson as the first president and Nui Robins as vice-president. The majority of the club's members were CMC members. (Arthur Dobson was the first European to discover and cross Arthurs Pass; the pass and the township are named after him.)

The site Giles had decided upon for the club's activities was in the basin between Mount Cheeseman and Mount Cockayne, about five kilometres from the Broken River bridge on the main highway. Nearby was a good slope for tobogganing and a lake that would become a 1000-square-metre skating rink in winter. With the slopes of Cheeseman and Cockayne, it really was the ideal location. (The ski area is actually on Mount Cockayne, not Mount Cheeseman.)

---

 **Mount Cheeseman**

*Location:* 112 km from Christchurch.
41 km from Springfield.

*Season:* Usually open by early July, closing late September.

*Elevation:* Mount Cockayne is 1847 metres high.
The platter lift takes you to 1840 metres.
The lodge is at 1570 metres.

*Vertical drop:* 277 metres.

*Terrain:* Beginner 20%, Intermediate 60%, Advanced 20%.

*Snowmaking:* None.

*Groomers:* One.

*Road toll:* None.

*Ski hire:* None.

*Lifts:* One learners' fixed-grip tow, one T-bar and a platter lift. Moderate charge, with family, learner and junior (under 18) reductions. Five-day ticket reductions are also available. Under 10s ski for free.

The 60 to 70 members of the club spent the summer of 1929–30 cutting a walking track from Broken River bridge to the site, and then began constructing what was to become known as 'Bottom Hut'. Some wood from the surrounding forest was used, but most of the material was carried by members, or dragged by horse and sled from the bridge. The hut was at an altitude of 1000 metres, and it as a 300-metre climb along a five and a half kilometre track from the bridge to the hut site.

Skiing began in the 1930 season. In those days, only the

## Mount Cheeseman

*Ski school:* Three instructors. Private lessons only, any time by arrangement Monday to Saturday. One to four people for one hour: $45 per person.

*Ski weeks:* 'Design your own ski holiday' scheme includes dinner, a bunk bed, breakfast, lift pass and ski lesson.
Prices are daily, a day being defined as from 4:00 pm one day to 4:00 pm the next.
July: $60 (Adult); $52 (Junior).
1 August–9 September: $76 (Adult); $67 (Junior).
10–30 September onwards: $60 (Adult); $52 (Junior).
If you book for five nights, you get your sixth night and following day's lift pass free.

*Accomm:* There are two lodges – the Top (day lodge) has 66 beds and Forest Lodge has 38. Transport from Forest Lodge is provided free for guests staying over school holiday weeks.

*Address:* Mount Cheeseman, PO Box 22-178, Christchurch.
Telephone: 0-3-379 5315.

*Snow report:* Press Inpho Ski Line 0-3-366 6644, then 1101.

hardest of the hardy 'crackpots' would become involved with the sport. It wasn't until 1938 that the 40-hour working week was introduced, so all CWSC members would be at work on Saturday morning. A day's skiing involved leaving Christchurch in cars at around 2:00 pm on Saturday. After travelling along the narrow gravel roads from Christchurch and fording most of the rivers, the convoy would rendezvous at the Springfield Hotel. From there, they would cross the steep and narrow Porters Pass Road, clearing snow as required, and arrive at Broken River by late evening. The walk up to the hut would take another hour or two, depending on snow, and they'd usually be in their bunks at Bottom Hut by about midnight.

To go skiing required walking through the bush behind the hut to the top of the toboggan run then up on to whichever snow slope looked most appealing. Nui Robins later recalled that: 'A good day's skiing consisted of two or three runs of about 300 feet vertical descent on a 30° slope. Then some smaller runs, the difficulty being that all uphill travel was by physical effort alone.' At the end of Sunday's skiing, skiers would walk out to their frozen cars and begin the long journey home, often arriving in Christchurch in the early hours of Monday morning. So much for an *après ski*.

In 1936, members built a four-bunk hut, named 'Robin's Nest' at 1600 metres, meaning that the keener skiers could climb to here on the Saturday night and get a few more runs in on the Sunday.

Little skiing occurred during World War Two, but over the summer of 1946–47, membership increased significantly and the club began making improvements. A road was bulldozed from Broken River to Bottom Hut, a middle hut with 21 bunks was built at 1200 metres, and members built a 50-metre long portable rope tow.

In 1950, the club built a 41-bunk top hut at 1600 metres. Robin's Nest gradually became redundant, and fell into disrepair. Its shell is still standing today and is passed on the way up the access road.

In 1978, the club became the first club ski area in the South Island to install a T-bar (Stratford Mountain Club on Mount Egmont also had one). It named the lift 'Fendalton Road', after a road in the more affluent part of Christchurch, the club having gained a bit of a reputation as the professional people's ski area.

This is an image the club has moved away from in recent years and, while you still often find yourself sharing the T-bar with a doctor, a lawyer or company director, the atmosphere nowadays is generally one of 'skiing' and not of what you do off the mountain. As, no doubt, the founders intended it to be.

Events in the club in recent years have included: a new forest

---

## GETTING THERE

**From Christchurch**
*By car*
Follow the instructions for Porter Heights, carrying on a further seven kilometres along Highway 73 to get to the Mount Cheeseman turn-off.

*Hitching*
Follow the instructions for Porter Heights, only there will probably be fewer people going to Mount Cheeseman so it would be an idea to be on the road by 7:30 am. Alternatively, phone the club's Christchurch office (0-3-379 5315) and ask if there's anyone going up who could give you a lift. Be prepared to chip in for petrol costs.

*Shuttles and buses*
Mountain Adventures runs a daily shuttle, making pick-ups on request in Christchurch between 7:00 and 7:30 am. A day's return fare is $27 (Adult); $25 (under 18s/Students). Bookings are essential. Phone 0-3-355 3320.

lodge in 1981, after the old Bottom Hut burned down; installation of a platter lift in 1984; and purchase of a groomer in 1993. These days, Mount Cheeseman is arguably the most popular club in the Canterbury region, with a membership of over 1000.

## The Ski Area

Mount Cheeseman's access road is quite possibly the most beautiful in the country. The lower half winds its way through native beech forest before rising above the bushline and giving spectacular views of the surrounding Torlesse and Craigieburn Mountain Ranges. From the car park, it's a 200-metre walk to the lodge, but you can drive there, drop your gear in the unload area, and then return to the car park.

The ski area is in a wide, southeasterly facing bowl and, while the vertical drop may not be very large, the beauty of Mount Cheeseman is the width of its bowl. From the top of the platter lift it's really a matter of traversing to your right, down a ridge towards the lodge, or to your left along the head wall of Mount Cockayne, and picking your route down. Grooming is carried out in the centre, flatter area of the bowl so, after a good snowfall, the slopes to either side remain covered in fresh, uncut powder. Perhaps an ulterior motive for naming the mountain 'Cockayne'?

For the absolute beginner, there is a small area just outside the lodge. It's a little restricted but, once the ski-legs have been attained, a novice may be capable of skiing from the top of the T-bar down the groomed slopes. There are a few short steeper pitches down the main trail, but most of these can be circumnavigated by using a cat-track. The T-bar has two get-off and get-on points on the way up, so if there's a section of the main trail you are finding success in, it may be an idea to do a few circuits. The top section of the trail seems to have the best gradient for the novice skier.

With its easy-to-use lifts and gentle, rolling groomed trails,

Mount Cheeseman is very popular with novice and intermediate skiers. Having said that, though, a short traverse in either direction from the top of the platter will give most advanced skiers a choice of challenging and varied runs. For the keener advanced skier who doesn't mind a short walk, the chutes way out left on Cockayne's headwall are well worth a few turns.

The ski-touring possibilities from here are fantastic. It's possible to go south over Mount Cheeseman and along the tops to the Mount Olympus ski area. Alternatively, to the north, it's possible to traverse along the tops of the Broken River ski area and beyond to the Craigieburn Valley ski area. Allow a full day for either of these trips, and check on snow conditions with ski patrol at Mount Cheeseman and the area to which you're heading.

# Mount Hutt

## History

Mount Hutt was named after John Hutt (1795–1880), the first chairman of the Canterbury Association. The Maori name for the mountain is Opuke.

The Mount Hutt ski area really came about as a result of an economic decline in the Methven–Rakaia region during the 1950s and 1960s. Locals had been observing the snow of Mount Hutt's south basin for years, and in 1969 the newly formed Lions Club decided that a study should be conducted to establish whether the basin could be turned into a ski area. A ski area was seen as a possible answer to the region's economic woes.

The studies were optimistic but a feasibility study into constructing a road up to the basin was not. The Lions Club contacted Peter Yeoman, an associate of an engineering and surveying firm, and Doug Hood, an Ashburton contractor. Both were keen to see the project go ahead and worked hard to establish a route up the mountain. Hood sometimes worked without pay, accepting shares in the unproven venture instead.

An initial road was established in 1970 and, in March 1972, the Mount Hutt Ski Field Development Co Ltd was formed, the Lions Club ceasing to be officially involved in the project. Over the winter of 1972, Willie Huber, a snow and ski area specialist from Germany who later became the area's manager, lived in a hut in the middle of the basin in order to further confirm the possibility of starting a ski area there.

With the help of voluntary work by Methven people, some road improvements, and the installation of two rope tows, the ski area was opened for limited skiing during the 1973 season. Impressed by the numbers attracted (up to 350 a day), the company officially opened the ski area on 16 June 1974. Things went well for the field and the price of a lift ticket was raised from 50c to $5 the following year.

By 1982, the area was running two rope tows, four T-bars and a triple chairlift. Methven was transformed into a unique farming–ski town, probably to the annoyance of the more vehement local farmers.

The first Federation International du Ski-sanctioned races on Mount Hutt were held in 1977 and the field has hosted several international ski teams over the years; the Canadian, Japanese, French, Swedish and USA teams have all spent southern hemisphere seasons based at Mount Hutt.

In 1990, Mount Hutt became the first southern hemisphere ski area to host the Alpine World Cup, no small feat for a field with such a short history and humble beginnings. The Mount Cook Company purchased Mount Hutt in May 1994. These days, as the largest field in the region, Mount Hutt attracts large numbers of local, national and international skiers every season.

## The Ski Area

The largest ski area in Canterbury, and the one with most facilities, Mount Hutt has something to offer every skier – from the nearly flat learners' area, to the narrow steep chutes of the Towers and South Face. Any standard of skier will enjoy their time at Mount Hutt.

The two platter lifts in the right-hand side of the bowl service excellent beginner/intermediate terrain, particularly to the left of the higher platter, where few advanced and faster skiers venture. The quad chairlift takes you higher on the mountain, giving you a choice of routes. Traffic between the top of the quad and the base of the Upper T-bars can get pretty heavy and it's wise to look up the mountain before making the traverse.

The smooth, wide run called Broadway begins at the base of the T-bars. This takes you over rolling terrain to the right of the top platter and down a short, steeper section before bringing you back to the base of the quad. Alternatively, from the top of

# Mount Hutt

*Location:* 25 km from Methven.
105 km from Christchurch.

*Season:* Snow conditions permitting, the season can start in early May and end in early November. Almost certainly open by early June through to mid-October.

*Elevation:* Mount Hutt itself is 2188 metres.
The base buildings are at 1585 metres.
The highest lift takes you to 2075 metres.

*Vertical drop:* 672 metres from the top of the Upper T-bar to the base of the triple chair, below the base buildings.

*Terrain:* Beginner 25%, Intermediate 50%, Advanced 25%.

*Snowmaking:* An air-water system means the snowmaking guns can be shifted around the mountain and snow can be (and usually is) made on all pisted runs.

*Groomers:* Four.

*Road toll:* None.

*Lifts:* Three rope tows, two platters, three T-bars, one triple and one quad chairlift.
High charge. Child, student and learner rates apply. Under 5s and over 65s free.

*Ski hire:* 800 pairs of skis (some executive) and snowboards.

| Full hire: | Day | $25 (Adult); | $17 (Child). |
| | Half day | $20 (Adult); | $15 (Child). |
| Part hire: | Day | $20 (Adult); | $15 (Child). |
| | Part day | $15 (Adult); | $10 (Child). |
| Snowboard: | Day | $30 (Adult); | $20 (Child). |
| | Half day | $25 (Adult); | $15 (Child). |
| Executive skis: | | $35. | |
| Clothing (full set): | | $20 (Adult); | $10 (Child). |

# Mount Hutt

*Specials:* 'Frequent Skier' cards, which cost $40 and entitle the holder to day passes for only $38. So, if you plan to ski at Mount Hutt for more than three days, get one of these.

'Ski Evolution' package (Day 1: ski hire, learner's lift pass, one lesson. Day 2: ski hire, lift pass, a two-hour group lesson. Days 3 and 4: ski hire, lift pass, two-hour lesson. Day 5: ski hire, lift pass) for $199 (Adult); $111 (Child).

'Starter' package with a guarantee (ski hire, a learner's lift pass and two 90-minute lessons) for $60 (Adult); $36 (Child).

'Learn to Snowboard' package (hire, a learner's lift pass and a two-hour lesson) for $75 (Adult); $50 (Child).

There are a number of other specials such as five-day packages, etc. To find out about these write to the address below, or phone the Mount Hutt Ski School 0-3-308 5075.

*Ski school:* Usually over 40 instructors.

Group lessons: All levels 10:30 am–12:30 pm; 1:45–3:45 pm. First timers 12:30–4:00 pm. Morning: $30 (Adult); $20 (Child). 1:45 pm: $27 (Adult); $18 (Child). Two lessons: $56 (Adult); $38 (Child). Four lessons: $108 (Adult); $72 (Child). Six lessons: $158 (Adult); $102 (Child).

Private lessons: $60 for one person for one hour. Each additional person $30. At 9:30 am: $45 for one or two people.

*Address:* Mount Hutt Ski and Alpine Tourist Co, PO Box 14, Methven. Telephone 0-3-302 8811.

*Snow report:* Phone the Press Inpho Ski Line 0-3-366 6644, then 1101.

# GETTING THERE

From Christchurch
*By car*
Take Highway 73, heading west, through the small townships of Yaldhurst and West Melton. Ten kilometres past West Melton you come to a turn-off to Hororata. This road, a shortcut to Methven and Mount Hutt, which almost every Christchurch skier uses, fords three rivers. These fords can be pretty treacherous after a good rainfall, so there's a sign just past the turn-off telling you if the fords are passable. Hororata is 20 kilometres along this road.

Carry on through Hororata along a long straight road until you come to the intersection with Highway 72. Turn left. Five kilometres later you'll cross the Rakaia River and from there it's another four kilometres to the turn-off to Methven (left on to Highway 77).

From the Methven turn-off it's another five kilometres to the Mount Hutt turn-off (on the right). The whole trip takes about an hour to Methven or an hour and a half to the Mount Hutt car park.

*Hitching*
You want to be somewhere along Riccarton Road by 7:30 am at the latest; the further along the road the better. Keep an eye out for cars with skis on their roof and smile!

This road also goes to the ski areas in the Craigieburn Range, so you can just sit back and go to whichever field your ride takes you to. If you definitely want to go to Mount Hutt, but your ride isn't going there, get a lift as far along Highway 73 as you can before the Hororata turn-off.

If it's locals who have picked you up they'll know where to drop you off. If they're not sure, just remember not to go off Highway 73 until the Hororata turn-off.

*Shuttles and buses*
The Snow and Surf Shop runs a shuttle that will go to either Mount Hutt, Porter Heights or Mount Cheeseman, depending on demand and snow conditions. It tends to go to Mount Hutt most frequently. The shuttle departs from the shop at 7:30 am and can make pick-ups if required. The shuttle arrives back in Christchurch at 6:15 pm. A return trip for an adult is $27; one-way $16. A student return trip is $24; one-way $13. Reservations are essential as these determine to which ski area the shuttle will go. For more information, or to book, phone 0–3–365 6604, or call into the shop at 85 Tuam Street.

The Skiers Express Snow Shuttle runs a daily shuttle, making pick-ups from within Christchurch between 6:55 and 7:10 am. The shuttle calls into McEwings Ski Hire on the way out of town so if you need gear you can hire it here, saving the hassle of the crowds in Mount Hutt's rental department. The shuttle leaves Mount Hutt at 4:00 pm, arriving back in Christchurch at 6:00 pm. An adult return fare is $29; student return is $25. One-way fares are the same as returns. Bookings are essential, so phone 0–3–379 6377.

The Mountain Mule shuttle makes daily trips, making pick-ups around Christchurch from 6:45 am, and has you on the mountain by 9:30 am. Adult return fare is $28; student $24. To book a seat, phone 0–3–385 8851.

Snowman Shuttles runs a daily shuttle to Mount Hutt. It starts making pick-ups from 7:00 am, arriving on the mountain by 9:10 am. It's $27 for an adult return trip; $24 for a student. There are no one-way fares. For bookings, phone 0–3–364 7223.

The Mount Cook Line operates a Mount Hutt Ski Bus service that makes daily trips to Mount Hutt. It departs from the Mount Cook Bus Terminal (40 Lichfield Street) at 7:00 am, stopping in the Square at 7:05, on Worcester Street (opposite Noahs Hotel) at 7:10, and a few other places in town. It's essential to make a reservation, and tickets must be picked up and paid for on the day prior to travel. Bookings can be made at the Visitor Information Centre (corner of Worcester Street and Oxford Terrace) or at one of the Mount Cook Line Travel Centres (47 Riccarton Road, 40 Lichfield Street, 91 Worcester Street). An adult return fare is $27; one way is $16. The student or Youth Hostel Association (YHA) member fare is $21 return; $13 one way. For more information, phone 0–3–379 0690.

The Ski Mount Hutt Express Ski Shuttle makes daily trips to Mount Hutt, leaving Christchurch at 8:15 am. An adult return fare is $35; $29 for a student or YHA member. One-way fares are negotiable. Also on offer is a $95 day package, which includes transport and the Mount Hutt beginner's package (learner's lift pass, a ski lesson and ski hire); and a $49 day package, which covers transport and ski hire. To book, phone 0–3–388 2042.

Leopard Coach Lines runs a daily trip to Mount Hutt, leaving the Square at 7:00 am and making pick-ups on the way (not door to door). An adult return fare is $25; student $20. One-way fares are negotiable. To book, phone 0–3–365 0194.

## From Methven

*By car*

From Methven drive north on Rakaia Gorge Road, Methven's main road. Three kilometres out of Methven you'll come to a sign-posted turn-off on your left. This road will take you directly to the access road, about ten kilometres away.

*Hitching*

If you're on Rakaia Gorge Road by 8:00 am you shouldn't have a problem getting a ride.

*Shuttles and buses*

Mount Hutt Tours runs three buses from Methven daily at 8:30, 9:00 and 9:30 am. They will pick you up from wherever you are staying. An adult return fare is $17; one-way is $11. Under 14s return or one-way is $10. From the toll gate the fare is $13 return; $10 one-way; or $9 for under 14s (return or one-way). Pick-ups from the toll gate are made at 8:30 am and every half hour until 10:30 am. Buses depart from Mount Hutt at 3:00 and 4:00 pm. Bus season passes are available. To buy a ticket call into the Mount Hutt Tours office (Rakaia Gorge Road) or phone 0–3–302 8611.

Mountain Transport run a mini-bus service to Mount Hutt daily. The adult return fare is $17; one-way $10. Child return fare is $10; one-way $8. Bookings are essential. Phone 0–3–302 8443.

Value Tours make a daily trip, making pick-ups around Methven at 8:00 am. The adult return fare is $17; $12 for a child. Bookings are essential. Phone 0–3–302 8112.

Bamfords also make a daily trip. Pick-ups around Methven are made at 8:00 am. A return fare is $17. Bookings are essential. Phone 0–3–302 8707.

the quad you can ski beneath the chairlift and turn right on the cat-track to the usually less-crowded slopes of Way Leggo, a good intermediate slope that can take you all the way to the triple chair's mid-station, or further to the base of the triple down an advanced route through a narrow gully called Log Chute.

From the top of the triple you have a choice of three equally steep runs. You can go to the left and on to the 2B slope, or take the steeper routes on the slopes beneath the chair, or traverse into the lower Towers region where you can pick your route down.

The longer Upper T-bar gives access to the more advanced runs on the mountain. From the top you can go to the left out along Virgin Mile, a large area with runs, often untracked, down into the bowl. Alternatively, you can keep a high traverse to the right and enter the top of Towers or South Face, both of which are advanced and sometimes gut-wrenching runs. Towers contains a number of chutes of varying widths for advanced skiers to play around in. A skier of less-than-advanced ability should not attempt either the South Face or the top of Towers.

Morning Glory, aptly named as it's the first slope to see the morning sun, is a wide cruising run, suitable for intermediates, which takes you to the top of the triple. If you're feeling like a fast cruising run, head over to Huber's Run. It's a wide semi-steep slope with a roll close to the bottom which, if you're going over at the right speed, is guaranteed to make you lose your stomach.

The lower sections of the mountain – International, Montezuma's and Log Chute – are almost a ski area in their own right. There's a lot of terrain down there, most of it ungroomed. A fantastic run is from the top of the triple chairlift, down the lower Towers and along the ridge line before descending on Montezuma's. The lower station of the triple chairlift closes at 3:30 pm and ski patrol have little compassion for anyone who turns up after that time, so don't be caught out. You will usually just have to walk back up to the carpark.

# Mount Olympus

## History

The South Island Ski Championships were held on Ball Glacier, Mount Cook, in the winter of 1932. To enter the championships a racer had to belong to a ski club. In the small Canterbury settlement of Windwhistle, a group of keen skiers who wished to enter the championships but didn't belong to a club, decided to form one. The group, of about a dozen, held a meeting and formed the Windwhistle Winter Sports Club (WWSC). And so it was that members of the newly formed club participated in the 1932 South Island Ski Championships.

By 1939, the club had developed an ice-skating rink on a pond in the Rakaia Gorge. The club by that stage consisted of 250 members, virtually all of whom were keen ice-skaters. Skiing in Canterbury at that time was more or less confined to the Canterbury Winter Sports Club on Mount Cheeseman and the Christchurch Ski Club at Temple Basin. In 1946, with the interest in ice-skating increasing, the WWSC became involved in setting up a rink on Lake Ida, at the southern end of the Craigieburn Range. It proved to be a good location, with Mount Ida keeping the lake in almost constant shade. It was the venue for many figure-skating and ice-hockey competitions.

Two years later, Ken Hall, a club member keen to establish skiing in the southern Craigieburns, went up the Ryton River in search of suitable slopes. He found the ideal location up a tributary of the Ryton, on the southern approaches of Mount Olympus. The club supported Hall's idea and, in early 1949, with volunteer labour, built a 12-bunk hut at the foot of the valley. Skiing on Mount Olympus began in the winter of 1949.

By 1951, with skiers starting to recognise the virtues of ski lifts, the club decided to install its first rope tow. That summer, members carried the tow up in pieces and began constructing it. The winter arrived early that year and work on the tow had to cease before it was finished. It was completed over the next summer and operational for the 1952 ski season.

As well as installing the tow during that summer, the club extended the road from Lake Ida up the Ryton valley to within a 90-minute walk from the tow. A prominent club member, Hugh Richards, was accidentally killed during blasting operations. Toward the end of that summer members built an 18-bunk lodge on the field itself, naming it the Hugh Richards Memorial Lodge.

##  Mount Olympus

*Location:* 125 km from Christchurch.
58 km from Methven.

*Season:* Usually open by mid-July, closing by mid to late October.

*Elevation:* Mount Olympus is 2097 metres high.
The top rope tow takes you to 1875 metres.
The base of the access tow is at 1434 metres.

*Vertical drop:* 441 metres.

*Terrain:* Beginners 10%, Intermediate 55%, Advanced 35%.

*Snowmaking:* None.

*Groomers:* None.

*Road toll:* None.

*Lifts:* Four rope tows.
Low charge, with student, learner and junior rates.

*Ski hire:* None.

*Specials:* On Saturday nights, you can get dinner, bed and breakfast in Top Hut for a low charge.

By the late 1950s, the club had cut a road further up the mountain and built an access tow from the end of it to the bottom of the main tow. The lodge has since been expanded to 40 bunks, and the number of organised ski weeks to the field has increased to ten. The busiest day on Mount Olympus in 1956 saw 22 skiers using the field, seven of whom had skied over from Mount Cheeseman for the day. Today, day-trippers can raise the total to over a hundred.

During the 1960s, the club consolidated its reputation as a small, sociable unit. Still based in Windwhistle, the club's annual

##  Mount Olympus

*Ski school:* Two instructors.
Lessons are included for people on ski weeks. Other people can negotiate a fee and time with an instructor.

*Ski weeks:* 8:00 am on Sunday to 5:00 pm the following Saturday: $385 (Adult); $315 (Junior); with a 10% discount for groups of six or more. The price covers lunch, dinner, bed and breakfast, lift passes and a two-hour lesson each day. To find out about dates or to book, phone 0-3-329 1823 or 0-3-318 0893.

*Accomm:* There are two huts – Bottom Hut in the lower car park and the main hut on the ski area itself. Unlike other club lodges, these two have a real mountain hut character to them. Bottom Hut sleeps 12 and the main hut sleeps 40. Both have electricity and log burners. Dinner, bed, breakfast, lunch, lift pass and lesson: $56 (Adult); $48 (Junior); $20 (Student).

*Address:* Windwhistle Sports Club, PO Box 25055, Christchurch.
Telephone: 0-3-318 0893

*Snow reports:* Seekers Snowphone 0-3-314 8722 or the Press Inpho Ski Line 0-3-366 6644, then 1101.

## How to get there

### From Christchurch
*By car*
The same as if you were going to Mount Hutt except, when you arrive at Windwhistle, where the road from Hororata meets Highway 72, continue west on the same road, over Highway 72, and follow the signs to Mount Olympus. From Windwhistle it's about 40 kilometres to Mount Olympis (about 16 kilometres unsealed). It's a good drive, first alongside the Rakaia River, then past Lake Coleridge and up into the Craigieburn Range.

*Hitching*
This is very difficult (mid-week it's impossible), but if you're determined then follow the directions for Mount Hutt, only be on the road by 7:00 am. If someone going to Mount Hutt offers you a ride, take it and get off at Windwhistle, from where you may be lucky and catch a lift to Mount Olympus. The best way of organising a lift is by phoning the club bookings officer (0–3–329 1823 or 0–3–318 6838), who may be able to put you on to a club member who's going up and has a spare seat. You may have to help out with petrol costs, and this can be negotiated.

*Shuttles and buses*
No companies run a regular service to Mount Olympus. If there are enough people interested in going, usually a minimum of eight, one of the Christchurch shuttle companies (see Mount Hutt section for details) may run a trip.

dances, which were held in woolsheds, became known as notoriously rowdy affairs and were actually cancelled for several years early in the decade.

The club today still relies strongly on its sociable reputation and the ever-present friendly atmosphere on the field. It is known in some circles as 'New Zealand's best kept-skiing secret'. In recent years, the club has been moving slowly with the marketing drive necessary to compete as a ski area. The area's relatively low profile, however, ensures that it is still kept somewhat secret. Things have changed since the 1960s, too. A toned-down version of the revelry that once held the district in awe of the club's annual dance occurs these days with regularity in the club's own lodges.

## THE SKI AREA

The first thing to do before heading to Mount Olympus is call the ski report. It's a long way to go just to find the road is closed.

The access road makes its way through a fairly barren landscape alongside the Ryton River up to Bottom Hut. On the way you pass a gate with a sign reading 'Drive on at your own risk'. The road really isn't all that bad provided you take it slowly. It may be necessary to get out every now and then to remove a larger rock from the road, but apart from these and the odd avoidable pot-hole, the road to Bottom Hut is no problem. Chains may be necessary to the hut, but are usually essential to get to the car park below the base of the access tow.

Occasionally, after a big dump of snow, the road between Bottom Hut and the top car park can be used only by four-wheel-drive vehicles with chains. A radio (with instructions on how to use it on the wall) at Bottom Hut should be used to call the main hut to find out the condition of the road, or to see if someone who can give you a lift will be coming up the road. During weekends, it's usually no problem getting a lift from Bottom Hut. Failing this, it's an easy 40-minute walk up to the access tow.

From the top car park, it's a short walk to the base of the access tow. There should be some tow belts there, so once you've donned your skis, help yourself to one of these, and get on the lift. This tow takes you right on to the area where the main hut, Learners' Tow and Main Tow are.

Beginners and 'never-ever' skiers will enjoy the wide and gentle beginners' area beside the lodge. The fireside hot drinks are never too far away. Once a novice skier has mastered the Learners' Tow, the next step is Main Tow, which has a few convenient spots to get off on the way up. The terrain below the lift's half-way mark is still gentle, particularly if you go further to the left in the base of the bowl. The more adventurous beginner might also find the Molly's Bump run well within their ability, being only a little steep in its very top section.

There are days at Mount Olympus when the advanced, powder-loving skiers believe they've found the perfect ski area. Fresh snow, less than 20 people on the whole area, and enough terrain to allow one to ski untouched snow for the entire day; and a day at Olympus can finish at 6:00 pm. If you do, in the very rare event, find yourself actually looking for fresh tracks, try dropping down the short, steep face behind the lodge to the base of the access tow. It's often one of the last places to be skied. That is, it could be up to a week after a snowfall before tracks appear there.

Bear in mind also that club members will not always be forthcoming with information on where to ski after the main runs have been tracked out. When faced by such queries, members will often just wink at you and have a little chuckle. By tradition it's then up to you to either follow them all day, or ensure that they are adequately supplied with refreshments in the lodge.

The Back Basin, with powder, is one of the country's best ski slopes. It's not necessary to catch Top Tow to be able to traverse to the Back Basin, but by doing so you will get quite a bit more of a vertical drop. It's a long, steep and unforgettable run to the base of the access tow. Few people do it just the once. The Main

Face is usually the first to get tracked out, and skiers usually end up racing each other back to the top of Main Tow and making the ever further traverse until it becomes necessary to ski all the way out and down Access Run.

The peak towering above the Main Basin is called The Sphinx. Occasionally, a group will climb the slope up to the col to the right of The Sphinx. It's about a half-hour walk and the skiing from the top down to Main Tow is a fantastic constant gradient, on which it's easy to make over 100 turns. From the top of Top Tow it's a short walk to the ridge line. This ridge carries on to the right and becomes Mount Olympus behind The Sphinx. From the ridge you get fantastic views of Harper River and the peaks of the Craigieburn Range.

There are excellent touring opportunities from Mount Olympus. From the col below The Sphinx, it's possible to enter Ryton Valley and ski down to below Bottom Hut, or to ski along the ridge to the Mount Cheeseman ski area. That route takes about three hours. Fit club members have toured as far as the Craigieburn Valley ski area (via Mount Cheeseman and the Broken River ski areas) and back in 16 hours. As club members will tell you, this is not a trip for the inexperienced or the ill-equipped.

# Porter Heights

## History

A natural Y-shaped valley, Porter Heights first caught the eye of skiers in 1966 when a Mr P. H. Willis spent a few winter days walking up the basin and skiing back down. Toward the end of the season, he and Mr A. Coberger climbed to the ridge at the head of the basin and skied the entire basin. Willis was impressed with the potential for developing the basin into a commercial resort, and soon got permission from the local runholders and the Crown Land Department to do so.

In April 1967, an access track was constructed from Highway 73 up to the basin and snow conditions were regularly observed by Willis over the winter. Things were looking good and a private company, Porter Heights Development Ltd, was registered by Willis in December 1967. There were 24 shareholders and a capital of $30,000. Work was carried out over the summer of 1967–68. An 18-foot-wide access road, car parks and a 1200-square-foot ski lodge were constructed; and three rope tows (a main tow running up the basin floor and two beginner tows purchased from the Whakapapa ski area on Mount Ruapehu) were installed.

On 15 June 1968, to the tune of Bavarian music and glühwein, Porter Heights was officially opened. It was the closest field to Christchurch and only the second commercial ski area in the Canterbury region.

Just 14 days later, an avalanche destroyed all of the area's facilities, including the ski lodge in which three employees were asleep. Two of the men were injured; the third, Chris Wormseley, was unhurt and managed to dig the other two out and build a shelter for them. He then made his way down the access road and summoned help. Porter Heights ski area was devastated.

Work began immediately on repairing the damage and the area was able to open again in late August with a 'shortened' tow. The season finished in late October. Operators took heed of the avalanche danger and duly increased safety measures. Avalanche control at Porter Heights these days is recognised as being some of the best in the country.

The 'Dome' cafeteria, built in Christchurch and flown to the field in July 1977, is an interesting construction. A bit of an eyesore in its surroundings, the Dome was designed so that it could withstand an avalanche. With the area's high standard of ski patrol, it's not likely to ever be put to the test.

Competing not only with the larger commercial area of Mount Hutt, but also with a number of smaller club areas, Porter Heights has spent the last 15 years constantly improving its facilities. All rope tows have been replaced by T-bars and a platter. There are now three groomers operating, while a snow-making system has been installed along the T1 lift line and beginners' area.

## The Ski Area

If you ask Christchurch skiers which Canterbury ski area is their favourite, 'Porter Heights with enough snow' is not an uncommon response. What they mean is not that Porter Heights doesn't get enough snow – with its snowmaking it always does. What they mean is that, when there is sufficient snow for skiing the whole area, it is hard to better. In the two runs – Big Mama and Bluff Face – it unquestionably has some of the best skiing terrain in New Zealand.

The natural progression as you go up the mountain – from the learners' area at the base, to the intermediate No 1 T-bar, up to the advanced No 2 and No 3 T-bars – is near perfect. The learners' area to the left of No 1 T-bar is an almost flat area, with an easy-to-use rope tow, and is an excellent site for the 'never-evers'. To the right of No 1 T-bar is a platter lift and beginners' area, suited to the skiers who have recently mastered the learners' area. A big advantage of both these areas is that they

##  Porter Heights

*Location:* 95 km from Christchurch.
35 km from Springfield.
105 km from Methven.

*Season:* Mid-June through to mid-October.

*Elevation:* No 3 T-bar takes you to the ridge line at 1950 metres. The base buildings are at 1340 metres.

*Vertical Drop:* 610 metres.

*Terrain:* Beginner 20%, Intermediate 40%, Advanced 40%.

*Snowmaking:* Down the centre of the basin, along the No 1 T-bar lift line and on the learners' area.

*Groomers:* Three.

*Road toll:* $6 per vehicle if someone is going skiing; $10 if not.

*Lifts:* A learners' fixed grip tow, one platter and three T-bars. Moderate charge, with youth, learners' and family reductions. Special passes for lift and equipment hire. Under 10s are free.

*Ski hire:* 400 pairs of skis and a few snowboards.

Adult ;Youth (school pupil).
Skis, boots and poles (daily): $25; $15.
Skis only (daily): $20; $10.
Boots only (daily): $15; $10.
Executive skis (daily): $25.
Snowboards: $10 hour; $15 half day; $25 day.
Big Foot: $10 half day; $15 day.

are separated by fencing from the No 1 T-bar area, and are consequently free of advanced, faster skiers.

The runs down either side of No 1 T-bar have a reasonably constant gradient from top to bottom and are excellent for

## Porter Heights

*Specials:* 'Frequent Skier Card' gives reduced lift passes and free use of the road. Cards can be bought from the ski area and most BP petrol stations in Christchurch.

'Beginners' Package' (a learners' lift pass, hire gear and one 90-minute lesson) is $45 (Adult); $25 (School pupil).

'Two for One' deal on Mondays means, if you buy one-day pass, Beginners' Pack or ski lesson, you get two.

*Ski school:* About ten instructors.
Group lessons: 10:00 am; 2:00 pm. 90 minutes.
$19 (Adult); $15 (Youth); $15 (Child).
Private lessons: One hour. $39 (Adult); $35 (Youth/Child). Each extra person $20.
Early Bird Private: 9:00–10:00 am. $35 (Adult); $30 (Youth/Child).

*Accomm:* A modern 40-bunk lodge on the access road is run by the Porter Heights Ski Club (separate from the ski area) and offers dinner, bed and breakfast for a moderate charge, with a reduction for students and children. There's a manager and a chef working in the lodge from June to October. Enquiries should be addressed to the Porter Heights Ski Club, PO Box 2473, Christchurch, or phone 0-3-379 7087 or 025-340 909.

*Address:* Porter Heights Ski Area Ltd, PO Box 536, Christchurch. Telephone: 0-3-379 7087.

*Snow report:* Phone the Press Inpho Ski Line 0-3-366 6644, then 1101.

either wide-cruising or short turns. It's a great intermediate run. No 2 T-bar takes you to just above the base of No 3 T-bar, at the top of Julian's Bowl. From here it's possible to ski down the steep Julian's Bowl, or the even steeper terrain to the left of No 2 T-bar, or the easy route down the cat-track to the top of No 1 T-bar. This cat-track is a blessing to intermediate skiers who enjoy the skiing on the groomed runs of No 3 T-bar, but who can't quite manage Julian's Bowl.

From the top of the No 3 T-bar, the mountain is yours. The first thing to do, however, is climb the short distance to the top. The view of Lake Coleridge and surrounding mountain ranges

## Getting there

**From Christchurch**

*By car*

Take Yaldhurst Road west out of the city. This becomes Highway 73 and takes you to the small township of Yaldhurst. Not far past Yaldhurst is a turn-off to the right signposted Old West Coast Road. This is a shortcut that will save you about ten kilometres. It's a long, straight road that joins back up with Highway 73 at Waddington.

From there it's ten kilometres to Springfield, from where it's another ten kilometres to the base of Porters Pass. The road over the pass is steep and winding, and can be icy in the mornings and evenings. Once over the pass, it's a further seven kilometres past Lake Lyndon to the Porter Heights turn-off. The access road is well maintained and an easy drive, provided it is not icy.

*Hitching*

You should be somewhere along Riccarton Road by 8:00 am; the further along the road, the better. Skiers using this road could be going to Mount Hutt or any of the ski is spectacular. To the south, you will see the northern slopes of Mount Hutt; further south you may be able to pick out Mount Cook. To the north, in the Craigieburn Range, you can clearly see the lodge and main lift line of Mount Olympus. Don't hang around too long though – first tracks on Big Mama aren't available all day.

It's a reasonably easy traverse (with a little climbing) along a ridge line to the top of Big Mama, but it's not until you're standing at the top of the slope that you realise just how long the run is. It's a huge 620 vertical metres from top to bottom – one of the largest vertical drops in one lift-accessed run in New

---

areas in the Craigieburn Range. If you get a lift with someone going to Mount Hutt or Mount Olympus, it's best to get dropped off at the Old West Coast Road turn-off. Porter Heights is the first field in the Craigieburn Range, and it must be passed to get to any of the others. So if your ride is going to another field – Broken River, Mount Cheeseman, Craigieburn Valley or Temple Basin – you can get dropped off at the Porter Heights turn-off. It won't be a problem catching a lift from there.

*Shuttles and buses*
The Snowman Shuttle makes a daily trip to Porter Heights, making pick-ups throughout Christchurch from 7:15 am and arriving on the mountain at 9:15 am. An adult fare is $22; $19 for students. There are no one-way fares. Phone: 0–3–364 7223.

Mountain Adventures also sends a shuttle daily. They make pick-ups in Christchurch between 7:00 and 7:30 am. The fare for an adult is $25; for students or youths (under 18) it's $22. They also have no one-way fares.

Zealand. If you're fit enough to enjoy long powder runs, Big Mama is heaven. If you prefer skiing chutes, traverse to the left from the top of No 3 T-bar to the Aorangi Chutes and The Leapers, where the terrain is steep, and the chutes narrow.

To ski the full Bluff Face, and some would say that's the only way, you have to traverse down McNulty's cat-track to the left of the top of the No 3 T-bar. When you reach the col on the cat-track, take your skis off and walk toward the summit of Allison Peak. Climb until you're high enough to make the traverse above the rocks at the top of Stellar Bowl. It's possible to traverse on to the face by going beneath these rocks but, by doing so, you miss out on the upper reaches of the face where fewer skiers venture. There is also some great chute skiing to be had up there.

The Powder Bowl and Crystal Valley Runs are both outside the ski area boundary. There is superb skiing to be had on both but, realistically, some walking is usually required to get back into the main bowl. Crystal Valley is perfect touring terrain and an excellent place to spend a day doing so. To ski Powder Bowl or Crystal Valley without informing ski patrol is just plain foolhardy.

# Temple Basin

## History

The east–west train route that passes through Arthurs Pass was completed in 1923. Until then, the crossing had been made on foot or by horse-drawn cart, usually by gold-fevered miners heading to the West Coast. With the advent of the train and the settlement of Arthurs Pass already established (it was where the workers who dug the Otira train tunnel lived), the area became one of the country's earliest tourist attractions.

Guy Butler, possibly one of the country's first tourist entrepreneurs, saw the potential in the region and purchased the old tunnel-workers' dining rooms and converted them into a lodge, enabling visitors to spend a night or two. Legend has it that, in 1927, he purchased every pair of skis available in Christchurch and Dunedin – all eight of them! He hired these out to his guests who used them in the immediate region and occasionally on the road over to Otira.

Oscar Coberger, a German ski instructor living in New Zealand, got wind of this and headed to the Pass in 1929, where he set up a winter sports shop with skis imported from Germany and started giving lessons. (The Coberger family has been linked with New Zealand's skiing ever since. Anton, Oscar's son, was largely responsible for setting up the Porter Heights ski area, and Annelise, Anton's daughter, won a silver medal in the slalom at the 1992 Albertville Olympics.) More and more tourists were coming to Arthurs Pass, and the Railways Department started running cheap (five-shilling) trips every Sunday, sometimes taking 1200 people in one day.

The Christchurch Ski Club was formed during the 1929 season and, by 1930, when it had 76 members, it decided that it would be an idea to check out some of the surrounding snowfields. The low altitude of the Arthurs Pass township was thought to be a disadvantage. The Temple Basin region was the obvious choice, and a rough walking track was formed through the bush up to the good skiing slopes. (Mount Temple and the basin are thought to have been named after Captain Temple of Geraldine, a painter of mountain scenes and a founder of the Canterbury Arts Society.)

## Temple Basin

*Location:* 8 km from Arthurs Pass.
85 km from Springfield.
163 km from Christchurch.

*Season:* Mid-June/early July through to mid-October.

*Elevation:* Temple Col is 1753 metres high.
Downhill Tow takes you to 1750 metres.
Base lodges are at 1329 metres.

*Vertical drop:* 421 metres.

*Terrain:* Beginner 20%, Intermediate 50%, Advanced 30%.

*Snowmaking:* None.

*Groomers:* None.

*Road toll:* None, as there is no road! There is a free goods lift to carry your gear up from the road.

*Lifts:* Four rope tows.
Low charge, with family and under-19 reductions.
These prices also include night-skiing (when operating).
You also need two belts: $3 day; $4 weekend; $8 week. A $10 deposit is refunded when you return them.

*Ski hire:* 130 sets of skis and some snowboards.
Full hire (skis, boots and poles):
$21 day; $34 weekend; $100 week.
Snowboards: $5 hour.

Much of the skiing in those early days came about due to the efforts of Coberger, who would guide tourists up to the basin, where he kept his skis. Once fitted into a pair, tourists would follow him up a slope and ski down, with Coberger instructing.

In 1933, club members built a corrugated-iron hut in the basin, at 1400 metres. The club continued to grow (although it

##  Temple Basin

*Ski school:* Three instructors.
Lesson times are very flexible.
Group lessons: $15 (Adult); $10 (Child).
Private lessons: $25 per hour.

*Ski weeks:* Lift passes, food, accommodation and instruction a for a week costs $355 (Adult); $315 (Junior). For more information, phone 0-3-355 9480.

*Accomm:* Two large lodges – the Temple Basin Ski Club Lodge and the Canterbury University Ski Club Lodge. Together they have enough bunks for 120 people. The TBSC Lodge has mainly four-berth rooms; the CUSC Lodge has mainly six -berth rooms. Both have large cooking and living areas. The CUSC Lodge is mainly used by university students, though it may take an overflow from the TBSC Lodge if space is available. The TBSC Lodge was renovated in 1994 and now offers some of the country's more extravagant on-mountain accommodation. It even has its own wine list! There is a low charge for a night's stay; a moderate charge for dinner, bed and breakfast. It may be necessary to book ahead.

*Address:* Temple Basin Ski Club, PO Box 1228, Christchurch. Telephone 0-3-355 9480.

*Snow report:* Phone the Press Inpho Ski Line 0-3-366 6644, then 1101.

was pretty quiet through the war years) and, in 1948, Dr Page, one of the founding members, built the club's first ski lift (only the second in the South Island). It was a short rope tow that ran off a Ford 10 petrol engine, and was a much welcome addition.

After establishing an accommodation base on the mountain, the club spent the following years developing lift facilities, installing four rope tows and a goods lift by 1984. These days, although it's an hour's walk (depending on snow cover) to get to the ski area, it has a large following of Christchurch enthusiasts, many of whom praise the walk as it deters the crowd and leaves them to ski what has been termed the 'no ski bunnies' ski area.

## GETTING THERE

**From Christchurch**

*By car*
Follow the instructions for Porter Heights and keep going west along Highway 73 for another 50 kilometres to the township of Arthurs Pass. From there, it's another eight kilometres to the Temple Basin car park on the right. The road to and from Arthurs Pass doesn't see much sun during winter, and can be treacherously icy in mornings and afternoons.

*Hitching*
The same as for Porter Heights, except that it would pay to be on the road earlier, say 7:00 am, because Temple Basin is further away. If you call the club's Christchurch office (0–3–355- 9480), they may be able to put you on to someone who's driving and has a spare seat.

*Shuttle and buses*
The Coast to Coast shuttle passes Temple Basin daily on its way to Greymouth. It leaves Christchurch at 8:00 am, passing Temple Basin at about 11:00 am. On its way back

Students from Canterbury University have been involved in skiing at Temple Basin since the early 1950s when they formed a ski club. The current University Ski Club hut is on the site of the original Temple Basin Lodge, the Christchurch Ski Club having moved to a new site a little higher in the basin.

## THE SKI AREA

There's a 40- to 60-minute (depending on the amount of snow) walk up to the ski area from the car park, but you don't have to carry your gear. A goods lift 500 metres further along the

> to Christchurch it passes Temple Basin at about 2:45 pm. A one-way fare is $25. Phone 0800–800 847 (toll-free).
>
> The Alpine Coach and Courier shuttle makes the same trip between Monday and Friday, only it leaves Christchurch at 3:00 pm, passing Temple Basin at about 5:00 pm. A one-way fare is $25. Phone 0–3–736 9834.
>
> *Train*
> You can catch the TranzAlpine from Christchurch to Arthurs Pass, then an Arthurs Pass taxi from there. The TranzAlpine leaves Christchurch at 9:15 am, getting into Arthurs Pass at 11:36 am. A one-way fare is $47. Contact New Zealand Rail 0800–802 802 (toll-free).
>
> **From Arthurs Pass**
> It's not difficult hitching to the ski area from Arthurs Pass. Christchurch skiers tend to pass through on their way to the basin from 8:30 am onwards. The Arthurs Pass Taxi Service (0–3–318 9266) runs trips to the ski area for $10.

highway, just over Arthurs Pass, will carry your gear to the top for free. The idea is to first drive to the goods lift and drop your gear off with the attendant there. It's advisable to keep your gear together so it goes up on the same trip. Once this is done, head back to the car park and commence walking. Remember, every ski area was like this once. As you climb, the views of Mount Rolleston (2271 metres) and the other peaks across the valley become better and better.

It's an easy walk up a rocky track to the lodges, though it can be awkward in icy or deep snow conditions. The first building you come to is the Lockwood Public Shelter, just above the top of the goods lift, where your gear should be by the time you get there. You can base yourself for the day at either the public shelter or the more luxurious Temple Basin Ski Club Lodge ($2 for the day), which is a short walk from the goods lift past the Canterbury University Ski Club Lodge.

You can hire tow belts and ski equipment from the Ski Hire office in the TBSC Lodge. Lift passes must be purchased from the small A-frame hut at the base of Temple Tow.

The Cassidy Lift services good terrain for beginners. From the top of the tow a short traverse to either side takes you to some interesting intermediate to advanced terrain, more so the further out you go. Beginners may find it a little hard-going from the top of Cassidy, but the beauty of rope tows is that they're easy to get off wherever you like. There is a good beginners' run from half-way up Cassidy. Beginners are likely to most enjoy this run and the lower slopes in the Temple Basin, from half-way up Temple Tow.

Temple Basin itself is a steep run toward the top, becoming gradually less so as it nears the bottom. To the left of Temple Tow is a fairly exciting run for advanced skiers, generally preferred by the less rock-shy.

The skiing in Downhill Basin is amongst the best in the country. More than a few skiers have been seen walking the track from Temple Tow early in the day, not to be seen again until their return as dusk nears. Downhill Basin is separated by a ridge and can't be seen from the rest of the ski area, making it a kind of a 'Hanging Rock' mystery to those in the lodges who see skiers continually disappear over the ridge.

The basin is wide, and has a huge option of routes to descend on. Advanced, intermediate, and the more intrepid beginner skiers, will all enjoy the skiing here. The upper third of the basin and the area to the right of the tow are relatively steep; the rest of the basin varies in gradient, with a few large undulations in the lower region. Because of its northerly aspect, Downhill Basin is in the sun for most of the day. The traverse from Downhill Basin, through the area called Upper Twin Creeks and back to the lodges, passes beneath a series of small bluffs and can be awkward in poor visibility.

From the top of Downhill Tow it's a short climb to the Temple Col, from where there's a fantastic view of the peaks of Arthurs Pass National Park. Dominating the view to the east is Mount Oates at 2009 metres. A traverse to the left from the top of Downhill Tow will take you over a ridge and into Bill's Basin. This is a huge expanse of snow in which first tracks are not usually difficult to obtain. There are numerous chutes at the bottom, through which you can ski and come out into Cassidy Basin. There are some very narrow chutes here. A further traverse on to the face of B'Limit opens up some exceptionally challenging terrain and should really be considered only by the more adroit skiers. The best way to ski this area is by hooking up with a club member who's prepared to show you around.

Night skiing is available, and in recent years has proved extremely popular with the over-nighters, who usually head out after a meal and a few glasses from the club's wine stock.

The ski-touring potential in and around Temple Basin is huge. If you plan to do some touring in the Temple Basin area, phone the club and check on local conditions before making the trip.

# ARTHURS PASS

Arthurs Pass was first used long ago by the Maori, who travelled over the Southern Alps in search of the valuable pounamu (greenstone) found on the West Coast.

During the West Coast gold rush in the 1860s, the people of Canterbury, on the other coast, were eager for the trade this gold could supply, and sought a route over the Alps. Arthur Dudley Dobson became the first European to 'discover' the pass in 1864. Both he and his brother George surveyed the Alps and were commissioned to make the final choice of route. When asked about possible routes, George declared, 'Arthur's Pass is the best route', and in so doing accidentally gave the pass its name.

A rough road was speedily built over the pass and ready by 1865. The township of Arthurs Pass started as a small hotel, serving beer and food to tired miners making the crossing. The road was slowly improved, and in 1923 a trans-alpine railway was constructed. (It is now regarded as one of the world's classic rail journeys.)

The township became a settlement for railway workers during the construction of the Otira train tunnel. Then, once the tunnel was completed, the workers were replaced by tourists using the new railway. It's still a very small town, with only about 60 year-round residents.

The town is set in a narrow valley, between two towering mountain ranges, and so does not receive a lot of direct sun during the day. Its main road (Highway 73) is lined with tiny old cottages, and in the centre of town is a building containing a store/cafeteria/petrol station. There's a **Youth Hostel**, 0–3–318 9230; and a backpackers' hostel (**The Mountain House**), 0–3–318 9258. Both have the essential pot-belly stoves and offer very good accommodation for a low charge.

At the eastern end of town is the **Chalet Restaurant and Guest House**, 0–3–318 9236, which does bed and breakfast. The cost is high (double room with private facilities), with a reduction for shared facilities. The **Alpine Motel**, 0–3–318 9233, at the western end of town, has rooms from a moderate to a high charge.

If you're looking for a meal you can try the **store cafeteria**, which serves hamburgers, fish and chips, etc (low charge) or the **Chalet Restaurant** with its fine service and exquisite dishes (high charge). The Chalet also has the only bar in town. It's a fantastic place, with a large open fire and warm surroundings.

Temple Basin is the nearest ski area to Arthurs Pass. But, as the ski area is about an hour's walk from the road, most people stay in the lodge on the mountain. You may, however, choose to spend a night in Arthurs Pass all the same. Either way it's worth checking out, and having a bit of a stroll around.

# CHRISTCHURCH

Canterbury is mostly too cold for traditional Polynesian horticulture, and so few Maori settled in the region. However, some small tribes did settle there, as it was well stocked with fish in the rivers, lakes and sea, and flocks of moas, large flightless birds (now extinct) that roamed across the plains.

The Ngai Tahu tribe, from the east coast of the North Island, gradually moved south, fighting and intermarrying with other tribes on their way. By 1800, the Ngai Tahu dominated the South Island, and one of their largest settlements was a pa (fortified village) at Kaiapoi, just north of Christchurch.

In 1770, James Cook, the first European to see the Canterbury coast, sailed past without setting foot on land. The first Europeans to land in Canterbury were the crew of the *Governor Bligh*, which landed on Banks Peninsula in 1815.

In the 1830s, the whale-hunting trade brought Europeans to the bays of Banks Peninsula. A French whaling captain, Jean François Langlois, 'bought' Banks Peninsula from the local Maori in 1838. He left for France, and returned with a shipload of immigrants in 1840, only to find that the British had annexed New Zealand. It was these people who settled the distinctly French township of Akaroa.

The Deans brothers, William and John, began farming on the Canterbury Plains in 1843. (They named the Avon River, after the river of that name in their home of Ayrshire, Scotland.) In the 1850s, the London-based Canterbury Association began sending migrants, known as 'Canterbury Pilgrims', to settle the city of Christchurch. Led by John Robert Godley, the association aimed to establish a traditional English community, with a class structure and an agricultural base. (The city was named after Godley's college at Oxford.)

By the 1870s, all farmable land on the plains and foothills had been leased out and turned into pastoral land. By 1880, there were over four million sheep in Canterbury, and more than 400,000 hectares of cultivated land. The city grew and gradually became the biggest city in the South Island.

These days, Christchurch displays a distinct contrast between old and new. The old is found in the classic Gothic revival architecture; the wide, tree-lined streets; and the grassy banks of the Avon in the city centre. The new can be found in the numerous bars, restaurants and cafés around town. It is a city with a kind of European feel to it and one that is capable of holding any visitor's interest for some time.

In the first week of August, Christchurch hosts its Winter Carnival, a series of fun events held in the city and on its surrounding ski areas. For a snow-lover there is no better time to visit Christchurch. You can spend your days participating in one of the events, or just skiing, and return to a city bar hosting the night's party, with fellow skiers and snowboarders. The number of events and venues is huge. They range from the Undy 500, a slalom race in which competitors wear nothing but their underwear, to the Formal Snow Ball, a black tie affair held in one of the city's classier venues.

# ARRIVAL

*By air*
Christchurch Airport lies about ten kilometres from the city centre. Buses leave Cathedral Square (usually called The Square) every half hour until 8:00 pm and are the cheapest way of getting to or from the airport. Alternatively, you can catch a shuttle bus, which will take you from the airport to your hostel or hotel for a higher fare. A taxi is the most expensive way of getting between the airport and city centre.

*By train*
The train station lies about four kilometres west of the city centre. Bus No 25 leaves from the corner of Clarence and Blenheim Roads (a five-minute walk from the station). Shuttles

and taxis are also available. Some hostels have shuttles waiting at the station and will give you a complimentary lift, provided, of course, you stay with them.

*By bus*
Each bus company has its own depot. If this is not near the city centre, buses will usually make a drop-off somewhere central, most often in The Square. The two major operators – Mount Cook Landline (0–3–379 0690) and Intercity/Ritchies (0–3–377 0951) – have depots very close to the centre of town. Mount Cook is at 40 Lichfield Street, and Intercity/Ritchies is at 471 Moorhouse Avenue. Both are within walking distance from most of the city's hostels. It won't be a problem catching a taxi from either depot.

*By shuttle*
Most shuttle companies will take you to wherever you want to go within Christchurch. If not, they will certainly be making a stop in The Square.

*By car*
With Highway 1 passing through the centre of Christchurch, it is difficult to get lost. Roads are well signed and, with the city's one-way system, it's quite easy to enter or leave the city (in some cases without actually trying to!). Provided you have some sort of city map, getting around town should be no problem at all. There are free maps available from the Information Centre on the corner of Worcester Street and Oxford Terrace. If you've hitched to Christchurch and been dropped off in the outskirts, you shouldn't be too far from a bus stop, at which a bus going to The Square should stop quite frequently. From The Square, most of the city centre is really within walking distance.

## SKI AND SNOWBOARD SHOPS

*Note:*
❏ The term 'etc' denotes that the daily rental charge gets progressively cheaper the longer you hire.

- Only the prices for a full set of equipment (skis, boots and poles) are listed here. All shops also hire out these items separately.
- All shops will want some kind of deposit before you can hire gear. Deposits usually requested are credit-card numbers, car licence-plate numbers and passports.

**Snow and Surf** (0–3–366 7351) at 85 Tuam Street has a good range of retail equipment and usually a fair range of second-hand skis and boots.

*Repair charges:*
Complete tune: $45.
Crystal glide and wax: $39.
Belt tune and fill: $35.
Edge sharpen and wax: $25.
Hot wax: $10.

*Hire charges:*
Skis, boots and poles: $20 (day); $35 (two days); $55 (three days) etc; $110 (week).
'Advanced skis': $30 (day); $100 (week).
Jackets or overalls: $15 (day); $25 (two days) etc; $75 (week).
Jackets and overalls: $25 (day); $40 (two days) etc; $105 (week).
Snowboards and boots: $30 (day); $50 (two days) etc; $100 (week).
Also hired out are touring skis, big feet, toboggans and roof racks.
The shop runs a daily ski shuttle to Mount Hutt, Porter Heights and Mount Cheeseman.

**McEwings Mountain Sports** has two shops in Christchurch – a retail and hire shop at 93 Cashel Street Mall (0–3–366 6211); and a hire shop at 200 Yaldhurst Road (0–3–342 8528), on the way to many ski areas. You can be fitted up at the central shop and pick up your gear from Yaldhurst if you wish. The central shop probably has the largest range of retail and second-hand skis in Christchurch.

*Repair charges:*
Full ski tune: $39.
Edge and sharpen: $18.
Hot wax: $9.
Crystal glide: from $20, depending on the number of passes your skis require over the stone.

*Hire charges:*
Skis, boots and poles: $20 (day); $38 (two days) etc; $130 (ten days).
Pants and jackets: $13 each (day); $25 each (two days) etc; $59 each (week).
Suit: $22 (day); $42 (two days) etc; $100 (week).
Snowboards and boots: $30 (day); $57 (two days) etc; $137 (week).
Demo/executive skis: $30 (day); $57 (two days) etc; $137 (week).
Ski mountaineering sets: $55 (day) etc.
Roof racks: $10 (day) etc.
Chains: $8 (day) etc.

**Victoria Ski Sport** at 130 Victoria Street (0–3–366 2018) has a good range of retail and second-hand equipment.

*Repair charges:*
Full ski tune with crystal glide: from $38, depending on the amount of work required.
Hot wax: $9.

*Hire charges:*
There are three rates – one day; weekend; week:
A full set (skis, boots and poles): $20; $35; $91.
Overalls or jackets: $13; $21; $54.
Overalls and jacket: $22; $40; $80.
Snowboards and boots: $25; $45; $110.

High-performance skis or demo skis: $30; $55; $140.

**Cobergers** (0–3–379 5174) at 15 Cranmer Square deals mainly with retail equipment. They have no equipment for hire, but they do do repairs.

*Repair charges:*
Crystal glide: from $35 to $49, depending on the amount of work required.
Sharpen and wax: $18.
Hot wax: $8.

**Ski Windsurf City** has two shops – a city shop (0–3–366 6516) at 64 Manchester Street; and a Yaldhurst Road outlet (0–3–342 5757) beside the Shell petrol station, just past the Yaldhurst Hotel. It's possible to get fitted out in the city shop and pick up the gear from the Yaldhurst one.

*Repair charges:*
Crystal glide: from $35.
Full tune, without crystal glide: $25.
Edge and wax: $18.
Hot wax: $8.

*Hire charges:*
Full set of gear: $22 (day); $40 (two days) etc; $113 (week with $18.50 a day after that).
Jackets or pants: $12 each (day); $22 (two days) etc.
Jackets and pants: $20 (day); $35 (two days) etc.
Students get a 15 per cent discount on any hire equipment.

**R & R Sport** have two shops – 81 Manchester Street (0–3–366 5100) and 81 Riccarton Road (0–3–348 3625). Both shops have large selections of second-hand ski gear. They also have a reasonable selection of new gear, particularly the Manchester Street shop. The Manchester Street shop doesn't hire out ski gear but does hire out snowboards and boots (soft bindings) for

$28 a day. A multi-day discount can be arranged. Inside R & R is Ruby's Ski Workshop. Ruby's motto is 'We can fix just about any damage inflicted on your skis or snowboard'.

*Repair charges:*
Hot wax: $5.
Edge sharpen: $9.
Ski base grind: $5.
Crystal glide: $30.
Patches: from $15.
Sole repair work: charged by the hour.
Snowboard grind and wax: $40.

*Hire charges from the Riccarton shop are:*
Full ski gear: $15 (day).
You may be able to negotiate a multi-day discount.

**Scuba Ski and Sailing** at 103 Manchester Street (0–3–365 1929) have a reasonable range of skis and ski paraphernalia.

*Repair charges:*
Hot wax: $5.
Base grind: from $15.
Edge sharpen: $12.
Sole repair: from $5.

*Hire charges:*
Full ski gear: $20 (day); $35 (two days); $80 (week).
Rates for longer than a week are negotiable.
Ski pants or jackets: $10 each (day); $50 (week).

## Snowboard shops

**Cheapskates** at 225b High Street (0–3–377 2942) is close to the Java Café, itself a popular shredder haunt.

*Hire charges:*
Boards and soft boots: $28 (day); $52 (two days) etc; $120 (week).

*Repair charges:*
Crystal glide and tune: $45.
Tune: $28.
Hot wax: $8.

**Wide Load** (0–3–366 5442) is upstairs in the Shands Emporium at 88 Hereford Street. As at Cheapskates, the staff there enjoy a good chat.

*Hire charges:*
Board and soft boots: $28 (day); student $25. Monday to Friday $115, or $125 over the weekend. Seven days $154.
Board only: $25 (day).
Boots only: $10.

*Repair charges:*
Base and edge grind: $35.
Edge sharpen: $8.
Hot wax: $5.

## PLACES TO STAY

**Rolleston House YHA** (0–3–366 9199) is on the corner of Worcester Street and Rolleston Avenue. It offers standard youth-hostel style accommodation, but the real beauty of this place is its location. It's across Worcester Boulevard from the Arts Centre (which really becomes the city's centre on weekends), handy to the centre of town, and a 20-metre walk from Hagley Park. Other bonuses include its off-street car parking and an on-call masseur who, for $20, will spend an hour curing any aching muscles. Costs are in the low price range.

**Cora Wilding YHA** (0–3–389 9199) at 9 Evelyn Couzins Avenue is named after the founder of the New Zealand branch of the YHA. One of the original Canterbury homesteads, it was converted to a hostel in 1966. Although it's a fair way from the centre of town, about a 25-minute walk, the quality of this place and its setting (a large garden in front and surrounded by tall trees) more than make up for any inconvenience. It's even possible to feel a little extravagant staying at Cora Wilding, and it's easy to see why the YHA hold their annual conferences here. Bunks are budget-priced, twins and doubles are in the low price range.

**Bealey International Backpackers** (0-3-366 6760) at 70 Bealey Avenue is a smallish 'quality' hostel, about a 15-minute walk from The Square. It has a TV room, a large kitchen, a laundry, a large back lawn and, best of all, a great log fire. The noticeboard here is fairly comprehensive and worth checking out if you're after something such as a car. There's a free shuttle service from the train and bus stations. Bunk rooms are budget-priced, twins and doubles in the low price range.

**Foley Towers** (0-3-366 9720) at 208 Kilmore Street is a five-minute walk from The Square. One of the original backpacker hostels of Christchurch, this place has a real 'laid-back' feel to it. The hostel actually consists of two large old townhouses and a modern motel-like extension. It has all the amenities as well as a couple of great back lawns. Bunk rooms are budget-priced, twins and doubles a few dollars more.

**Frauenreisehaus** (0-3-366 2585) at 272 Barbadoes Street is a women-only hostel. A ten-minute walk from The Square, it's in a great old two-storey place. It has a German library and the latest German magazines (there are some Japanese books and magazines, too). It has free washing machines, a good drying room, free tea/coffee, free local phone calls, a good pool table, TV, Cable TV, video, and bike hire for $3 a day. Bunks are budget-priced, with twin or double rooms a few dollars more. Single rooms are slightly more expensive again.

**Dreamland Hostel** (0-3-366 3519) is at 21-23 Packe Street, off Bealey Avenue between Madras and Barbadoes Streets. It is a couple of converted houses, about a 15-minute walk from The Square. It does have a homely atmosphere about it, and is likely to appeal to you if you're after a 'mellow' place to stay. It has a fireplace that is kept regularly stoked and, if you need cooling (or freezing), there's always the swimming pool out the back. There is a free pick-up service from the inner city, and sometimes from the train station. Bunks and rooms (twin and double) are in the budget range.

**Round the World** (0-3-365 4363) at 314 Barbadoes Street is the newest backpackers' hostel in Christchurch. It was purpose-built in April 1993. Looking more like a hotel, or a block of townhouses, it lacks a little of the character the other places have, but it does have all the mod cons, and is kept very clean (almost sterile, in fact). It's a ten-minute walk from The Square, and is one of the few hostels in Christchurch with facilities for the disabled. A bunk in a dormitory is budget-priced; in a twin room, low.

**Meadowpark Holiday Park** (0-3-352 9176) is at 529 Cranford Street. Five kilometres north of The Square, this is really a place to stay if you have your own transport, or don't mind catching a bus (Nos 1 or 4) to the centre. It's basically a large holiday camp with a variety of accommodation, the backpackers' part being a number of three-bed, budget-priced cabins. Cooking, shower and toilet facilities are in their own separate blocks. A big plus for this place is its spa, sauna and heated swimming pool, for which there is a small charge.

**Charlie B's** (0-3-379 8429) is at 268 Madras Street, a two-minute walk from The Square. With loads of off-street parking, this place offers the cheapest beds in town in their dormitories. The dorms are pretty big but, if you're on a tight budget, this is the place to stay. Bunks in rooms that sleep two, three or four are also budget-priced; single rooms just hit the low price range. As well as being cheap it has a games room, pool table, Sky TV and videos, a back garden and a few great open fires. It's quite easy to get attached to the routine of skiing all day and playing a quiet game of pool in front of a roaring fire by night. Another bonus is the complimentary pick-up and drop-off service.

**Croydon House** (0–3–366 5111) at 63 Armagh Street, although primarily a bed and breakfast outfit, does offer 15 beds for backpackers' accommodation. It's a two-minute walk from The Square and a shuttle will make pick-ups and drop-offs to the train and bus stations. There's a good warm kitchen, a washing machine you can use for free, and a lounge area with Sky TV. There are budget beds in shared rooms or low-priced singles. A night in the B&B part is moderately priced.

**Stonehurst Hotel** (0–3–379 4647) at 241 Gloucester Street is a huge 160-bed backpackers' Mecca. There are two big advantages of staying at this place: the free nightly beers from the in-house bar; and the great '$5 for all you can eat' Continental breakfasts, served from 6:00 am, in plenty of time to get to the slopes. You can also get a decent-sized cooked dinner for a moderate charge. It's a kind of 'hostel meets hotel' type of place. There are budget bunks, budget twins and doubles, low-priced singles. Rooms with a TV and private bathroom that sleep four are budget-priced, while twins and doubles are low-priced.

**Backpackers Inn** (0–3–379 46205) at 50 Cathedral Square is quite possibly the most central hostel in any city in the world. If you're planning on spending most of your nights in Christchurch 'on the town', this is the place for you. It's above 'Baileys Bar', one of the Irish bars in the city and a popular haunt for locals and travellers alike. The hostel has 150 beds in double, twin and dorm (five–six beds) rooms. Every room has its own toilet and shower. There's a TV room, kitchen, dining room and a common room with a couple of pool tables. A bed in any room is in the budget price range.

The **YMCA** (0–3–365 0502) at 12 Hereford Street offers accommodation to anyone, not only young men. It's in a new building across the road from Hagley Park, and a five-minute walk from The Square. The rooms and bunks are good and facilities include a fitness centre, gymnasium, aerobics classes, squash courts, a climbing wall and a sauna! If you're thinking of spending a week or two in Christchurch, this place should certainly be on your list. Bunks are budget-priced, singles and doubles are in the moderate price range. If you stay for three nights or more you get a 10 per cent discount. It would be an idea to book ahead, and almost essential during the August school holidays.

**Pavilions Motor Lodge** (0–3–355 3554 or 0800–805 555, toll-free) at 42 Papanui Road, is a 15-minute walk from the town centre, and not far from Hagley Park. It has a range of rooms, all in the high price range. Most rooms have a kitchen; all have tea- and coffee-making facilities, a fridge, minibar, TV and en suite. It has a spa pool, sauna, laundry, and a licensed restaurant and bar. Bookings are essential.

**Towers Hotel** (0–3–348 0613 or 0800–650 101, toll-free) is on the corner of Deans Avenue and Kilmarnock Street, over the road from Hagley Park, and a ten-minute walk from the city centre. It has a range of high-priced rooms, all with TV, radio, telephone, fridge, tea- and coffee-making facilities, en suites and a mini bar. There's also a laundry. Breakfasts can be served in your room. Bookings are a must.

**Grange Guesthouse** (0–3–366 2850) at 56 Armagh Street is a great Victorian mansion offering bed and breakfast accommodation. It's very central, about a five-minute walk from Cathedral Square. There are twin/double and single rooms, each with en suite and complimentary tea and coffee. All are in the high price range. There's a laundry and a cosy guest lounge/TV room. Breakfasts are English or Continental.

**Windsor Hotel** (0–3–366 1503) at 52 Armagh Street is a five-minute walk from The Square. It is a traditional bed and breakfast place, with shared bathroom facilities, a laundry, complimentary tea and coffee, and a lounge/TV room. With prices ranging from moderate to high, depending on the number of beds in the room, this offers good, affordable accommodation.

**Aotea Motel** (0–3–379 1311) at 302 Bealey Avenue has a range of ten modern units. With at least two people per unit the cost is moderate. Each unit has a kitchen with full cooking facilities, a TV, radio and telephone. Breakfasts can be brought to your room. There's a laundry, and a courtesy coach to and from the airport and bus or train station. It's a ten-minute walk from The Square.

**Château on the Park** (0–3–348 8999) at 189 Deans Avenue is one of the city's prestige hotels. It's just over the road from Hagley Park, and a short distance from the city centre. For a high charge, you get an exquisite room with tea- and coffee-making facilities, a refrigerator with a minibar, a colour TV, radio, shower and bath. The whole place is done out in a medieval theme, with a restaurant called 'Camelot', a brasserie called 'Lamplighter', and a bar called 'Den of the Little Red Foxes'. It also has a heated swimming pool. There's a complimentary shuttle service into The Square, and the reception staff are basically able to organise anything you'd like.

**Noah's Christchurch Hotel** (0–3–379 4700 or 0800–654 994, toll-free), on the banks of the Avon about a minute's walk from The Square, is probably the most luxurious place to stay. It's where royalty and pop stars stay. It has everything you'd expect from a 4.5-star hotel, and service is superb.

## PLACES TO EAT

In Christchurch, it's really a matter of deciding what cuisine you feel like and then choosing the restaurant. Listed here are a number of places with a variety of cuisines, all offering good value for money.

**Rita's Burritas** (0–3–379 2387) at 818 Colombo Street serves good-sized, moderately priced Mexican dishes between 5:30 and 10:00 pm. It's a small place with just a few tables, so if you want a table book ahead. Takeaways are available. It's licensed to serve beer and wine or you can bring your own. There's a charge of $1 per person if you BYO.

Just down the road (834 Colombo Street) from Rita's is **South of the Border** (0–3–379 7808), another Mexican restaurant. There's more seating here but the prices, although still in the moderate price range, are a little higher. It's strictly BYO, for which they charge $1 per head. Hours are 6:00 to 10:00 pm.

If souvlakia or doner kebabs are more to your liking, there's no shortage of restaurants. **Costas Souvlaki Bar** (open 11:00 am to 6:00 pm) in the Armagh Food Fair (142 Armagh Street) make arguably the best and most affordable souvlaki and kebabs in town, all in the low price range. For a more substantial Greek dining experience at moderate prices, try **Santorini Greek Ouzeri** (0–3–379 6975) on the corner of Gloucester Street and Cambridge Terrace. Open from 5:00 pm until late, it's a large place with a great setting – an inside mezzanine floor painted to look like a Greek courtyard. There is often live Greek music. It's usually busy so book. For a good-sized, low-priced Turkish meal visit the **Topkapi Turkish Kebab House** (0–3–379 4447) at 185 Manchester Street. There's a wide selection of kebabs, and you can sit on large Persian cushions around low tables if desired. This BYO restaurant is also quite busy, so book. Takeaways are available. Hours are 11:00 am to 11:00 pm; closed on Sundays.

There are two excellent, moderately priced Thai restaurants to choose from. The **Mythai** (0–3–365 1295) at 84 Hereford Street serves great meals and has an authentic atmosphere. It's BYO, and it may be necessary to book ahead. The **Sala Thai** (0–3–365 5447) is a little further from the centre of town, on the corner of Colombo and Kilmore Streets. The atmosphere is similarly authentic, and the food just as good. It's also BYO. Both of these restaurants are open between 5:00 and 11:00 pm.

For possibly the largest servings in town, and certainly one of the livelier atmospheres, head to the **Lone Star Café** (0–3–365 7086) at 26 Manchester Street; open from 5:30 pm until late. The mains are moderately priced but are huge. It's a big place with a Western/cowboy theme, and is almost always packed. If you haven't booked a table it usually means waiting in the bar, which isn't all bad, for up to an hour. It's licensed, but you can BYO wine.

**Winnie Bagoes** (0–3–366 6315) at 83 Lichfield Street is a popular pizza bar that seems to be constantly busy. This is more than likely because of the inexplicably good, moderately priced pizzas (the 'crocodile' variety is a specialty) and the fine wine list. It has a bar, and is also a good spot for just a drink. Hours are 11:30 am to 12:00 midnight.

**Six Chairs Missing** (0–3–366 4197) on New Regent Street was apparently named after a mishap in furniture delivery. A small place with a pleasant informal atmosphere, it is known as one of the best dining spots in town. The wine list is good, and it's also BYO. Most mains are in the high price range. It's open every day except Sunday: for coffee and snacks between 10:00 am and 5:00 pm; for evening meals from 6:00 pm to midnight. Bookings are vital for the evenings.

**Scottelis Pizzeria** (0–3–374 5812) on the corner of Oxford Terrace and Armagh Street is a kind of a pizza-bar-meets-café-meets-wine-bar place. Open from 11:00 am until late, its pizzas are very good and moderately priced. Bookings are advisable. Just down Armagh Street from Scottelis is **The Winery**, a pleasant spot with one of the city's best wine lists (albeit a little pricey).

**Sala Sala Restaurant** and **Sushi Bar** (0–3–366 6755), which is the outright winner of 'The Perplexing Restaurant Door' award, is a very authentic Japanese restaurant (the kind of place in which you just hate asking for a fork), serving exceptionally tasty meals in the moderate price range. It's on the corner of Gloucester Street and Oxford Terrace, and bookings are essential. It's licensed (no BYO), and open from 12:00–2:00 pm and 6:00–10:00 pm.

**Tiffanys Restaurant** (0–3–379 1350) on the banks of the Avon has possibly the finest setting of all inner city restaurants. With its silver service, great wine list and fabulous food, it rates fairly highly as a place to dine. Meals are in the high price range. It's licensed and BYO (bottled wine only), and open from 11:00 am until late. Bookings are essential.

**Il Felice** (0–3–366 7535) at 56 Lichfield Street has a distinctly Mediterranean air to it. The walls are covered with great murals, dining is by candlelight, and the meals are truly excellent (the Seafood Chowder especially). Mains range from moderate to high in price. It's BYO and licensed. Open from 6:00–11:00 pm, bookings are essential.

**Spagalimis Pizza Restaurant** (0–3–379 7469) is a ten-minute walk from the centre of town, at 155 Victoria Street. It has a casual, relaxed atmosphere, and serves fantastic pizzas in three sizes from low to moderately priced. Open from 11:00 am until late, it's licensed and BYO. Booking ahead is advisable.

If you feel like a good steak, and you're a Beatles fan, head for

**Sergeant Pepper's Steak House** (0–3–365 3686) at 750a Colombo Street. The walls are covered with 'Fab Four' memorabilia and more often than not there's Beatles music playing (any Beatles song at your request). For a moderate price, you can have your steak any way you like; or if steak's not your thing, they also do fish and chips.

For something a little different, try the **Zydeco Café** (0–3–365 4556) at 113 Manchester Street. Open from 6:00 pm until late, it's a Cajun restaurant, and serves what is probably the spiciest food in town. A small, popular place, it's great for a quiet evening. The meals are moderately priced and it's BYO. Bookings are advisable.

Even more different is the **Pyramids of Sahara Egyptian** Restaurant, a few doors down from the Zydeco Café. It's an authentic place, right down to the occasional belly dancer, and the meals are moderately priced. It's BYO and open from 5:00 pm to 12:00 midnight.

## HAPPENING PLACES

In recent years, Christchurch has developed something of a café culture. Gone are the days of leaning on formica tables and walking through a smoke-filled room on sodden carpet to a grumpy barman. The quality of coffee has made quantum leaps, too. To best savour this renaissance, try one of these:

**Le Café** in the Arts Centre on Worcester Avenue.

**Boulevard Bakehouse**, also in the Arts Centre, and famous for its pumpkin and chocolate muffins.

**Java Café** on the corner of High, Manchester and Lichfield Streets – a kind of 'alternative' place, with fantastic banana smoothies served in old fruit jars.

**Café d'Fafo** on Hereford Street – a little pricey, but a strong contestant for the city's best brew.

**Espresso 124** in Cashel Street – it's also a very Continental delicatessen.

**Bardelli's**, also in Cashel Street, and one of the 'places to be seen'. It's also a bar that serves good, low-priced pasta dishes.

**Mainstreet Vegetarian Café and Bar** at 840 Colombo Street – fantastic vegetarian meals, as well as home to some pretty great fruit cakes. It also has a bar.

For beer connoisseurs, there are two bars that must be visited – the **Loaded Hog** at 39 Dundas Street, and the **Dux de Lux** at 41 Hereford Street. Both brew their own range of beers. The Loaded Hog is a little way from the heart of town but the beer alone is worth the short trip. There's live music every Friday and Saturday night. The Dux is in an old building in the Arts Centre. It has a great garden bar and live music every Thursday, Friday and Saturday night. It's certainly one of the most popular bars in town and seems to be a real melting pot.

**Kickin' Jazz** at 633 Colombo Street is a laid-back bar/café, popular with the city's night-owls. It's open from 6:00 pm until late, and can often still be busy at 1:00 in the morning. Jazz plays (sometimes a live band) while groups of people chat, play chess or backgammon, or just look out the window on to the street below (it's upstairs). Just the place to hang out following a full-on day in the mountains.

**Joe Bolidos**, just down the road from Kickin' Jazz (look out for the billboard), is also upstairs, but aside from that, the two have little in common. On entering Joe Bolidos, you could be excused for feeling like you've just stepped on to the Starship Enterprise's entertainment deck. There's a lot of sheet metal, an orbiting Flash Gordon-style spaceship, a round pool table, and occasionally the odd person who looks as though they've taken this whole 'spaced out' theme a little too seriously. It's one of a kind and certainly worth a look. Open from 6:00 pm.

The **Fin Bar** at 144 Gloucester Street is probably the most authentic of the Irish bars. The walls are covered in the appropriate paraphernalia (Irish stuff), and there's live (Russian) music (just joking, it's Irish) every night but Sunday. It can get quite loud and, if you have a strong fear of dancing on floors that feel like they're about to collapse, stay away. Open from 4:30 pm until late, with happy hours 4:30–6:30 pm. Bands start at 8:00 pm.

**Coyotes** at 126 Oxford Terrace has a great Mexican-style decor, and is particularly popular with the portable-phone-toting sect. It is one of the busiest bars in town, and lends itself well to a lively *après-ski* atmosphere. It's open from 10:00 am until late.

The **Edge Bar and Café** on Hereford Street is an enormous place with a caf´ at its front, a circular bar in the middle, and a large dance floor out the back. It can get very busy, with live music on Friday and Saturday nights. Week days it is open from 10:00 am until late; Saturdays and Sundays it opens at 6:00 pm. A reasonable standard of dress is required.

**Jolly Poacher** is a bar with an English theme on Victoria Street (over the road from the casino). It's an authentic place with an emphasis on the English passions of fox hunting, grouse shooting and darts (one of the city's more well-used dartboards resides here). Good, low-priced bar meals are available, and the bar has been known to give away a glass of glühwein to anyone presenting a day ski pass. Open from 11:00 am until late.

For a taste of Olde Christchurch, go to **The Civic Bar** at 198 Manchester Street. It's in a grand, old building with chandeliers and a library of old books. The walls are covered with photos of old Christchurch and there's a snooker table you can play on for free. It's a great place to spend some time having a quiet drink if the weather's bad. What's more, the prices are more reasonable than some of the trendier places in town.

The **Hofbrauhaus** is Christchurch's own German beer-drinking hall and, as such, is usually not the place to go for a quiet drink, particularly on Thursday, Friday or Saturday nights. The atmosphere is friendly and loud, often with live accordions and German drinking songs. Prices here are also very reasonable. It's at 112 Lichfield Street, over the road from the Java Café. Hours are 5:00 pm till late every night.

**Bailies Bar**, beneath Warner's Hotel in The Square, is Christchurch's 'downtown' bar, with its own contingent of locals and usually quite a few travellers. There's nothing outstanding about the place, but being the closest bar to the city centre keeps it pretty lively. On Friday and Saturday nights, there's live music and standing room only.

If you find yourself with some spare time, and have the inclination, head over to Lyttelton (buses go there) and visit the **Wunderbar** (0–3–328 8818). It's located above the Supervalue Supermarket on London Street, and is a totally, totally eccentric place. Any description seems to do it an injustice – it really must be seen in person. It's open from 5:00 pm to 3:00 am midweek, and 1:00 pm to 4:00 am on weekends. They do a great cabaret show.

## SERVICES

*Medical:* Christchurch Hospital is on the corner of Riccarton Avenue and Oxford Terrace: 0–3–364 0640; Emergencies 0–3–364 0270.
There's an urgent pharmacy (open until 11 pm every day) on the corner of Bealey Avenue and Colombo Street: 0–3–366 4439.
To see a private doctor, refer to the listing in the front pages of the telephone book. To find out which doctor or medical centre is closest to you phone 0–3–365 7777.

If you prefer natural healing, try the Herbal Dispensary at 220 Kilmore Street: 0–3–365 1906.

*Police:* The central police station is on the corner of Hereford Street and Cambridge Terrace: 0–3–379 3999. In emergencies, phone 111.

*Post Office:* The central branch of New Zealand Post is in Telecom Mall, The Square: 0–3–353 1899.

## INFORMATION

Most hostel or hotel receptions will be able to provide you with general and tourist information. If you require more, try the following places:

❑ The Information Centre on the corner of Worcester Street and Oxford Terrace: 0–3–379 9629.

❑ Trailblazer's at 96 Worcester Street: 0–3–366 6033. It has ski reports from around the South Island ski areas running continuously on a TV screen.

❑ YHA Head Office on the corner of Gloucester and Manchester Streets: 0–3–379 9970.

## GETTING AROUND

Christchurch is flat, making it easy to get around by foot or bicycle. You can hire a bike for a day from Trailblazers (96 Worcester Street) for $20. If you don't fancy walking or cycling, you can catch a bus or a taxi.

There's a good bus network with stops all over town. Every bus route makes its way to and from The Square. There are three different bus stops in The Square, so check the timetables, or ask a bus driver to find out if you're at the right one. For all bus information, phone Businfo 0–3–366 8855.

Like buses, there is always a group of taxis around The Square. If you don't happen to be in The Square, but need a taxi, phone 0–3–379 9799 or 0–3–379 5795. If you catch a taxi, ask for a concession card. Most companies have these. They're free and entitle you to a cheaper fare when you travel with that particular company. The old trams that cruise around doing the 'city loop' are $3 per hour, and a trip on one of these is the best way to come to grips with the inner-city layout.

There are plenty of car rental outfits in Christchurch. Rates and conditions vary, with the better-known companies charging a little more than the others. It's an idea to call a few before hiring, and negotiate as you see fit. Listed below are a few of the rental companies:

Avis Rent-a-Car, 26 Lichfield Street: 0–3–379 6133.

Budget Rent-a-Car, corner Oxford Terrace and Lichfield Street: 0–3–366 0072.

Economy Rental Cars, 519 Wairakei Road: 0–3–358 7410.

Hertz Rent-a-Car, 48–50 Lichfield Street: 0–3–379 9888.

McDonald Rent-a-Car, 171 Armagh Street: 0–3–366 0929.

NZ Rent-a-Car, 27 Lichfield Street: 0–3–379 6880.

Pegasus Rental Cars, 127 Peterborough Street: 0–3–365 1100.

Shoestring Rentals, 17 Wise Street: 0–3–338 6636.

For campervan rentals, try Maui Tours of New Zealand, 530–544 Memorial Avenue: 0–3–358 4139; or Newmans Holidays, 530–544 Memorial Ave: 0–3–353 5600.

## Travelling on

*Domestic airlines*
It's possible to fly from Christchurch to most major centres in New Zealand with one of the following airlines:

Air New Zealand, 702 Colombo Street, Triangle Centre: 0-3-353 4899.

Ansett New Zealand, Clarendon Towers, 78 Worcester Street: 0-3-379 1300.

Mount Cook Airlines, 91 Worcester Street, 47 Riccarton Road or 40 Lichfield Street: 0-3-379 0690.

*Train*
Trains from Christchurch go north to Picton (via Kaikoura), south to Invercargill (via Dunedin), or west on the famous TranzAlpine journey to Greymouth (via Arthurs Pass). The New Zealand Rail Travel Centre is at 574 Colombo Street. The Railway Station is on Clarence Street, Addington. For any train enquiries or reservations, phone 0800-802 802 (toll-free).

*Shuttle and bus*
Allans Coachlines runs services to Methven: 0-3-358 9110.

Atomic Shuttles runs services to Queenstown, Picton and Dunedin: 0-3-322 8883.

Catch-A-Bus runs services to Dunedin, Queenstown and Wanaka: 0800-508 000 (toll-free).

Coast to Coast Shuttle runs services to Springfield, Arthurs Pass and Greymouth: 0800-800 847 (toll-free).

Hanmer Connection runs services to Hanmer: 0-3-315 7575 or 025-332 088.

Intercity/Ritchies runs services to destinations throughout the South Island: 0-3-377 0951.

Ko-op Shuttles runs services to Dunedin and Picton: 0-3-366 6633.

Midnight Express runs services to Nelson and Picton: 0-3-548 0400.

Mount Cook Landline runs services to destinations throughout the South Island: 0-3-379 0690.

Southern Link Shuttles runs services to Dunedin, Picton and Queenstown: 0–3–379 9991.

*International airlines*
Air New Zealand, 702 Colombo Street, Triangle Centre: 0–3–353 4899.

Ansett New Zealand, Clarendon Towers, 78 Worcester Street: 0–3–379 1300.

British Airways, 152–156 Hereford Street: 0–3–379 2503.

Japan Airlines, Level 11, Clarendon Towers, 78 Worcester Street: 0–3–365 5879.

Qantas Airways, 119 Armagh Street: 0–3–379 6500 or 0800–808 767 (toll-free).

Singapore Airlines, AMP Building, Cathedral Square: 0–3–366 8003.

United Airlines, 152 Hereford Street: 0–3–366 1736.

# METHVEN

A Scotsman, Robert Patton, bought land on the plains beneath Mount Hutt in 1869. He named it after his home town of Methven in Scotland. Methven remained a relatively quiet little farming town until 1974, when the Mount Hutt ski area opened. Since then, Methven has gradually evolved into a resort town and one of the Southern Hemisphere's major ski areas. It's a small place (a ten-minute walk in any direction from the town centre to its outskirts) and, while it certainly has that ski-town feel to it, it's still in many ways the farm-town that it was.

The town goes through a transformation every autumn, many of the restaurants and hostels opening just for the skiing months. Every taste is catered for – from takeaway joints to à la carte restaurants, and from the quiet hotel pubs to the bouncing VeeTees bar/nightclub.

If you go to Methven expecting a Queenstown equivalent, you'll be disappointed. Perhaps Methven's greatest quality is that, unlike Queenstown, it has retained its original small-town ambience.

## SKI AND SNOWBOARD SHOPS

**Wombats** (0–3–302 8084) on the corner of Bank Street and Rakaia Gorge Road has a wide range of new and second-hand ski gear.

*Hire charges:*
Skis: $18 (day); $32 (two days); $16 each day after that.
Demo skis: $30 (day); with boots $35.

*Repair charges:*
Full tune: $40.
Race tune (to personal requirements): $60.

Edge and wax: $20.
Hot wax: $10.

**Big Als** (0–3–302 8003) is in the Mall on the corner of Chertsey and Rakaia Gorge Roads.

*Hire charges:*
Skis for a day: $20 (Adult); $15 (Youth, under 17); $10 (Child).
Snowboards (with hard or soft boots) for a day: $38 (Adult); $30 (Youth); $15 (Under 12s).
Ski gear and clothing for a day: $36 (Adult); $29 (Youth); $17 (Child).
Multi-day rates are available on all hires.

*Repair charges by the 'Ski Surgeon':*
Hand tune: $49.
Full tune: $39.
Edge wax and p-tex: from $8.
Edge sharpen: $12.
Hot wax $8.

## PLACES TO STAY

**Alpenorn Chalet** (0–3–302 8779) at 44 Allen Street, a five-minute walk from the town centre, should not be overlooked if you're planning a stay in Methven. It's a little more expensive than other hostels, although still in the low price range. But for the price you can enjoy possibly the best *après-ski* setting in town. Adjoining the back of the chalet is a glass conservatory with a spa pool, lounge suites and a pot-belly stove. With a drink in hand, you can sit back in the pool and watch the lights of groomers and snowmakers at work on Mount Hutt. After a day's skiing it's hard to beat. The kitchen/living room area has a log burner, television and stereo. Washing and drying machines can be used free of charge, and there's an electric blanket on every bed. For a low price, you can have a hot breakfast. Rooms are either single or double, and weekly rates are negotiable. There's only room for 14 guests, so booking ahead is a good idea. The spa pool can be used by non-residents for $5 per person.

**Agnes Rose Lodge** (0-3-302 8556) at 10 McKerrow Street is a two-minute walk from the town centre. It has a great living room/kitchen area with a pot-belly stove and good views of Mount Hutt. There's also another living-room area with a log burner and stereo with a huge selection of LPs; very pleasant *après-ski* atmosphere. An added attraction of this hostel is that you can cook your meals on an old coal range, and to see this thing in action is a real experience. There are laundry facilities, a ski-tuning area and a Border Collie called 'Tahoe' that'll keep you entertained for as long as you have the energy. It's budget-priced, with linen included. There are only 21 beds, so book ahead.

**Docs Place** (0-3-302 8560) at 261 Forest Drive is also a two-minute walk from the town centre, and used to be the local doctor's surgery. It's a smallish hostel with a friendly atmosphere. The kitchen and living area are in one room, revolving around a log burner and dining table. This is the kind of place you arrive at alone and leave with a handful of friends. There's an extra-large back lawn with a volleyball net and, after a fresh snowfall, a game or two is essential. There are no laundry facilities but it's just a short walk to the town laundrette. The cost is low.

**Mount Hutt Bunkhouse** and **Lampard Lodge** (0-3-302 9050 or 0-3- 302 8270) at 8 Lampard Street are two houses just five minutes' walk from the town centre. There's a good-sized common room with a log burner in the Bunkhouse, while Lampard Lodge has a smaller living room with a log burner. Everyone usually congregates in the Bunkhouse living room, where all the meeting and *après-ski* activities tend to occur. There's a TV in both houses. The washing and drying machines are in the Bunkhouse and cost $1 a load in each. There are also two drying rooms and ski-tuning facilities. The cost is in the low price range.

**Pinedale Lodge** (0–3–302 8621) on the corner of Alford and Allen Streets, a five-minute walk from town, has possibly the best fireplace in Methven. It's in the common room, along with a stereo and a pool table that you can play for free. Adjoining the common room is a large dining room and kitchen. The lodge itself is an old, colonial-style house, with large rooms and a high roof. There are ski-tuning facilities, and a load of washing will be washed and dried for $6. Nightly charges are low, and a weekly rate is negotiable.

**The Bedpost** (or Mount Hutt Accommodation) (0–3–302 8508) consists of two houses at 177 Rakaia Gorge Road, Methven's main road. A five-minute walk from the centre of town, this is a homely place that has a reasonably large lounge with an open fire in the main house (Carlyn Lodge). There are ski-tuning facilities, a drying room, washing and drying machines you can use for free, and even a dish-washing machine. There are facilities for the disabled. A night is in the low price range, with a lesser charge if you have a sleeping bag and don't require linen.

**Forest Lodge** (0–3–302 8116) at 140 Forest Drive is a well-priced bed and breakfast place. It has a great lounge area with a large open fire, a TV, and even a piano. It's just a short walk from the centre of town. It has a restaurant, a spa pool, a drying room, and ski-tuning facilities. There are twin, double, and multi-share rooms, and a night's stay, including breakfast, is in the moderate price range.

**Centrepoint Resort Hotel** (0–3–302 8724; fax 0–3–302 8870) on Rakaia Gorge Road, at the southern end of the town, is Methven's largest hotel. It has an excellent à la carte restaurant (Les Alps), a cocktail bar, and Montezuma's nightclub/bar. Its three new outdoor hot pools, in which you can enjoy a drink and watch the moon ascend over Mount Hutt, are certainly one of its greatest attractions. Non-residents can use the pools for a small charge ($4). All rooms are in the high price range, and bookings are essential.

**Southern Cross Hotel** (0–3–302 8464) on Racecourse Avenue has single, double, twin, triple and family-size rooms. The bar/lounge has a pool table, a piano, a TV, a video, and is a great, cosy hangout after a day's skiing. There's also a restaurant, spa, sauna and drying rooms. The cost is in the high price range.

**Mount Hutt Motels** (0–3–302 8382) at 207 Rakaia Gorge Road is a complex of ten self-contained units. Each unit sleeps from two to eight people, and has an oven, microwave and fridge. There's a communal lounge with a TV and a radio, and video units are available. Perhaps the place's biggest asset is its outdoor spa pool. There's also a guest laundry, and electric blankets in every room. The cost is in the high price range.

For a completely luxurious stay in Methven, check out either the **Beluga Lodge** (0–3–302 8290) at 40 Allen Street, or the **Powderhouse Ski Lodge** (0–3–302 910) at 3 Cameron Street. To stay a night in either usually requires booking well in advance. Both places have spa pools, en suites for every room, drying rooms, and great lounges and dining rooms. These are 'top-of-the-line' places, where no request is too great, and the cost falls in the high price range.

## PLACES TO EAT

The **Last Post Café** (0–3–302 8259) on Rakaia Gorge Road was the old post office. These days it's a restaurant with a Western/cowboy type theme, and is a great place for a meal after a day on the slopes. The food is not strictly of the Western/cowboy variety, with the choice of mains pretty good.

Inside the café is the restaurant and 'Grumpys Bar', a good place for a quiet brew and a chat to Grumpy himself. The restaurant is often busy and booking ahead is essential. The charge is moderate. Hours are 5:00 pm until late.

The **Epic Eatery** (0–3–302 8888) at 32 Forest Drive has a great *après-ski* atmosphere, complete with wood and brick surroundings and two open fires. It's BYO and serves moderately priced Mexican cuisine. Open from 5:00 pm until late, it's best to book ahead.

**Uncle Dominics Pizza and Kebabs** (0–3–302 8237) is in the shopping centre on the corner of Rakaia Gorge Road and Forest Drive. You can buy takeaways or eat in. There's a TV with ski videos playing constantly, making it a good place to hang out while eating your pizza or kebab. You can get a reasonable, low-cost meal here from 5:00 pm until late.

**Eagle Rock** (0–3–302 8222) in the Value Tours building, below VeeTees bar/nightclub, is a good place for a quiet beer and a salubrious pasta dish before making the trip upstairs to the night's revelry. The cost is low to moderate. It's a good idea to book a table.

The **Blue Pub** (0–3–302 8046) is the place to go if you're famished. For a moderate charge, there's an 'all-you-can-eat' smorgasbord every night. You just don't visit Methven without dropping in to the Blue Pub. Hours are 11:00 am until late.

For fish'n'chips, **Woodsys**, on the main road, is the place to visit. It's open from 11:00 am until late.

## HAPPENING PLACES

It could be argued that a night on the town in Methven is incomplete without a visit to **VeeTees** bar/nightclub (0–3–302

8252), upstairs in the Value Tours building on the main road. It has everything a ski-town bar should have – crowds, good music, a pool table, inexpensive meals, and nights (Tuesday) when you can get cheap beer. Drinks are significantly less expensive and the SkiFlix video is shown on a big screen. Virtually the whole town flocks to the bar to watch this video, taken on Mount Hutt over the past week. There's a fair chance you'll see yourself. The very generous meals are in the moderate price range.

The **Blue Pub**, New Zealand's famous bastion of the *après-ski* drink, is a popular stop for skiers on the way back to their accommodation. On a sunny afternoon, the footpath in front of the hotel is usually covered with basking skiers and their jugs of liquid refreshment. Across the road is the Canterbury Hotel, known as 'The Brown Pub', which is where the locals go for a quiet drink.

**Munchies Café** on the main road serves good home-made food for a low to moderate price. With its wood burner, and cheap bottomless cups of coffee, it is a good place to simply hang out and watch the world pass by.

The **Dry Creek Tavern and Steakhouse** (0–3–302 8515), in the shopping centre on the corner of Rakaia Gorge Road and Forest Drive, is a good place for a quiet beer in a relaxed, fireside atmosphere. The restaurant serves good steak meals for a moderate charge.

## SERVICES

*Medical:* The Methven Medical Centre is on the corner of Chertsey and Rakaia Gorge Roads (the main intersection in the town centre): 0–3–302 8105. Methven Pharmacy is in the mall: 0–3–302 8103.

*Police:* The police station is on Chertsey Road: 0–3–302 8200 or 0–3–302 2020. In emergencies, phone 111.

*Post Office:* The town's postal centre is in the Gifts Galore shop in the mall: 0–3–302 8463.

## INFORMATION

The Methven Information Centre is in the Value Tours building on the main road: 0–3–302 8955; PO Box 16.

Big Als ski shop is another place to go for local information, Big Al himself being an authority on most local matters.

For Mount Hutt information and the day's conditions, see the window of the Mount Hutt town office on the main road, just down from VeeTees: 0–3–302 8811.

## GETTING AROUND

Because it's a short distance from any one point to another, walking is really the best way to get around. Another option is hiring a mountain bike from Big Als. To rent a car contact Allright Rental Cars in the Gifts Galore shop in the mall: 0–3–302 8463; or NZ Rent a Car at the Methven Travel Centre on Forest Drive: 0–3–302 8106.

## TRAVELLING ON

*By shuttle and bus*
Allans Coachlines runs services to Christchurch:
0–3–302- 8106.

Intercity/Ritchies runs services to Wanaka, Queenstown and Christchurch: 0–3–302 8044.

# SPRINGFIELD

Although you wouldn't know it now, Springfield was once a sizeable settlement. Originally called Kowai Pass, it became a rural centre in the early nineteenth century. Once a route was established over Porters Pass, the town became the last stop for people heading west from Christchurch. In 1863, George Willis built the original Springfield Hotel. He was succeeded in 1865 – by which stage the Arthurs Pass road to the West Coast had been completed – by J. H. Bailey, who built a new hotel, the first on the present site. This burnt down on 5 January 1880, the same day the railway reached Springfield from Christchurch. The present hotel was built in 1895 by W. J. Cloudsley, who enlarged it to 40 rooms and built the hall next door capable of holding 500 people. The early 1900s were Springfield's boom years. A locomotive depot was built, and the town became a railway settlement.

In 1923, the Otira train tunnel through Arthurs Pass had been completed, and there was no longer as great a need for Springfield's railway depot. The real demise, however, occurred in the 1950s with the advent of the diesel locomotive. The town's depot gradually became redundant and the town returned to its rural origins, only now with a train station.

The **Springfield Hotel** remains the hub of the town, and is probably busier now after a good day's skiing than it ever was during the locomotive days. Being on the only road between Christchurch and five of Canterbury's ski areas, the hotel is a kind of bottleneck for the *après-ski* drink. It has a huge fireplace, a pool table, and serves great hot chips. There's also a good selection of hot meals available. After a hot spring day in the mountains, it's very, very hard to pick a better place to be than on the hotel's patio with a long cold drink.

If you're looking to stay a night in Springfield, try **Smylies**

Hostel (0–3–318 4840). It's on the main road at the eastern end of town. The rooms are warm, and there's a TV room, a great open-plan kitchen, a dining room, and a living room with a large fireplace. It has a Japanese spa bath that is pure bliss. The cost of a night's stay is low, and a cooked breakfast is $5. The Springfield Hotel (0–3–318 4812) also has a number of rooms, varying from low to moderate in charge.

For a good cup of coffee or a light snack, try the **Te Kowai Coffee and Crafts Shop** across the road from the hotel. Also across the road are the town's supermarket/cafeteria and a petrol station. Car chains can be purchased, not hired, from the petrol station.

Although Springfield is hardly a bustling ski town – in fact, it hardly looks as though it has any connection with skiing at all – the friendliness of the local farmers, and Porter Heights staff, who live in the town, make it a great place to spend a night or two, all the same.

# South Canterbury/ North Otago

## Ski Areas

Awakino 225
Fox Peak 233
Mount Dobson 240
Ohau 246

## Resorts

Fairlie 254
Kurow 259

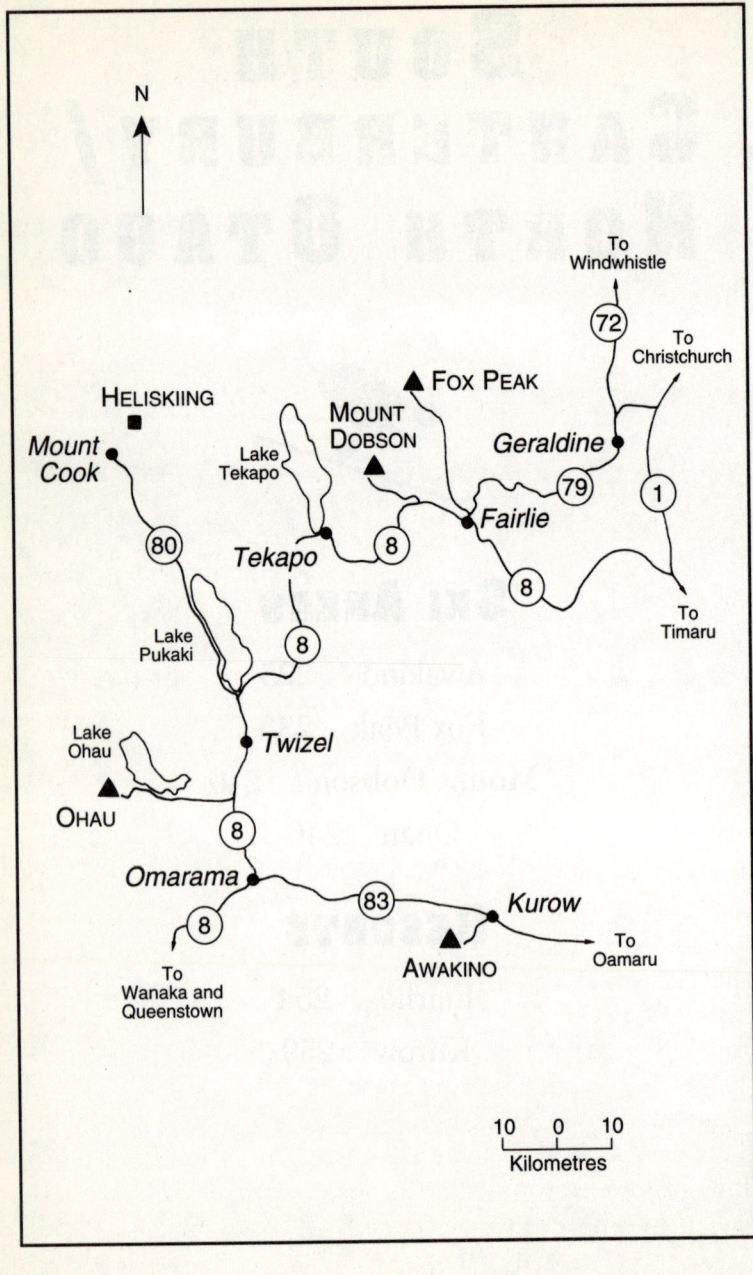

# AWAKINO

## HISTORY

Spurred on by very heavy snow, a group of 20 keen people in Oamaru met on 19 June 1939 to discuss the formation of a ski club. The nearest ski areas in those days were on the Ball Glacier at Mount Cook, and a small slope on the Rock and Pillar Range in Central Otago. The group looked at the possibility of skiing in North Otago, nearer to Oamaru.

A local mountaineer, H. T. Stevenson, gave the group a quick lecture on 'Mountains and Matters Pertaining to Mountains', then a committee was elected with Rodney Williams as president, and Brian Patterson as secretary. After some further discussion, the name Waitaki Ski Club (WSC) was chosen, Waitaki being the name of the county in which Oamaru lies.

The club made several ski trips in that first season to some slopes 30 kilometres west of Oamaru at Danseys Pass. They had only a few pairs of skis, so people had to take turns or use a toboggan.

After World War Two began later that year, it wasn't long before many of the Waitaki Ski Club were away on service. Petrol rationing began shortly afterwards. In 1940, the remaining members made two trips to Ball Glacier and one to Queenstown, where they competed for the Wigley Cup on Coronet Peak. The next year, they made another two trips to Ball Glacier and a number of trips to Danseys Pass, where they had gained permission to modify an old roadmen's hut to their purposes. The club became officially affiliated to the Federated Mountain Clubs and the Ski Council that year.

There was no activity at all between 1942 and 1944, but in the winter of 1945, with members returning from the war and the lifting of travel restrictions, ski trips recommenced. Members made two trips to Ball Glacier and one to Danseys Pass, where they discovered that their hut had blown down, and there wasn't any snow.

In 1946, membership of the club was starting to pick up, and the goal of the season was to find a 'skiing ground'. The club president, Williams, recalled a climbing trip he had made in

## Awakino

- *Location:* 11 km from Kurow.
  100 km from Ohau.
  180 km from Wanaka.
  239 km from Queenstown.

- *Season:* Usually open by early July and closed by early October. Only open during weekends, unless there's a ski week going on. Phone the club to confirm that it's open.

- *Elevation:* The highest peak on the area is Rocky Top (1935 metres) above Ridge Tow.
  The Main Lodge is at about 1500 metres.
  The day lodges are at about 1700 metres.
  The top of Ridge Tow is at about 1900 metres.

- *Vertical drop:* Approximately 400 metres from the top of Ridge Tow to the Main Lodge.

- *Terrain:* Beginner 5%, Intermediate 60%, advanced 35%.

- *Snowmaking:* None.

- *Groomers:* None.

- *Road toll:* None.

- *Lifts:* Four rope tows. Low charge, with junior reduction.

- *Ski hire:* None.

- *Specials:* For $38.50 you get a night's accommodation in the lodge, dinner and breakfast, a lift pass, and a lesson.

1939 to Mount Kurow in the Saint Mary Range. He had actually climbed Mount Bitterness and Fosters Peak by mistake, but as he was carrying skis he skied from the peaks down to the West branch of the Awakino River. He made two further trips to Mount Kurow in 1940, and it had occurred to him then that the

## Awakino

*Ski school:* Qualified club members do the instructing. Lessons are designed to cater mainly for people staying on a ski week, but you should be able to negotiate a lesson and a price.

*Ski weeks:* A ski week ($230) covers accommodation (Sunday–Saturday), lift passes, instruction on each day, and all dinners and breakfasts. Usually run from the beginning of July until mid-September. For details, phone the club on 0–3–436 0771 or 0–3–439 5464. You must book three weeks in advance.

*Accomm:* The Main Lodge is the smallest ski club lodge in the country. It has two bunkrooms, with a total of 40 bunks. The lodge has a kitchen with coal and electric ranges (and cooking and dining facilities), a dining room, showers, and flush toilets. The cost is in the budget range.

*Address:* The Secretary, Waitaki Ski Club Inc, PO Box 191, Oamaru. Telephone: 0–3–439 5464.

*Snow reports:* The only way of finding out what conditions are like is by phoning the club on 0–3– 436 0771.

area was suitable for skiing. Consequently, on Queens Birthday 1946, he made another trip to the area, this time with the intention of finding a skiing ground for the club. It was on this trip that the site of the present ski area impressed him. (The first skiing in the Saint Mary Range had actually occurred in 1934, when European labourers working on the Waitaki River's hydro dams had taken hand-made skis up to the slopes.)

The weekend following Williams' trip he took a group of 11 members up the Awakino Valley, where they skied a number of slopes, including the present ski area. Members were impressed with the skiing but, wanting to be sure, they made further expeditions throughout the Saint Mary and other nearby mountain ranges. By August 1946, the club had judged the West Awakino Valley as being by far the most suitable, and they decided to extend the existing farm road (from which the area was a two-hour walk) and build a hut. Members approached these tasks with great enthusiasm, and the first working party began work on the weekend of 16–17 August.

The first ski week was held between 31 August and 8 October. The club hadn't built the hut by that stage, and members stayed in a hut further down the valley, making a two-hour walk to the

## GETTING THERE

**From Kurow**
The township of Kurow, where the access road to Awakino begins, is halfway along Highway 83 which runs between Omarama (on Highway 8) and Highway 1 on the east coast. If you're driving it's easy, if you're hitching it can be difficult, especially from Kurow. If you're hitching, phone the club as they may know of someone who could give you a lift. There are no shuttle services running.

snow each day. Most skiing occurred at the site of the present hut, where a box of provisions and a primus were kept. Over the summer of 1946 members worked hard constructing bridges and cutting a road up to the site of the proposed hut. Once the road had reached the site, they began work on the hut. Funding for the hut was raised by members running raffles in Oamaru, and from a Government grant of £150.

The Awakino Hut was completed by early May 1947. Earlier, on Anzac Day (25 April), members working on the hut had climbed the mountain now known as Fosters Peak to unveil a cross that had been erected the previous weekend. The cross, which still stands, was erected to the memory of Colin Foster, the only WSC member to die in the war. (The other cross in Glacier Basin was erected in 1983, in memory of Michael McCabe, a club president.)

With the hut erected and membership increasing, things progressed for the club and the Awakino ski area. In 1948, a day shelter (now used as a storage shed) was erected in the Awakino Basin, and in 1949 the first tow was installed. Between 1951 and 1956 a club member, Herbie Familton, was in the New Zealand ski team. In 1955, additions were made to the Awakino Hut, enabling it to sleep 50. The Main and Learners' Tows were installed in the 1960s, and the new day lodge and the Ridge Tow were put in in 1989, in time for the club's 50th anniversary celebrations.

These days, the club, with around 200 members, is the smallest in the country. The ski area continues to have a strong, but small, following amongst North Otago people, but generally maintains a fairly low profile.

## THE SKI AREA

Probably the ski area that has changed least since skiing began there over 50 years ago, Awakino exudes the feeling of skiing in a timeless place. Most importantly, this is how club members favour it, and rightly so – it's an extraordinary place.

From Kurow, it's about an 11-kilometre drive through farmland to Awakino's bottom car park (only the first few kilometres of the road are sealed). The road, which is flat and generally well kept, has a number of gates along it that you will have to open and close; there can be up to seven of these. The land you travel through is typical of Central Otago – dry, barren, and covered in golden tussock.

Before you go to Awakino, phone the club and make sure it's going to be open (it is on most weekends and over the school holidays). If you're driving, ask what condition the road is in. Two-wheel-drive vehicles are not to proceed past the bottom car park and, depending on road conditions, low-clearance four-wheel-drive vehicles may not be allowed either.

Beyond a locked gate at the car park, the road continues to the lodge. On the other side of this gate, there is a collection of antique-looking four-wheel-drive vehicles, amongst them a Mark 1 Land Rover. Don't let the appearance of these machines fool you; each of them is capable of tremendous feats and all are worthy of the respect bestowed upon them by club members.

If the club knows you're coming, they will probably arrange for one of these beasts to give you a ride to the lodge (depending on when you arrive). There is no charge, but donations for the vehicle's up-keep will be accepted. Just the knowledge that one has helped keep a Mark 1 Land Rover operable is satisfaction enough for many donors. From the car park to the lodge is about a ten-minute drive, or a 40-minute walk, depending on snow cover. The lodge is relatively small compared to others. From the lodge's balcony there is a fantastic view down the Awakino River Valley and of the Hakataramea Plains in the distance.

Any club member should be able to organise a tow belt for you in the lodge. Once you've got one, and your ski gear is on, make your way over to the access tow – a short walk up the road from the lodge. It's an idea to take your lunch etc up to the ski area, where there are a couple of day lodges in which to base yourself.

There is no ski lift in New Zealand with more character than Awakino's access tow. It is run by an old parked-up tractor – a piece of machinery that fosters at least a hint of affection in all who see it. Once you feel suitably acquainted, hook on to the rope and make your way up to the day lodges. One of the day lodges is just a shelter with tables and chairs; the other has cooking facilities, and even a TV. Beside the shelter is New Zealand's highest pay phone at 1700 metres. As you make the traverse from the access tow you pass the club's tiny original day shelter, which resembles the abandoned buildings left by Scott in the Antarctic.

From the top of the access tow it's a short traverse to the left to the day lodges. If you didn't buy a day pass in the main lodge, there will be a club member in one of the day lodges who will sell you one. In front of the lodges is the Beginners' Tow, a short rope tow on a gentle gradient, ideal for absolute beginners. The base of Main Tow is a short ski from the lodges and runs up the area's main slope, Waitaki Face, which is a wide, steepish run. You can get off Main Tow halfway up, at the top of Waitaki Face, or carry on to the top of the lift from where you can go to the left, down into Glacier Basin (it's not really a glacier), or to the right and take Ridge Tow to the Ridge. Ridge Tow, which is sometimes buried in snow, may not be operating. It is used over the school holiday period and during lean snow years.

Glacier Basin is a long, wide valley on a gentle slope, with a number of possible routes down it. It is not often that the basin is completely covered with snow, and route-finding through the rocky patches is usually required. The best way to ski the whole basin is to get to the top of Ridge Tow and traverse, or walk, along the ridge to the head of the basin (from the top of Main Tow it's about a 20-minute walk). The headwall of the basin offers superb skiing, especially after a fresh snowfall or a strong southerly wind, which tends to fill this area with light wind-blown snow.

For chute skiing, traverse further along the ridge to Fosters Peak, on the other side of the basin from Main Tow. There are three main, and a number of smaller chutes here; all are equally steep and take you back into Glacier Basin.

From the ridge above Ridge Tow, it's possible to ski off the back of the ridge, down to Hut Creek and then traverse back around on Waitaki Face; this is a great run. Once you're on the ridge, you'll see that the potential for touring in the region is huge. If you're making a trip, make sure someone in your party has at least basic avalanche knowledge.

# Fox Peak

## History

In 1926, a young Timaru man, Lud Mahan, was asked if he would like a job at Mount Cook. He was keen, and suspected the job would involve wool-pressing, or shearing, or something similar on the Mount Cook sheep station.

As it turned out, Mahan was actually given a job at the Hermitage Hotel involving general duties – guiding tourists, backpacking stores to huts, painting the roof, washing dishes, killing pigs, and so on. These were pioneering days for the New Zealand tourism industry, which at the time consisted largely of young free-spirited men like Mahan taking parties into nearby mountain ranges. The Hermitage guides' motto was 'We tread the untrodden snow, ourselves as pure.'

Mahan and fellow guides would spend weekends taking tourists up to Mueller Hut in the Sealy Range, below Mount Ollivier (1917 metres). Near the hut, in a hole between two rocks, were stored pairs of ash skis. The guides would take the tourists up on to the slopes of Mount Ollivier, tie these skis to their feet and tell them to 'bend their knees and point the skis straight downhill'. Countless people first experienced skiing on these slopes and, by 1928, large parties were coming to Mount Cook for the ski-guiding. Trips became longer, up to a week or ten days, and other slopes were skied in the Ball Hut, Tasman Saddle, and Hooker Hut regions.

In 1929, someone at a party suggested the guides form some sort of ski club. An unofficial club, 'Gugnuncs', was formed. A tongue-in-cheek forerunner to what would eventually become the Tasman Ski Club, the Gugnuncs became quite enthusiastic and actually wore 'club' blazers of red, white and blue stripes, with a golden lion on the pocket.

In 1931, Alf Brustad, one of the Norwegian guides employed

by the Hermitage for their skiing and guiding abilities, took Mahan and fellow guides, Dan Bryant and Lin Murray, on a day-long traverse of the Southern Alps from Mount Cook to Tekapo. During the trip, which was considered a marathon journey in those days, Brustad asked Mahan, 'Why don't you boys start a ski club and call it the Tasman Ski Club after the Tasman Glacier?'

The first meeting to form the club was held in September 1931. Dr W. R. Fea was elected club president. There were 14

## Fox Peak

*Location:* 29 km from Fairlie.
198 km from Christchurch.
159 km from Methven.

*Season:* Usually from early July to mid to late October.
Open weekends from the start of the season, and all week from early August until mid-September.

*Elevation:* Fox Peak is 2332 metres.
The top of Apex Tow is at 1850 metres.
The base area is at 1170 metres.

*Vertical drop:* 680 metres.

*Terrain:* Beginner 15%, Intermediate 60%, Advanced 25%.

*Lifts:* Four rope tows, plus an access tow. Moderate charges, with student reductions. Learners' Tow is free.

*Snowmaking:* None.

*Groomers:* One.

*Road toll:* None.

*Ski hire:* None.

*Specials:* A 'Weekender' (Saturday night accommodation and tow foundation members, one of whom was Harry Wigley (later Sir), son of Rudolph Wigley of the Mount Cook Group.

During the early 1930s, New Zealand was feeling the impact of worldwide depression and any available money was spent on necessities. The majority of the Tasman Ski Club members were from Timaru, and the nearest skiing at the time was in the Mount Cook region. But, while skiing was tenaciously considered a necessity by some members, they could not really justify the cost of petrol to get to Mount Cook.

## Fox Peak

fees for both days is $55 (Adult); $37 (Secondary school student).
Special rates are also available for large or educational groups.

*Ski school:* Two or three instructors.
Private lessons: $25 per hour.
Group lessons (10:00 am; 2:00 pm): $10.

*Ski weeks:* Sunday to Saturday, and include a bed, all meals (dinner, lunch and breakfast), tow fees and a lesson each week day: cost $275. Special rates for large or educational groups. For enquiries or bookings, write to the address below or phone 0-3-615 7290.

*Accomm:* All accommodation is in the Fox Lodge, three kilometres below the ski area, with room for 50 people. It's a modern, well-furnished lodge, with great views. A night's accommodation, supplying your own sleeping bag, is in the budget range. Bookings are essential.

*Address:* Fox Peak Ski Club, PO Box 368, Timaru. Telephone: 0-3-688 1749.

*Snow reports:* Phone the Fox Peak snow report 0-3-688-0044.

In September 1932, Mahan, Murray, and Fea made a trip from Timaru to the top of Fox Peak with the objective of finding a suitable slope for skiing and a site for a hut. They skied from the top of the peak and found a good place for the hut. In December, a large committee visited the area and decided to build on the site of the present hut. Permission to build was granted by the land owner, Mr S. P. Bray, a keen supporter of the idea. In those days, there weren't many like Mr Bray, who is quoted as saying: 'There are much worse things that people from the towns could do than go up to the mountains to ski.'

The first hut was built during the Easter and May holidays of 1933. Until 1946, most people worked a six-day week, so a ski trip to Fox Peak involved leaving Timaru on Saturday afternoon, climbing to the hut that night and skiing on Sunday, leaving for home in the afternoon. Some members would catch the train to Fairlie and cycle from there to the river, then make the climb to the hut.

Club members now spent most of their skiing time on Fox Peak, but still made the occasional trip to the Mount Cook region, where Ball Glacier had become the most popular site for skiing. In the early 1930s, two professional English skiers – Harold Elworthy and Barry Caulfield – spent seasons at Mount Cook and taught members of Tasman Ski Club the intricacies of the sport. Members learned well and, in the 1933 New Zealand championships at Ball Hut, the Tasman Ski Club picked up places in all events; the Wigley brothers, Harry and Sandy, showing some of the class that would establish them as two of the country's best skiers. It was shortly before these championships that the club decided to allow women to join, which worked to their advantage at the championships, where the club's female members also did very well.

The war years were quiet for the club, which had 35 of its members on active service in the Middle East, and many others in other parts of the world in the air force and navy. In 1949, things started picking up again, with the hut being extended. Then, in 1950, the club's first tow, built by C. W. F. Hamilton (of

Hamilton jet-boat fame) was installed. Rope for the tow was given to the club by the Mount Cook Company.

Like other club areas around the country, development was truly under way once the first tow had been installed (and the war had ended). A top hut, on the area itself, was constructed in 1957; two further tows were installed in 1965, with another one in 1967. From 1969 to 1972, the area was commercialised and run by a private operator before eventually reverting back to the club. The Apex Tow was installed in 1981 and a 'Bombardier' groomer was purchased in 1984. The groomer caught fire and rolled quietly into what is now known as 'Bombardier Valley' in 1990 (a replacement was purchased in 1992). The Tasman Ski Club changed its name to Fox Peak Ski Club in 1991.

## GETTING THERE

**From Fairlie**

*By car*

Head north on Highway 79. About a kilometre out of town you arrive at Clayton Road on your left. Take this road and follow the Fox Peak signposts. The access road is 22 kilometres down Clayton Road. There's a gate, which must be kept closed, at the beginning of the access road, and from here it's about 7 kilometres to the ski area.

*Hitching*

Be on the road out of Fairlie by 8:30 am, walking the short distance to Clayton Road if possible. It's not always easy catching a lift (although it's easier on weekends), and it may be an idea to phone the club, 0–3–688 3779, to see if someone can pick you up on their way.

*By shuttle*

There are no shuttle services to Fox Peak.

# The Ski Area

Fox Peak ski area is huge. It's larger than many commercial areas and, of the club areas, is probably second only in size to Craigieburn Valley. The area also has a comparatively large vertical drop of 680 metres.

The access road off Clayton Road, which is mostly unsealed, is about 10 kilometres long and also unsealed. The road crosses the North Opuha River on a one-lane wooden bridge before crossing a small culvert and starting its climb. It's kept in quite good shape, but has been known to become a bit bumpy in places. About half-way between the bridge and the ski area, you pass Fox Lodge, the main on-mountain accommodation (there are a few privately owned huts on the area itself). From the lodge, the road starts climbing steadily and makes several hairpin turns. As you climb, you get great views to the east of surrounding plains and mountain ranges, with the Pacific in the distance.

Fox Peak has five rope tows – the access, Meadow, Tasman, Apex and Skid Row. Tow belts for these can be hired from the ticket office at the base of the area. The access tow is basically redundant these days as it's easy to drive up to the car park.

Meadow Tow is the area's 'shirt-front' lift, accessing a wide slope that is suited to intermediate skiers. From the top of Meadow it's about a 100-metre traverse to your left to the bottom of Tasman Tow. Tasman Tow is over a kilometre long and opens up some great advanced and intermediate skiers' terrain. The runs to the right of the tow are quite steep, as are those to the immediate left. Further out to the left is Happy Valley, which offers superb skiing. It's a slight gully with slopes on either side; it's possible to find a slope to suit your liking. With its northeasterly aspect, Happy Valley gets the early sun and keeps it well into the day. The same goes for the rest of the mountain, too, with the exception of South Basin, where the access slopes remain largely in the shade.

From the top of Apex Tow you have some of the best skiing

terrain in the country below you. Both North and South Basins are enormous expanses. South Basin has a fairly consistent gradient from top to bottom, while North Basin consists of dips, rolls and wide faces. Intermediate skiers will enjoy the skiing in both basins, but of the two the South Basin is the easier.

Skid Row Tow is the only tow in the country that can be used without a lift ticket. As a slope to learn on it's great. Add that to the fact that it's free and Skid Row is perfect. At the bottom of the slope are a few picnic tables and, on a sunny day, the first-time skier could not choose a better place to learn.

There is great ski-touring potential from the area. A trip to the summit of Fox Peak is very rewarding, with great runs back to the ski area down the peak's eastern or northern slopes. The ridge leading north from the peak is full of short, steep chutes that, although they take a bit of time getting to, can be worthwhile. Snow caving on the upper slopes of Fox Peak is a tremendous experience, with fantastic views of sunset and sunrise, as the sun rises over the Pacific and sets behind Mount Cook and the Southern Alps. Check the weather forecast and avalanche hazard with ski patrol before heading out.

# MOUNT DOBSON

## HISTORY

Mount Dobson came about as the result of one man's vision. That man, Peter Foote, was a mechanic who ran an earth-moving and farm machinery repair business in Fairlie.

A keen skier, Foote would often look up to the Two Thumb Range from his workshop, aware that somewhere in those mountains there was certain to be a ski area waiting to be developed. After a few trips into the range, he found the perfect site on Mount Dobson in 1972 and applied to the Government to establish a ski area there. At that stage the Government didn't have a formal policy regarding the development of ski areas, and put the application aside for two years while such a policy was devised. Foote carried out snow observations over the 1973 and 1974 seasons and, when a policy was finalised by the end of 1974, he was confident a ski area on Mount Dobson would be a success.

Following the completion of a policy, a further two years of bureaucratic feuding ensued over construction of the access road. The matter was finally put to rest and, in February 1976, work began on the road. Foote's earth-moving machinery – three bulldozers and a grader – were put to the task of cutting the 15-kilometre access road, which included two bridges, 70 culverts, six cattle stops, and the planting of 26,000 trees. Peter worked well into the night, and Fairlie residents became accustomed to his bulldozer headlights glaring from the mountains as they went to bed. Peter's wife, Shirley, when she wasn't busy with their three young sons, spent time mixing concrete for the culverts or planting trees.

From the beginning, the Footes were aware that it would be a time- and finance-consuming business. But because they wanted to do things their way, not the way a group of directors thought they should, they chose not to form a public company. Consequently, development of the area was a little slower than it may have been with financial backing, and at times work on the road would have to cease to allow income to be earned from outside work.

When the road was completed in early 1979, two bulldozers were sold and the money used to construct two rope tows and a day hut. The Mount Dobson Ski Area was officially opened to the public in September 1979.

---

## GETTING THERE

**From Fairlie**
*By car*
Drive west on Highway 8 toward Tekapo. After about ten kilometres you arrive at a sign-posted turn-off on your right. It's an unsealed road, with the toll gate a short way along. It's possible to leave your car here and take the Mount Dobson shuttle which makes pick-ups daily at 9:15 am. Returns are $12 (Adult); $10 (Youth/child).

*Hitching*
It's quite easy getting a lift from Fairlie. Try being on Highway 8 no later than 8:30 am. If you get a lift with someone who's not going up the mountain, get as close to the turn-off as you can, where it may be a bit easier (remember, people have to stop at the toll gate).

*By shuttle*
Mount Dobson Ski Area Transport has a bus departing from outside the Ski Shack Shop in Fairlie daily at 9:00 am. Returns are $14 (Adult); $12 (Youth/child). Prior to arriving in Fairlie, the shuttle passes through Timaru, Temuka and Geraldine, and it's possible to book a trip from these places too. To book, phone 0–3–693 9656.

The area proved to be popular in its first season, particularly with novice skiers, and over the summer of 1979–80 the car park was extended and further buildings were constructed. Foote purchased a groomer following the 1981 season and, by early 1982, when the time had come to improve the lifts, he had no problem getting the necessary backing to install the learners' platter lift. Such was the confidence that Mount Dobson was going to succeed. And it did.

##  Mount Dobson

*Location:* 25 km from Fairlie.
187 km from Christchurch.
147 km from Methven.
138 km from Lake Ohau.
86 km from Timaru.

*Season:* Usually from early July until mid-October.

*Elevation:* The top of the T-bar is at 2010 metres.
The car park is at 1692 metres.

*Vertical drop:* From the top of the T-bar to the base of Platter 2 is about 400 metres.

*Terrain:* Beginner 20%, Intermediate 60%, Advanced 20%.

*Snowmaking:* None.

*Groomers:* Two.

*Road toll:* $5.

*Lifts:* One T-bar, two platters and one beginners' fixed grip. Moderate charge, with youth (under 16) and child (under 12) reductions.

*Ski hire:* A full set of equipment for a day: $20 (Adult); $16 (Youth); $12 (Child).

In 1984, the T-bar was installed, doing away with the rope tow, and making the area entirely user-friendly for beginners. By then, Mount Dobson had firmly established its niche as a great family and novice ski area with Canterbury skiers. In 1985, a second platter lift was installed to open up the huge West Basin, and the ski area, now complemented with more terrain and challenging slopes, began to attract advanced skiers in greater numbers.

 **Mount Dobson**

*Specials:* A 'Beginners Package' (a Platter 1 lift pass, lesson, and rental): $40 (Adult); $30 (Youth); $20 (Child).

An 'Intermediate Package' (a Platter 1 lift pass, lesson, and rental): $63 (Adult); $49 (Youth); $34 (Child).

An 'All Lifts Package' (an All Lifts pass, lesson, and rental): $72 (Adult); $53 (Youth); $39 (Child).

*Ski school:* The Badenoch Ski School.

Group lesson (90 minutes; 11:00 am, 1:30 pm): $20 (Adult); $15 (Youth/child).

Private lessons available all day (60 or 90 minutes): $40, $60 (Adult/youth); $35, $55 (Child).
Each additional person $10.
An Early Bird private lesson (starting at 9:30 am and 10:00 am): $35 (Adult/youth); $30 (Child).
For more information, contact Ski School Director, Mount Dobson, Fairlie; or phone 0-3-685 8039.

*Address:* Mount Dobson Ski Area Ltd, Fairlie, South Canterbury. Telephone: 0-3-685 8039)

*Snow reports:* Phone the Mount Dobson Snow Phone on 0900-39 888 (costs 65c per minute) or listen to any local radio station.

Mount Dobson has built a large partisan-like following in Canterbury, and is responsible for basically changing the whole atmosphere of Fairlie during the winter months. It's still a young ski area (a point perhaps most evident by the temporary-looking base buildings), and relies largely on hospitality, for which it has gained an excellent reputation.

## THE SKI AREA

If someone was to design a ski area specifically for beginner and intermediate skiers, it would come out looking something like Mount Dobson.

The access road is 15 kilometres, one of the longest in the country. It's a good road – wide, not too steep, and well graded. The road climbs to 1692 metres, and the car park is New Zealand's highest.

The ski area is in a wide, sunny basin that is basically split in half by the small bluff on the left of the T-bar. This gives Mount Dobson two distinct parts – the East and the West, accessed from the top of the T-bar by East Trail and West Trail respectively. The majority of skiing is done in the eastern part. This is because skiing in the West requires two lifts to get back to the top, whereas skiing in the East requires just the T-bar. Platter 2 must be used to get back to the T-bar from the West.

On the left of Platter 1 (the country's longest platter lift), is a very long and wide learners' area, ideal for 'never-evers' and beginners. There are two spots to unload on the way up the T-bar, and the runs down from both are on gentle slopes, so beginners needn't feel restricted to just the learners' area. The top section of the T-bar is on a steep slope, alongside Shirt Front, which can be a demanding run, especially in icy or mogul conditions.

The intermediate and more adventurous beginner skier should try heading out West. Easy Run is a wide, groomed run on a mostly gentle slope, and lacks the crowds of the M1 or Out East runs. Half Pipe is a long, narrow gully, not a half pipe in the strictest terms of the word, and it's not uncommon to see snowboarders and skiers enjoying screaming from side to side down the gully.

On a powder day, and Mount Dobson gets a few, it is best to traverse on either East or West Trail and pick a route down into the basin. Bluffs is one of the first slopes to lose snow, and on a powder day is arguably the mountain's best run, so get in quick! The slopes way out west, past Easy Run, are excellent but short, unless you ski to below Platter 2 and walk back up. When you see the untouched slopes below the platter, the temptation to continue skiing may be too much and the walk may seem worth it.

There are some good touring areas to explore out to the west of Easy Run. You'll see the slopes out there as you drive up to the field, and it's possible to walk up to the access road after skiing them. If you're planning to make a trip out that way, try spotting a route back as you're driving up. Ski patrol will give you avalanche hazard information before you set off.

If you can organise someone to pick you up on the road, there's a route out past Sunny Run that is worth taking as the day's last run. It will take you over a wide slope and down a narrow gully to the road. Don't do this run without checking on conditions with ski patrol.

# OHAU

## HISTORY

People from around the world were visiting the Southern Alps as early as 1870. In 1883, the Government, recognising the area's recreational and tourist potential, offered finance to open up a route to Mount Cook. This done, the Government declared land in the area a Recreational Reserve.

In 1887, a group of Timaru businessmen built the first hotel, called the Hermitage, at Mount Cook. The business failed in 1894, mainly because it was then a three-day journey from Christchurch (one day by train to Fairlie, and two on coach from there), and because it was expensive, at £10 for a seven-day trip.

Lake Ohau was mentioned as a worthwhile excursion from the Christchurch–Mount Cook route as early as 1884. In 1889, a bridge was built over the Ohau River, and a livery service between Kurow and Pukaki began, meeting with the Fairlie–Hermitage coach at Lake Pukaki. This opened up the Ohau region a little more, and the occasional tourist would make the day trip from Pukaki to Ohau.

Between 1894 and 1900, the Government commissioned a number of investigations in search of a mountain pass over the Southern Alps. The only crossing then was Arthurs Pass, in the north, so if another was found in the south it would enable tourists to make the round trip from Christchurch, via the West Coast, back over the divide, to the Hermitage, and back to Christchurch. Many of these investigations were carried out in the Hopkins Valley, at the head of Lake Ohau. (A suitable pass was never found, and it wasn't until the Haast Pass highway was finished in 1965 that the round trip could be made.)

The possibility of a main-divide road being constructed along the shores of Lake Ohau led to considerable interest in the area.

This interest continued after the road plan was scrapped and, in 1916, Rudolph Wigley's Mount Cook Motor Company included Lake Ohau in its Grand Motor Tour. At this stage the company was already making trips between Christchurch, Wanaka and the Hermitage.

While more and more people were visiting Lake Ohau, the majority of tourists were still visiting just Mount Cook. The Mount Cook Company took over the lease of the Hermitage from the Government in 1921. In its first year under the company's control, 1000 people visited the Mount Cook region. Wigley kept the Hermitage open throughout the winter months and, largely because of the rising popularity of skiing, the region was attracting 15,000 a year by 1943.

In 1944, the Hermitage reverted to Government control. The Mount Cook Company by that stage was concentrating mainly on the development of Queenstown and Coronet Peak, and its transport services throughout the South Island. In the early 1950s, Harry Wigley succeeded to his father's business. The previous decade, Harry had flown over, and tramped into, every basin in the Ohau Range. He had noted then that the basin below Mount Sutton, above Lake Ohau, had great potential as a ski area.

In 1948, Harry Wigley bought land on the Western shore of Lake Ohau, and with buildings obtained from the Pukaki hydro-electricity construction site, built the Lake Ohau Lodge. By 1951, the lodge could accommodate 70 people and had a number of tourist attractions, such as horse-riding, fishing, tramping, and cruising on the lake on the launch *Thelma* (the shell of which now lies on the shore below the lodge). Many of the lodge's visitors were those who used to stay at the Hermitage when it was run by Rudolph Wigley.

It was undoubtedly always Harry Wigley's intention to develop a ski area in the basin above the lodge, which he'd spied in earlier years, and in 1953 he established the Ohau Ski Field. The construction of a steep four-wheel-drive track up to the basin was started. (A new road, along a different route, has since

# Ohau

Location: 134 km from Fairlie.
140 km from Wanaka.
211 km from Queenstown.
320 km from Christchurch.

Season: Usually open by early July and closed by mid-October.

Elevation: The top station of the T-bar is at 1825 metres.
The ridge above it is at about 1860 metres.
The base of the Platter lift is at about 1400 metres.
The day lodge is at about 1450 metres.

Vertical drop: 425 metres.

Terrain: Beginner 20%, Intermediate 50%, Advanced 30%.

Snowmaking: None.

Groomers: One.

Road toll: None.

Lifts: One T-bar, one platter and one fixed grip.
Moderate charge, with youth (17 and under), child (12 and under) and student reductions. Under 5s, free. Over 65s, 50% discount.

Ski hire:

|  |  | Adult | Youth | Child |
|---|---|---|---|---|
| Full set: | Day | $25 | $20 | $15 |
| Full set: | Half day | $15 | $12 | $10 |
| Snowboard: | Day | $30 | $25 | $20 |
| Snowboard: | Half day | $20 | $15 | $10 |

Specials: A 'Beginners Package' (a Platter and fixed grip lift pass, hire, and a lesson):
$40 (Adult); $30 (Youth); $20 (Child).

Ohau offers a 'guarantee' on snow and weather

 Ohau

conditions. If conditions do not meet your expectations, you will get a full refund if you return your lift pass no more than 40 minutes after purchasing it.

*Ski school:*

|  | Adult | Youth | Child |
|---|---|---|---|
| Class lesson: (90 minutes) 10:30 am; 1:45 pm | $25 | $20 | $15 |
| Private lesson: (One hour) | $45 | $45 | $45 |

Each additional person $10.

*Accomm:* Lake Ohau Lodge, at the base of the mountain, is a fantastic place to stay. Everything, including the views, facilities and meals is superb, and a night's accommodation can be as affordable, or as plush, as you like. For a low charge, you can share facilities and supply your own bedding. For a high charge, you get private facilities, underfloor heating, dinner and breakfast. There is a moderate charge for a full three-course meal in the lodge's restaurant, bed and a cooked or Continental breakfast. It is possible to dine in the restaurant without staying in the lodge.

For what you receive at the lodge, be it accommodation or food, the prices are exceptional. For enquiries or bookings, phone or fax 0-3-438 9885, or write to the address below.

If you stay in the lodge, you get specially priced lift passes (adult $30; student $25; youth $15; child $10). If you stay for five nights and ski five days, you're offered a free day's skiing and the sixth night's accommodation.

*Address:* Lake Ohau Lodge, Lake Ohau, PO Box 51, Twizel. Telephone: 0-3-438 9727.

*Snow reports:* Telephone or fax 0-3-438 9885.

been constructed.) In June 1953, five local runholders, who were keen skiers, advanced the Mount Cook Company £100 each to produce a rope tow in return for free skiing for life. The rope tow, which Bill Hamilton constructed and the runholders helped install, was operational for the 1953 season.

Skiing occurred on a small scale for several seasons, and development on the area was slow. A day hut was built in the basin in 1955, the road was completed in 1956 and, in September 1959, the area had an official opening.

The lodge was sold to the Eames family in 1959, although the Mount Cook Company continued to run the ski area until 1963, by which stage the majority of the company's resources were required at the booming Coronet Peak. The Ohau ski area was consequently sold to the Eames family.

The lodge and ski area were both run as a family business by the Eames, whose hospitality was widely acknowledged, and visits to both lodge and ski area increased rapidly during the

## GETTING THERE

Whether driving, hitching or on a bus, the only way of getting to Ohau is on Highway 8, turning west at a turn-off halfway between Omarama and Twizel. If you're driving, this is simple. If you're hitching or on a bus, you'll have to be dropped off at the turn-off and hopefully catch a ride up to the lodge. This may not be particularly easy, but if you're there in the morning your chances are better, especially on weekends.

**From the lodge**
A shuttle departs from the lodge daily at 9:15 am. A return ticket is $10 (Adult); $5 (Youth/child). There's usually no problem getting a seat but, if you want to book ahead, phone 0–3–438 9885.

years they were there. In 1978, they purchased a T-bar, but during its installation ran into financial trouble and subsequently sold the ski area.

A public company, Lake Ohau Skifield Ltd, purchased the ski area in early 1979, completing the installation of the T-bar, and installing a platter lift and a fixed grip rope tow. The 1980s were not good years for the Ohau ski area. Combined with a number of poor seasons, and carrying the debt of its developments (the area came close to winding up in 1983), the ski area went through several changes of ownership.

This all changed in 1989 when both ski area and lodge returned to a family business operation, this time run by the Neilsons. The superb atmosphere in the lodge and on the ski area is probably as close as one can get to that which Rudolph Wigley established at the Hermitage and Ball Glacier over 60 years ago.

## THE SKI AREA

Skiing at Ohau is not just a day's skiing. Some would say that unless you've spent a day at the Ohau ski area and a night in the Ohau Lodge, you've yet to experience the best of what skiing is in New Zealand.

Seemingly in the middle of nowhere, about half-way between Queenstown and Christchurch, many skiers make the mistake of visiting Ohau for a short time en route between those centres. The 'Ohau experience' is best enjoyed by staying a night or two in the Ohau Lodge, at the base of the mountain, on the shore of Lake Ohau. For the most relaxing *après-ski* atmosphere in New Zealand, the lodge has no equal. At night in the bar, it's possible to sit back in a comfortable chair, in front of a roaring fire, and look out over the opalescent Lake Ohau to Mount Cook. Even the lodge's two spa pools have great views.

If you're travelling on a budget, but enjoy the occasional extravagance, make a stay in the Ohau Lodge such an occasion. What's more, the experience far exceeds the cost.

The only way of getting to Lake Ohau is via a 20-kilometre sealed road off Highway 8, 42 kilometres south of Twizel. From the lake it's a further 10 kilometres up the unsealed access road; the views of the lake and the Mackenzie Country become more spectacular the higher you climb. The condition of the road varies from excellent to jarring, depending on when it was last graded. Chains can be hired ($20) from the base of the access road, or from the lodge.

Apart from the two learners' areas (one fixed grip, one platter) at the base of the ski area, and the wide groomed Boulevard Run, the terrain is generally steep. Left of the T-bar is the steepest part of the ski area, and Escalator is the steepest run on the mountain. The strong-nerved should consider traversing further than Escalator, past the rocky bluff, and descend to the platter lift.

The face above the day lodge, with Sun Run on it, offers some steep runs and, because it gets sun early in the day, is often the best place to ski in the morning. The other face, with the Exhibition and Escalator Runs, remains in the shade until late in the day. It's not uncommon to have great spring skiing on Sun Run with Exhibition and Escalator remaining firm. Advanced skiers are likely to enjoy the variety. After a fresh snowfall, it's a different story; both faces are fantastic skiing. A race for fresh tracks at Ohau is not uncommon, but it rarely approaches the ferocity of similar races at other areas.

A walk to the ridge above the T-bar is worth it for the views alone. To ski Ridge Run is good enough reason for making the walk several times. From the ridge you get a good view over the Maitland Valley to the Barrier Range. The highest peak in the range is Mount Saint Mary (2332 metres) to the southwest. The peak towering above the southern face of the ski area is Mount Sutton at 1999 metres. A great run is to make a few turns on Ridge Run then traverse as high as possible on to the face above Sun Run and descend to the day lodge.

The learners' area above the day lodge is a wide slope with an excellent gradient for 'never-evers'. Once progressing from there, a skier may be able to ski down the cat-track to the more challenging runs on the platter lift. Be warned though: from the platter you must either walk back up to the day lodge or take the T-bar to the top. While the Boulevard is definitely a beginners' run, it does get a little steep in places (below Top Flat). Boulevard does give the less-confident skier a good reign of the mountain and few ski areas have such an easy run from their highest point. The T-bar is 1033 metres long, the longest in New Zealand.

The Luge is a great run down a gully, while Shirt Front is a wide, groomed slope suitable for wide, cruising turns. The small group of rocks to the right of The Luge offer some good 'mini-extreme' type skiing down some short steep pitches. Intermediate skiers are likely to find both the Luge and Shirt Front Runs challenging.

The Ohau Range, in which the Ohau ski area lies, is generally a steep range of mountains and consequently ski-touring in the region can be tricky. A recommended trip from the ski area is to head south on the ridge past Mount Sutton to Dumbell Lake. Ski patrol will give you an avalanche-hazard forecast before you head out.

# Fairlie

The settlement of Fairlie started in 1865, when James Litster built an accommodation house on the banks of the Opihi River. In those days, the route into the interior was along the Tengawai River and through Mackenzie Pass, to the south. Litster encouraged bullock drivers to travel a little further north and stay in his house. Faced with the option of either sleeping under their wagons beside the Tengawai River or staying at Litsters, the house soon became quite popular.

Litster's brother-in-law, David Hamilton, came to give him a hand in running the house, and it was Hamilton, from Fairlie, Scotland, who named the place Fairlie Creek. The name stuck until 1892, when it was shortened.

Burkes Pass, another entrance to the interior basins, had been discovered in 1855. It was to the west of Fairlie and, being an easier crossing than the Mackenzie Pass, the Government chose Burkes Pass as the official route. A small settlement (named Burkes Pass) was started to the east of the pass.

Fairlie, however, had started to become something of a rural centre and, in 1884, the Government ran a branch railway from Timaru as far as Fairlie. This effectively put an end to further developments at Burkes Pass and shifted all attention to Fairlie. The 'Fairlie Flyer' made the Timaru–Fairlie service until the line was removed in 1968. Fairlie's railway station was shifted to the Fairlie Museum Complex in 1979, and these days there's little evidence of there ever having been a railway.

By the time the railway was removed, Fairlie was firmly established as the largest town in the area. It has been associated with skiing since the early 1930s, when it was a stopping point for members of the Tasman Ski Club on their way to Fox Peak. However, it wasn't until 1979, with the opening of the Mount Dobson ski area, that the town began showing any real sign of being involved with skiing. These days, far from a hustling, bustling ski town, Fairlie remains a welcoming laid-back, rural centre.

## Ski shops

The **Ski Shack** (0–3–685 8088) on Main Street is very well stocked with a wide selection of equipment.

*Hire charges:*
Full ski gear for a day: $20 (Adult); $16 (Youth); $12 (Child).
Snowboards: $25 (day).
Executive equipment is also available.

*Repair charges:*
Charges vary according to the amount of work required.

## Places to stay

The **Rimuwhare Country Retreat** (phone/fax 0–3–685 8058; 53 Mount Cook Road) is at the western end of town, en route to Mount Dobson. Built in 1889, it was originally the doctor's residence. Behind the colonial-style house, there is a group of fully equipped units (fridge, kitchen, bathroom and underfloor heating). There are two- and three-bedroom units, with the cost varying from low to moderate, depending on how many people share. The in-house bar is small and comfortable with a large open fire, and its restaurant is one of the best in the region; certainly the best in Fairlie (see Places to eat). Bookings are essential.

**Aorangi Motel** (0–3–685 8340) at 26 Denmark Street has seven units sleeping two to seven people for a moderate charge. Each unit has full kitchen facilities, a TV, radio, telephone, tea- and coffee-making facilities and electric blankets. A great bonus is the spa pool, which non-residents can use for $3 an hour. Cooked and Continental breakfasts are available.

The **Allandale B & B and Backpackers** (0–3–685 8708) is at 10 Allandale Road. The bed and breakfast section has double rooms (linen and towels provided), and a homely lounge area with TV, stereo and log burner. Tea and coffee is available, and a night's stay is in the low price range; budget if you don't have breakfast. A cooked breakfast or evening meal is available for a low charge. The backpackers' section consists of two seven-bed dormitories and a living room with full kitchen facilities and TV. A night's stay is in the budget range. The lodge has two resident Sydney Silkies who love playing 'fetch' in the large back garden.

## PLACES TO EAT

The **Rimuwhare Country Retreat Restaurant** (0–3–685 8058) at 53 Mount Cook Road offers the finest meals in town. The menu lists dishes that range from the exotic to the more traditional local fare. The restaurant has won several cuisine awards, is moderately priced, and the food really is very good. There's a large open fire. It's fully licensed. Book ahead.

The two café/takeaway shops on the main road – **BB Stop** and **Toms Diner** – both serve a range of dishes as well as fish'n'chips. Both are low to moderately priced, and the coffee is usually pretty good. Bookings are not usually required.

The **Sunflower Centre** is a health food and crafts shop at 31 Main Street. There's a good choice of healthy meals (the vegeburgers are excellent) and the dining area is full of craft work of all sorts. Herbal teas are available in abundance, and the banana smoothies are something else. You can get a good-sized meal for a moderate charge.

## HAPPENING PLACES

There are two pubs in Fairlie – the Gladstone Grand Hotel and the Fairlie Hotel. Both are on Main Street. The **Gladstone**

Grand, known as 'The Bottom Pub', is the smaller of the two. It's blessed with a pool table and quite possibly the ugliest carpet in the country. It tends to be frequented mainly by the local farmers and the occasional skier. It's a great place to meet the locals, many of whom seem to have started playing pool at a young age. Bar meals at low to moderate prices are available.

The **Fairlie Hotel**, known as 'The Top Pub', tends to be where the majority of skiers head for their *après-ski* drink. The carpet is marginally better, as are your chances of winning a game of pool, although the Mount Dobson staff are also quite proficient on the felt. Low to moderately priced bar meals are available here, too.

The **Silverstream Hotel** is a charming-looking building about seven kilometres west of Fairlie, toward Mount Dobson. It's a popular place to stop following a descent of the Mount Dobson access road. Among other things, it has on its wall a map of the European Alps (to the right of the deer's head and below the stuffed salmon). It has the seemingly obligatory pool table, and also serves low to moderately priced bar meals. The garden bar is great in spring time.

## SERVICES

*Medical:* The Fairlie Medical Centre is on Ayr Street: 0–3–685 8211.
Pharmacy on Main Street: 0–3–685 8164.
*Police:* The police station is on Kirke Street: 0–3–685 8400. In emergencies, phone 111.
*Post Office:* L & L Hardware on Main Street acts as the Fairlie Postal Agency.

## INFORMATION

The Sunflower Centre, 31 Main Street: 0–3–685 8258.

## Getting Around

Fairlie's a small town in which a walk from end to end takes no longer than 15 minutes.

## Travelling On

Atomic Shuttles runs services to Christchurch and Queenstown. To book, phone Christchurch 0–3–322 8883 or 025–353 834.

Catch-A-Bus Shuttles runs services to Christchurch, Wanaka and Queenstown. To book, phone Dunedin 0–3–477 7900 or 0800–50 8000 (toll-free).

Intercity/Ritchies runs services to destinations throughout the South Island. Located at BB Stop, 81 Main Street: 0–3–685 8139.

Mount Cook Landline runs services to destinations throughout the South Island. Located on Main Street: 0–3–685 8311 or 0800–800 287 (toll-free).

# Kurow

Kurow is a small rural centre in the Waitaki Valley. The valley was long ago used by east coast Maori as part of their route to the west coast in search of pounamu (greenstone).

In the late 1800s, the land in the Waitaki, much of which had been cleared of bush by the Maori during their moa-hunting days, was turned into sheep and cattle runs by Europeans, and the township of Kurow developed. (The moa, a large flightless bird, is now extinct.)

In 1928, work began on the Waitaki hydroelectric dam, seven kilometres upstream from Kurow. Completed in 1935, the Waitaki was followed by Benmore (completed in 1966) and Aviemore (completed in 1968) dams, both further upstream on the Waitaki River. The region was full of dam workers during these periods, and Kurow was at its busiest.

These days, Kurow – with its two supermarkets, two pubs and two petrol stations – is still the largest town in the Waitaki Valley. It's busiest during the summer months, the Waitaki River being popular for fishing. In the winter, it's quieter, although you wouldn't know it by visiting either of the pubs, which tend to be just as busy year-round.

Other than a sign-post on the main road indicating 'Awakino Ski Grounds 11 km', there is little evidence of the ski area at all and, while most people in Kurow know of Awakino's existence, very few have actually skied there.

If you find yourself spending a night in Kurow, the **Kurow Holiday Park** (0–3–436 0725) at the western end of town offers a good range of accommodation, from a budget backpackers' dormitory to moderately priced tourist flats. The more upmarket **Kurow Motels** (moderately priced) on the main road, 0–3–436 0655, has a choice of shared or private facilities, with a TV in each room.

Both pubs, the **Kurow** and the **Waitaki**, have single, double and twin rooms available for a low price. They're both fairly typical country New Zealand pubs with friendly, laid-back atmospheres. The Kurow (0–3–436 0850) is the smaller of the two and seems to be less rowdy than the Waitaki, which has two large pool tables, and a TV that more often than not has horse racing on it. Both pubs serve hot meals and are perfect for an *après-ski* drink after a day on Awakino. For food there's also a takeaway shop at the western end of town which makes a good batch of fish and chips, and burgers. There's an Information Centre on the main road: 0–3–436 0819.

# Central Otago

## Ski Areas

Cardrona 263
Coronet Peak 272
The Remarkables 280
Treble Cone 288
Waiorau Nordic 295

## Resorts

Queenstown 301
Wanaka 318

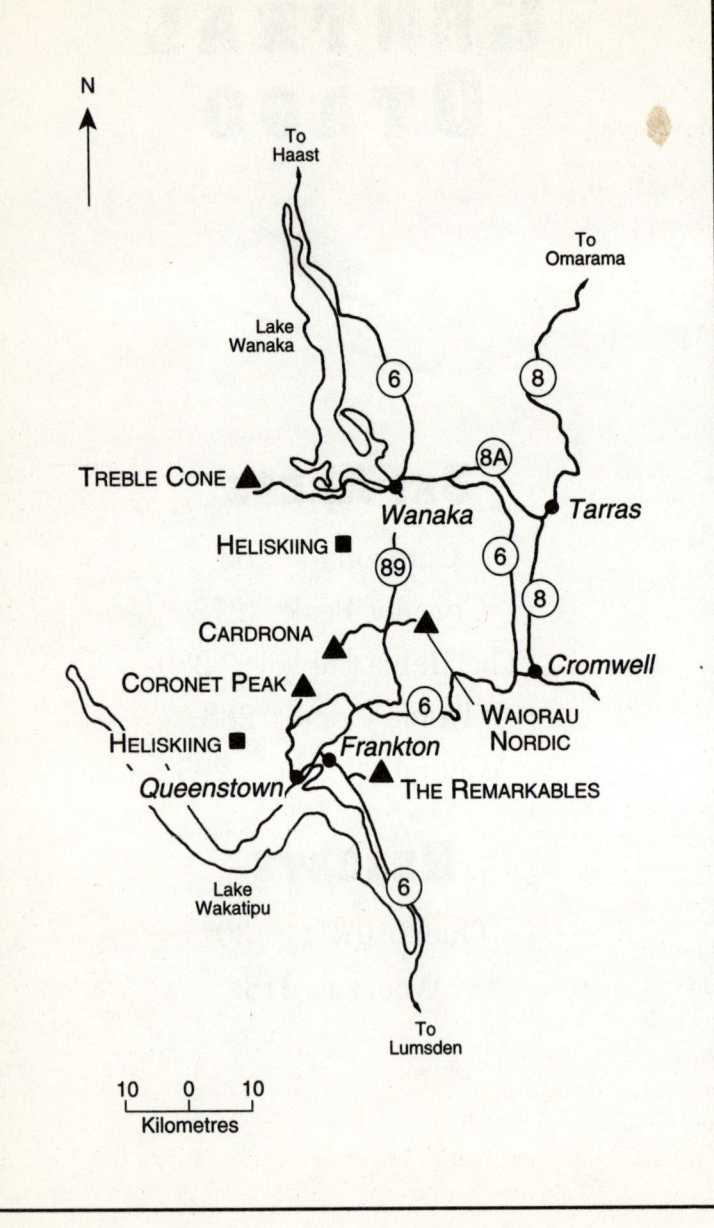

# CARDRONA

## HISTORY

The history of the Cardrona ski area is really a 'success story' of phenomenal proportions. There are four main reasons for this. First, the man who started the area, John Lee, had great foresight and determination. Secondly, the area's location between Queenstown and Wanaka is ideal. Thirdly, the land on which the area has developed is freehold, meaning it's free from many of the bureaucratic, restrictive, and time-consuming processes necessary when developing land leased from the Government (developments must, however, gain local Council, Department of Conservation, and Landcorp approval). Fourthly, and most importantly, Cardrona caters fantastically to the beginner and intermediate skiers, who generally spend more money at an area than advanced or expert skiers. Also central to Cardrona's success is the reputable good nature of its staff, a fact noted by many a visitor over the years.

Lee's family had been in the Cardrona region for some time, his great uncle helping to build the Kawarau dam in the quest for gold in the late 1800s, and his father being one of the returned soldiers who settled on sheep-runs in the valley in the early 1920s.

In the late 1960s and early 70s, there was a marked population decline in rural New Zealand. Cardrona Valley, with a population of 21, was feeling the effects of this decline – the school bus service had been terminated, the two-day-a-week mail service was under threat of closing, and the valley road was being down-graded. Lee, who farmed Waiorau Station in the valley, was determined to restore these community services and cease the valley's decline.

In 1970, he purchased Cardrona Station with the idea of developing a ski area on Mount Cardrona, although he was not himself a skier. The Mount Cook Company had conducted a study of the area in 1954 and found the mountain to have potential as a ski area. Developing a ski area on Cardrona was one of two options Lee had in mind to fix the valley's problems. The other option, his first, was to develop a cross-country ski area on the Pisa Range. But, because the Pisa Range was on Crown land, he knew it would take years of negotiation before the idea was approved. He did, however, eventually start the area, Waiorau, in 1989.

Following the purchase of Cardrona, Lee began researching ski areas. His wife, Mary, and other locals would walk, or catch a chopper, up to the slopes of Mount Cardrona and spend the day skiing. Lee would walk up to look at the area, and monitor snow and weather conditions. Reports from those who skied there were exceedingly favourable and, in 1974, Lee started pushing an old farm road further up the mountain. This proved to be fairly difficult and costly.

The road continued its slow climb up the mountain and, in 1976, a renowned Austrian ski-lift engineer, Reinholdt Zauner, first visited Cardrona. He told Lee: 'I hate to see a man who is sitting on a goldmine and doesn't know it.' The following year, a 200-metre portable rope tow was put in the main (MacDougall's) basin, and on some weekends 30 to 40 people were skiing the area.

In 1980, a 1000-metre rope tow was bought from Mount Hutt. The road had reached 'Tow Hut Corner' by this stage, and the tow ran from there up to the main basin. The 1980 season was not a particularly good one but, although the area opened for only three weeks, it attracted 1100 skiers. The area was largely run by volunteers who did odd jobs in return for free skiing.

It was about this time that Lee started requesting that the Council keep the Crown Range road open year-round. The road runs between Cardrona and Queenstown and used to close for winter. If the ski area was going to succeed, this access from Queenstown was essential.

The next ski season lasted six weeks, closing in early September due to farming commitments. During that time there were 4000 skier days, and this success encouraged further business partners to join the team. Some skiers were having trouble with the ungroomed snow, and the queues were sometimes up to half an hour long, so a small groomer and a 300-metre learners' tow were purchased. These helped but, in 1982, the area attracted 10,000 skier visits (due largely to Lee keeping the Crown Range road open to secure visits from Queenstown skiers), and it was obvious that the area needed to increase its lift capacity. Several times during the season a 'Full Capacity' sign had to be put out at the toll gate.

Over the 1983–84 summer, Lee and partners invested more capital and, with a loan, installed the La Franchi double chairlift. They also got electricity to the area and bought another groomer. Even with these developments the 'Full Capacity' sign was still required. In July 1983, the council finally agreed to keep the Crown Range road open.

Over the following summer, the Lee's Leap cat-track was cut, opening up the large Captain's Basin area, named after a wild horse who lived in the basin and who had for years proved very difficult to round up for the annual Wanaka rodeo. The 1984 season was a poor one for many ski areas, but not Cardrona, which attracted 50,000 skier visits.

After that season, Lee and partners decided to form a public company, Cardrona Ski Area, to invite further investment and to increase its financial resources. It was the first ski area to be listed on the stock exchange. With an injection of capital, the company built a new base building and installed the country's first quad chairlift, MacDougall's. The 'Full Capacity' sign was put away.

Early in 1986, the Captain's quad chairlift and a cafeteria were installed in Captain's Basin. There were 78,000 skier visits during the 1986 season. In the 1987 season, Cardrona attracted 101,000 skier visits, an increase of about 1000% since 1977.

The share-market crash of 1987 saw some big changes in the

# Cardrona

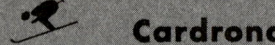

*Location:* 35 km from Wanaka.
57 km from Queenstown (via Crown Range).
146 km from Queenstown (via Cromwell).
311 km from Dunedin.

*Season:* Opens early June, closes early to mid-October.

*Elevation:* Mount Cardrona itself is 1934 metres high.
The top of Captain's Quad chairlift is at 1890 metres.
The bottom of La Franchi chairlift is at 1600 metres.
The base buildings are at 1700 metres.

*Vertical drop:* 390 metres.

*Terrain:* Beginner 25%, Intermediate 60%, Advanced 15%.

*Snowmaking:* Yes.

*Groomers:* Two.

*Road toll:* $9.

*Lifts:* Two quad chairlifts, one double chairlift, one platter lift and a fixed grip tow. High charge, with reductions for learners and over 60s. Under 5s free.

*Ski hire:* Full set: Day: $26(Adult); $20 (Child, 17 and under).
Half day: $20(Adult); $10 (Child).
Executive: Day: $40; $28  Half day: $28; $21.
Snowboard: Day: $42; $29  Half day: $29; $22.
Hour: $13; $10.

*Specials:* A variety of Beginner Packages that include a Learners' lift pass, hire and lesson/s. Day packages include 'All Lifts' passes for one or two days, and one lesson on each day. Days need not be taken consecutively. Prices are as follows:
1 lesson: $36 (Adult); $26 (Child). 2 lessons: $48; $35.

# Cardrona

2-day: $124 (Adult); $80 (Child).
1-day beginner's snowboard: $55 (Adult); $45 (Child).
A 'Cardrona Club Card' (discounted lift passes for multi-day skiing): $25 (Adult); $20 (Student); $12 (Child).

*Ski school:* Numerous programmes/clinics such as the three-day Top ski programme, Women's workshops, Perfection clinics, and so on. For more information, contact the ski area at the address below.

Standard group lessons (10:30 am and 2:00 pm):
1 group lesson: $30 (Adult); $20 (Child).
2 group lessons: $56 (Adult); $37 (Child).
4 group lessons: $96 (Adult); $64 (Child).

Private: $62 (hour); $130 (half day); $260 (day).
A sunrise (9:30 am) or sunset lesson (3:00 pm): $52.
Each additional person (maximum three) $22.

*Accomm:* The clocktower building in MacDougall's Basin has four luxury apartments, each sleeping up to eight people, with their own kitchen, living room, bathroom and terrace overlooking the ski area. Nowhere else in New Zealand is this type of accommodation available on a ski area. In June and October, an apartment costs $225 per night; July, $285; August $375; September, $450. Booking is absolutely essential: phone 0-3-443 7411 or 0-3-443 7341, or fax 0-3-443 8818.

*Address:* Cardrona Ski Resort, PO Box 117, Wanaka. Telephone: 0-3-443 7341.

*Snow reports:* Phone the Cardrona Snowphone on 0900–34444. The following radio stations also have reports: Resort/Central Radio (at 6:50 am), QFM 92.0 (at 6:45 am) and 4XO (at 7:45 am).

organisation, and early in 1988 half of the company was sold to Vealls Investments. In 1990, Vealls bought the remaining 50%, and John Lee was no longer involved with the area.

## Getting there

**From Wanaka**

*By car*

It's well sign-posted from Wanaka township but, if you have any problems, just ask someone to point you in the right direction. The toll gate is a 23-kilometre drive south of the town along Crown Range road (Highway 89). From the toll gate, you climb a 12-kilometre, unsealed road to the ski area.

*Hitching*

Head along MacDougall Street as far as the corner of Tenby Street. There will undoubtedly be a group of people already as this is the 'recognised' hitching point for getting to Cardrona. Try being there by 8:00 am and be prepared for a bit of competition.

*By shuttle*

Goodsports run two daily trips, making pick-ups in Wanaka at 8:30 am and 9:00 am. An adult return fare is $20; a child's (10 and under) is $15. Bookings are essential: 0–3–443 7966.

Edgewater Resort runs a daily trip, making pick-ups in Wanaka at 8:15 am. An adult return fare is $20, a child's (10 and under) is $15. Bookings are essential: 0–3–443 8311.

**From Queenstown**

*By car*

There are two ways — a short way and a long way. The

Lee had a goal from the beginning: to turn his father's greatest liability, snow, into an asset. This he did, and today the Cardrona ski area and the Cardrona Valley both show signs of going from

---

short way is via the Crown Range road. It is mostly unsealed and, in icy or extremely muddy conditions, it may be closed. The long route involves a drive through Cromwell and Luggate to Wanaka, from where you head south on the Crown Range road.

*Hitching*
It's not easy but, if you're determined, be on Skippers Road, just past the turn-off from Shotover Street, by about 7:30 am. Chances are you'll get a lift with someone going to Coronet Peak. If so, get a ride as far as the Coronet Peak access road. If you can't get a ride to Cardrona from there, take a lift with anyone going to the Crown Range road turn-off or, better still, to Wanaka. The rest is fairly straightforward from either spot.

*By shuttle*
Kiwi Discovery makes a daily trip to Cardrona, making pick-ups and leaving Queenstown at 8:00 am. Departs from Cardrona at 4:00 pm. An adult return fare is $28; $17 for children. Bookings are essential: 0–3–442 7340.

Kawarau Rafts make a daily trip to Cardrona. A bus makes pick-ups around Queenstown and departs at 8:00 am. A return adult fare is $28; $17 for children. Bookings are essential: 0–3–442 9792.

Mountain Tours and Transport makes a trip at 8:00 am, or as required. A return adult fare is $26; $16 for children. Bookings are essential: 0–3–442 6341 or 025-340 298.

strength to strength. In 1994, the ski area built the first commercial on-mountain accommodation on a New Zealand ski area. Lee presently owns and operates the Waiorau Nordic ski area, across the valley from Cardrona ski area. Vealls Investments continue to develop the ski area, and Cardrona's future under this company is looking as bright as ever.

## THE SKI AREA

The access road to Cardrona comes off the Crown Range road, a partly unsealed road connecting Wanaka to Queenstown. On this road is the 'township' of Cardrona, consisting of a few houses, a small church, and one of the most famous pubs in the country, the Cardrona Hotel. About two kilometres north (toward Wanaka) of the hotel is the toll gate and access road to the Cardrona Ski Area. From the toll gate it's about a 12-kilometre drive on the unsealed access road to the ski area.

Over the years, Cardrona has gained a reputation as a ski area suited primarily to beginner and intermediate skiers. This reputation is well earned as it has fantastic beginner and intermediate trails, and families seem to thrive on the area's friendly atmosphere. In Arcadia Chutes, however, Cardrona has some of the best chute skiing in New Zealand. It is almost conceivable that Cardrona's reputation as a beginner–intermediate ski area is being purported by Wanaka's advanced skiing fraternity. This kind of information keeps the chute-poachers away and, as it is, few skiers venture into the Arcadia region.

Both the Irish Pipes and White Star chutes are steep, long and narrow in places. Once you reach the flat area before the next set of chutes you get another choice of routes down to the Comeback Trail. This flat area is also a good spot to stop and have a look back up the mountain and choose your next route through the Arcadia Chutes. In poor visibility, it pays to ski with caution in this part of the ski area.

The MacDougall's quad is one of a few chairlifts in the

country that a first-time skier could go to the top of, and ski down without too much difficulty. It won't be a cinch though, and novice skiers have a long, wide beginners' area, with a gentle gradient, on which to hone their skills before attempting MacDougall's. Above the beginners' area is an artificial snowboarders' half-pipe.

The step up from the MacDougall's quad is Captain's quad, where the terrain is a little steeper, particularly toward the top. The easiest way to get to Captain's is along the Shaun's Way cat-track, but on a powder day Scum Valley and Swaggerman is the route to take. The Captain's bowl is full of wide, groomed trails, excellent for intermediate skiers. Chute-loving skiers will enjoy the Tulips and Secret Chute region. There are a number of narrow chutes in the rocks, and while they're not as long as those in the Arcadia region, they are certainly worth a few (jump) turns.

The slopes beneath the La Franchi chairlift are the steepest groomed runs on the area, the Sluice Box being the steepest of these. When northern hemisphere ski teams (Norwegian, Canadian, Japanese) visit Cardrona, much of their training is done on these slopes. Caution is required at the intersection of Sluice Box and All Nations. There's a bit of a blind corner there and it pays to keep an eye out for skiers coming down the other run. Last Shot Bowl and Valley View are long runs down shallow gullies; fantastic skiing on a powder day.

From almost anywhere on the ski area you have a view across Cardrona Valley to the Pisa Range, on which the Waiorau Nordic ski area lies. From the top of MacDougall's quad, along the Skyline Run, there are views down Soho Creek and the Arrow River toward Arrowtown and Queenstown. It's also possible to see The Remarkables and Coronet Peak from here.

# CORONET PEAK

## HISTORY

Rudolph Wigley was a farmer from South Canterbury who had two great passions – motor cars and mountains. He's considered a pioneer of motoring in New Zealand, having made many adventurous journeys in some of the first motorised vehicles. In 1906, he became the first to drive from Timaru to the Hermitage, at Mount Cook, using a De Dion vehicle.

The Hermitage Hotel had been built in the late nineteenth century and by the early 1900s the Mount Cook area was attracting tourists from around New Zealand and all over the world. It was during these years that Wigley formed the Mount Cook Motor Company and began a regular transport service to the Hermitage from Christchurch and Timaru. Because most guests visited the area in the summer, which was a short season, his business ran at a loss. In 1922, amid some political squabble, Wigley took over the lease of the Hermitage from the Government.

Wigley started running the Hermitage all year round, and soon recognised the need to attract more people during the winter. In 1922, accompanied by two guides, he made the first winter ascent of Mount Cook, achieving nationwide media promotion of the area's winter sports. (It would be 50 years before the next winter ascent of Mount Cook.)

The other winter sport Wigley introduced to entice visitors was skiing. In those days it involved guides taking parties up on to the Mueller and Ball Glaciers for a day's skiing. It was these guides, working for the Hermitage, who would later form the Tasman Ski Club and start the Fox Peak ski area.

Through the 1930s, the Hermitage and Mount Cook Company prospered, with more and more people heading to Mount Cook for their summer and winter holidays. Skiing, in particular, was taking off, with professional instructors from Europe introducing New Zealanders to the sport. Things were going well for Wigley and, in 1936, with son Harry, he formed Queenstown–Mount Cook Airways, flying people from throughout New Zealand to Queenstown, which was rapidly gaining recognition as a great holiday spot. Sandy Wigley, Rudolph's other son, became general manager of the company's Queenstown branch in 1938. It was Sandy who saw the potential of skiing in the Queenstown region, and it was he who, having held trials on the Crown Range and Skippers Saddle, decided on Coronet Peak as the best location for a ski area.

The first mechanised transport of skiers on Coronet Peak occurred in 1938, when people skied from the present base lodge site down to the flats, and drove back up to Skippers Saddle for another run.

In 1944, the lease of the Hermitage reverted to the Government, which had no intention of developing skiing in the Mount Cook region. This would have proved ruinous for the Wigleys' bus service to the region, so they began concentrating solely on Queenstown. In 1947, Bill Hamilton was hired to install Coronet Peak's first rope tow. (Hamilton also designed the steel 'nutcracker' device that was used to grip the rope, and connected by rope to a belt around the skier. This device is still used on many club ski areas around the country.) All spare hands in the Mount Cook Company were sent to Queenstown and, in June 1947, Coronet Peak was officially opened.

The rest is history. Queenstown became bigger and bigger, as did the interest in skiing, and so too did the Mount Cook Company. In 1962, the company began flying scheduled DC-3 flights between Christchurch and Queenstown. In 1964, a double chairlift was installed, and a new base lodge built on Coronet Peak. In 1970, a platter lift was installed, followed three years later by a triple chairlift. In 1991, Air New Zealand became the 100 per cent shareholder of the Mount Cook Group. The latest development on Coronet Peak was the installation of a detachable quad chairlift in 1994.

## Coronet Peak

*Location:* 18 km from Queenstown.
71 km from Wanaka (via the Crown Range).
110 km from Wanaka (via Cromwell).

*Season:* Usually opens early/mid-June and closes mid-October.

*Elevation:* Coronet Peak is 1650 metres high.
The base buildings are at 1220 metres. The top of Express Quad, the highest lift, is at 1640 metres.

*Vertical drop:* 420 metres.

*Terrain:* Beginner 20%, Intermediate 45%, Advanced 35%.

*Snowmaking:* On most groomed runs.

*Groomers:* Five.

*Road toll:* None.

*Lifts:* One detachable quad chairlift, one triple chairlift, one double chairlift, one T-bar, one platter and a fixed grip rope tow. High charge, with student, child (16 and under), novice, learner and night-skiing reductions.

*Ski hire:* Full ski sets:
Recreation: Day: $28 (Adult); $19 (Child). Extra days: $19; $16. Under 5s: $15 (day); $6 (hour).
Performance: $39 (Adult); $33 (Child).
Snowboards (Adult/child): $20 (half day); $35 (day); $30 (additional days).
Insurance against damage/breakage: $2 per day.

*Specials:* Multi-day discounts:
3 Time Anytime Pass: $155 (Adult); $80 (Child).
5 Time Anytime Pass: $242 (Adult); $123 (Child).
These passes can also be used at The Remarkables.

## Coronet Peak

The 'Starters Pak'(two lessons, rental equipment, a 'Learners Lift Pass' and a 'Guarantee' (for adults only) that you will be linking turns by the end of the day): $60 (Adults); $36 (Child).

A 'Snowboard Starter Pak' includes a novice pass.

*Ski school:* Endless programmes and clinics: The 'Penguin Club' for 4–6 year olds, Technical Ski Courses, Women's Weeks, Dual Mountain Ski Weeks (with The Remarkables Ski Area), Race Training, and so on. For more information, write to the address below, or phone 0-3-442 4600, or fax 0-3-442 4605.

Class lessons (two hours, starting 10:30 am; 2:00 pm):
1 Session: $35 (Adult); $23 (Child).
2 Sessions: $62 (Adult); $38 (Child).
4 Sessions: $118 (Adult); $74 (Child).
6 Sessions: $174 (Adult); $105 (Child).
10 Sessions: $260 (Adult); $158 (Child).

Private lessons (Adult/Child): $80 (hour); additional person: $40.
Early Bird (9:30 am): $70; additional person: $35.
All day (5 hours): $365; additional person: $105.

*Address:* Mount Cook Group, PO Box 359, Queenstown.
Telephone: 0-3-442 4640.

*Snow reports:* You can phone the Coronet Peak/Remarkables Snowphone on 0900–34444 (costs 99c per minute), listen to any local radio station, or phone or visit any of the Queenstown or Wanaka ski shops.

# Getting there

**From Queenstown**

*By car*

From anywhere in town you should head to Skippers Road, which leads north. Six kilometres out of Queenstown you pass the Arthurs Point pub, the second oldest in the country, before crossing the Shotover River. After a further six kilometres along the road you arrive at the Coronet Peak turn-off. From here it's a seven-kilometre climb up the sealed access road.

*Hitching*

Most people hitch from Skippers Road, just past the turn-off from Shotover Street. It's quite easy to get a lift from there. The earlier the better, but at about 8:30 am is the best time.

*By shuttle or bus*

The Mount Cook Line runs two buses up every day, departing from the Mount Cook Line Ski Centre on Church Street and making pick-ups from a number of hostels, hotels and motels. One departs at 8:30 am, the other at 10:30 am. Returns are $20 (Adult); $14 (Child, 16 and under). To book a seat, phone 0–3–442 4640.

Kiwi Discovery runs two buses daily. They make pick-ups and depart Queenstown at 8:30 am and 10:15 am. Return trips are at 2:00 pm or 4:00 pm. Return fares are $19 (Adult); $13 (Child). To book, phone 0–3–442 7340.

Mountain Tours and Transport run two daily shuttles. Pick-ups start at 8:30 am and at 10:30 am. A return fare is $18. To book a seat, phone 0–3–442 6431 or 025–340 298. Trips will be made at other times depending on demand.

Kawarau Rafts make a daily trip at 8:00 am for $19 return. They will also run one at 10:00 am depending on demand (minimum four people). To book a seat, phone 0–3–442 9792.

## From Wanaka

### By car
The shortest route from Wanaka to Coronet Peak is via the Crown Range Road (Highway 89). It's unsealed for part of the way and, while it may be the shortest route, it is not always the quickest. Mud or snow can make the road impassable. At other times it will be passable only in a four-wheel-drive vehicle. There's a sign on the road as you leave Wanaka that tells you what condition the road's in. If it's impassable, you'll have to go the long way via Cromwell and the Kawarau Gorge on Highway 6 (110 kilometres, compared to 71 via the Crown Range Road). The Crown Range Road joins Highway 6 just before the turn-off (on the right) to Arrowtown. Take this turn-off, and it's a 13-kilometre drive to the ski area turn-off.

### Hitching
Catching a ride from Wanaka to Coronet Peak is not always easy, as few people make the trip. Your chances are actually better if you go the Cromwell way. That way you're likely to get a lift with someone going to Cromwell, or Queenstown, in which case you can get off when they turn off. Most people using the Crown Range Road will be going to Cardrona. If you're hitching from Cromwell, be on the road by 7:30 am.

### By shuttle
There are no shuttle services. The Wanaka-based shuttle operators usually run a trip to Coronet Peak if Cardrona and Treble Cone are closed.

From running a small transport service between Timaru and Mount Cook in the 1920s, to operating a nationwide air and bus service, and three of the country's biggest ski areas (Coronet Peak, The Remarkables, and Mount Hutt) in the 1990s, no single company has made a larger contribution to New Zealand's tourism industry than the Mount Cook Group.

## The Ski Area

Coronet Peak has the only sealed access road in the South Island. Although this makes for easier driving, it also means it can be very slippery in icy conditions. Consequently, chains are still often required. If you're driving to Coronet, try getting there as early as possible. The earlier you arrive, the closer to the lifts you can park, and the sooner you'll be skiing what has been termed 'New Zealand's premier ski area'.

Coronet Peak was the country's first real ski destination and, since its beginnings, it has remained at the leading edge of New Zealand's ski industry. The developments that have occurred at Coronet Peak, and the area's increasing popularity, can be attributed to the same reason that skiing began there in the first place – great skiing. And the reason skiing is great here is, not least, because of the terrain. Unlike many New Zealand ski areas, which lie in concave-type terrain (basins or bowls), Coronet Peak is spread across the side of a mountain and has a more convex shape. There are seemingly limitless ways of getting down Coronet Peak.

The learners' area is made up of wide, groomed runs and has its own chairlift. A big advantage of the learners' area is that it is one large area, rather than a number of small ones. It is also in an area of its own and, as such, is more or less used only by beginners.

There are a number of wide, groomed trails on the mountain. These vary in gradient, but almost all of them are suitable for a strong beginner or intermediate skier. The M1 is the easiest route from top to bottom and there is probably no better-named trail in New Zealand. It can get quite crowded, and it pays to slow down when approaching trail intersections. The areas of ungroomed snow between the trails are full of rolls and dips, making for more exciting skiing if you've had enough of the trails.

On a powder day it pays to get to the area very early. Queenstown has no shortage of powder-mad locals and there are days when, after two or three runs, you'll turn around to look up the mountain and see nothing but tracks through fresh powder. But you won't see the locals; by that stage they'll all be out on Sarah Sue or the region between Exchange Drop and Rocky Gully.

The Back Bowls are the steepest section of the mountain and the untracked stuff tends to last a bit longer out there. One of the best runs for advanced skiers is down the Back Bowls, then back to the ridge, which is just within the ski-area boundary. Traverse along the ridge toward Rocky Gully and descend to the Aeroplane Run when you see a route you like the look of.

For mogul-keen skiers, the slope to your left of the triple chairlift, below mid-station (which is very rarely used) is one of the best patches of moguls in the country. On the way up the chairlift, it's almost always possible to observe someone destroying their knees.

Because of the good skiing available, and its popularity, Coronet Peak is often crowded. So, if you want to ski here, be prepared to queue for the lifts. People from around the world base themselves in Queenstown for a winter, many just to be able to ski Coronet Peak. It's worth the queuing.

# THE REMARKABLES

## HISTORY

In 1970, the Mount Cook Group (see Coronet Peak) saw the need for another ski area in the Queenstown region. Its Coronet Peak area, with 120,000 skier days a year, was close to capacity. The low altitude of Coronet Peak (1650 metres) was also recognised as a disadvantage, as was its lack of flatter, learners' terrain. (Since then, lift developments, snowmaking, and land works have disposed of these problems.)

So the company looked at three potential areas for developing a new ski area – the Wye, Doolans and Rastusburn Valleys. The ideal site had to be within a half-hour drive of Queenstown, be easily accessed, and have good beginner and intermediate skiers' terrain. The Wye was too steep; the Doolans were too far away. The Rastusburn, however, fitted all these criteria, and it was here that the company chose to develop. Having made the decision, however, it took ten years before development actually commenced. These years were full of bureaucratic dispute between the Mount Cook Group and the Government, and involved newly instituted environmental legislation.

The proposed ski area was given the name The Remarkables, after the range in which the Rastusburn Valley lies. In October 1973, the company made formal application to the Government's Lands Department for a lease of the Rastusburn Basin. The Lands Department requested that the company prepare an Environmental Impact Report (EIR), outlining the environmental impacts of the proposed development. The EIR, submitted by the company in December 1975, was one of the first in New Zealand.

The Lands Department had reservations about the new ski area, its primary concern being the visual impact of an access road across the renowned western face of The Remarkables (for which the range is named). In April 1976, a Government body, the Commission for the Environment, published an audit of the EIR, outlining matters that the company would need to investigate further prior to gaining consent. In June 1977, the company submitted another EIR, a huge document containing a comprehensive study of the environment, and how the impact of the ski area on the environment would be minimised.

Finally, in April 1980, seven years after the first application, approval was granted. The company called for tenders for construction of the road, which wasn't actually started until August 1983. The road climbs 1280 metres over 13.9 kilometres, and was completed in June 1984. Every tussock removed was carefully replanted to reduce the road's visual impact.

Once the road was in, work began on the base building and two chairlifts – the Shadow Basin quad and the Alta double. In July 1985, The Remarkables ski area was opened to the public. By July of the following year, the area had an additional chairlift, the Sugar Bowl quad, and several fixed grip tows for beginners. The company's budget for the area in 1973 was about $4 million. The total cost, due largely to changes in planning and design, but also to the years of investigation, was closer to $13 million.

The Remarkables offers fantastic skiing, not only to beginners and intermediates; as a compliment area to Coronet Peak, it's perfect. When viewing The Remarkables from Coronet Peak (the top of which is only 50 metres above The Remarkables car park), it is readily apparent why the area came about.

# THE SKI AREA

Anyone who tells you that The Remarkables ski area is good only for beginner and intermediate skiers is simply wrong.

**The Remarkables**

Location: 24 km from Queenstown.
83 km from Wanaka (via the Crown Range).
122 km from Wanaka (via Cromwell).

Season: Usually open by late June and closed by early October.

Elevation: Double Cone, the highest peak above Lake Alta is 2324 metres high.
The top of Shadow Basin is at 2050 metres.
The top of Sugar Bowl is at 1870 metres.
The base buildings are at 1730 metres.

Vertical drop: 320 metres from the top of Shadow Basin to the base buildings. Probably close to 450 metres from the top of Shadow Basin to the road via Homeward Run.

Terrain: Beginner 30%, Intermediate 40%, Advanced 30%.

Snowmaking: Yes.

Groomers: Two.

Road toll: $9.

Lifts: Two quad chairlifts, one double chairlift, and two fixed grip learners' lifts. High charge, with student, child (16 and under), learner and afternoon reductions.

Ski hire: Full ski sets:
Recreation: Day: $28 (Adult); $24 (Child). Extra days: $18; $15. Under 5s: $15 (day); $6 (hour).
Performance: $39 (Adult); $33 (Child).
Snowboards (Adult/child): $19 (half day); $32 (day); $27 (additional days).
Insurance against damage/breakage: $2 per day.

Specials: Multi-day discounts:
3 Time Anytime Pass: $148 (Adult); $74 (Child).
5 Time Anytime Pass: $239 (Adult); $120 (Child).

##  The Remarkables

8 Time Anytime Pass: $352 (Adult); $178 (Child).
12 Time Anytime Pass: $483 (Adult); $242 (Child).
15 Time Anytime Pass: $564 (Adult); $282 (Child).
All passes can also be used at Coronet Peak.

The 'Starters Pak' (two lessons, rental equipment, a 'Learners Lift Pass' and a 'Guarantee' (for adults only) that you will be linking turns by the end of the day: $60 (Adults); $36 (Child).

A 'Snowboarding Starter Pak' (half-day snowboard rental, one hour's instruction): $53 (Adult); $42 (Child).

*Ski school:* Endless programmes and clinics: The 'Penguin Club' for 4–6 year olds, Technical Ski Courses, Women's Weeks, Dual Mountain Ski Weeks (with the Coronet Peak Ski Area), Race Training, and so on. For more information, write to the address below, or phone 0-3-442 4600, or fax 0-3-442 4605.

Class lessons (two hours, starting 10:30 am; 2:00 pm):
1 Session: $32 (Adult); $20 (Child).
2 Sessions: $60 (Adult); $36 (Child).
4 Sessions: $115 (Adult); $70 (Child).
6 Sessions: $168 (Adult); $102 (Child).
10 Sessions: $256 (Adult); $150 (Child).

Private lessons (Adult/Child): $72 (hour); Additional person: $27.
Early Bird (9:30 am): $53; Additional person: $25.
All day (5 hours): $320; Additional person: $75.

*Address:* Mount Cook Group, PO Box 359, Queenstown. Telephone: 0-3-442 4640.

*Snow reports:* You can phone the Coronet Peak/Remarkables Snowphone on 0900-34444 (costs 99c per minute), listen to any local radio station, or phone or visit any of the Queenstown or Wanaka ski shops.

Anyone who has skied the very narrow, very steep Elevator Chute will confirm this, as will anyone who has skied down the long and exhausting Homeward Run. To say, however, that The Remarkables is one of the best areas for beginner and intermediate skiers is indisputable.

## Getting there

**From Queenstown**

*By car*

Head toward Frankton (the route to Invercargill) on Highway 6. When you reach Frankton (six kilometres), turn right with Highway 6. The Remarkables access road (14 kilometres long) is four kilometres away.

*Hitching*

The best way to catch a lift is to be somewhere along Frankton Road (past Suburb Street would be best) by no later than 8:00 am. If you catch a lift with someone who's going only as far as Frankton, take it. From there it'll be easier getting a lift (beside the airport). Any car with skis on is almost guaranteed to be going to The Remarkables.

*By shuttle*

Mount Cook Line runs two buses up every day, departing from the Mount Cook Line Ski Centre on Church Street (8:30 and 10:30 am), and picking up from a number of hostels, hotels and motels. A return fare is $19 (Adult); $13 (Child). Buses leave the ski area at 3:00 and 4:00 pm. To book a seat, phone 0–3–442 4640.

Kiwi Discovery runs a daily shuttle, making pick-ups in town and departing at 8:15 am. A return fare is $19 (Adult); $13 (Child). Buses leave the ski area at 2:00 and and 4:00 pm. To book a seat, phone 0–3–442 7340.

Beginners who have skied a day or two will find the runs from the Alta and Sugar Bowl chairlifts well within their ability. There are very wide groomed slopes down both. Shadow Basin isn't much different, but there are some steeper and narrower sections that will challenge the less-confident skier. The

---

Kawarau Rafts runs a daily shuttle, making pick-ups in town and departing for the ski area at 8:00 am. A return fare is $19 (Adult); $13 (Child). The shuttle leaves the ski area at 4:00 pm. To book a seat, phone 0–3–442 9792.

Mountain Tours and Transport runs a shuttle, making pick-ups in town and leaving at 8:30 am; other times as required. A return fare is $18. To book a seat, phone 0–3–442 6341 or 025–340 298.

### From Wanaka

*By car*

Few people drive from Wanaka to The Remarkables. The route is the same as for Coronet Peak, only instead of turning off to Arrowtown carry on along Highway 6. Take the Frankton turn-off to the left 12 kilometres away, and it's a four-kilometre drive to the access road.

*Hitching*

Follow the instructions for Coronet Peak, only stay on Highway 6 instead of taking the Arrowtown turn-off. It will not be easy hitching, but if you can make it as far as the Frankton turn-off by 9:30 or 10:00 am, the rest is easy. Start hitching from Wanaka at around 7:00 am.

*By shuttle*

There are no shuttle services between Wanaka and The Remarkables. You may be able to charter a van for a day. Phone the Wanaka shuttle operators for more details.

beginners' area in front of the base building is a large area with a very gentle slope. For someone who is learning to ski there are few places as good to start on as The Remarkables beginners' areas.

For the advanced skier, the Shadow Basin is really where it's at. The chutes off The Highway (Expressway, Hour Glass and Rainbow Warrior) are all short and steep, good practice grounds before heading over to the Alta, Escalator, and Elevator chutes. The Escalator and Elevator are both very demanding runs, the Alta chutes a little less so. All of these will bring you out on to the large flat area that is the frozen Lake Alta. It's quite a feeling to ski across the snow-covered lake, with the large rocky bluffs above you.

The walk up to the chutes from the top of Shadow Basin chairlift takes about ten minutes. From the top of the chairlift it's also worth making the walk up to the lookout. It's at the top of the steep Remarkables face, and the views of Lake Wakatipu, Queenstown and the surrounding peaks are spectacular. If you were to take one photograph of the Queenstown region, this is where you'd take it from.

The Homeward Run was a heliski run before the ski area started, and is one of the longest and most enjoyable runs on any ski area in the country. Fresh tracks are available for days after a fall of powder. The Homeward Shuttle (seats about 30) makes trips every 20 minutes from the base of the slope to the base of Shadow Basin chairlift. On a good day, skiers will make this circuit for hours and hours.

While the Sugar Bowl chairlift accesses mainly intermediate and beginner slopes, the advanced skier who is prepared to walk a bit will find some great runs. The Gallipoli Chutes and surrounding slopes are steep and infrequently skied. It is not possible to ski to the top of the chutes, contrary to the trail map, and from Water Race it's about a five-minute walk.

A 15-minute walk up the northern face of Sugar Bowl opens up one of Queenstown's local skiing fraternity's favourite runs. It doesn't appear on the trail map because it's out of bounds, and is only occasionally opened by ski patrol. It's known as Toilet Bowl, and takes you down a long face to the road, from where it's a short walk to the Homeward Shuttle's pick-up point. If it's open and the snow is good, don't miss the opportunity. (If the snow is heavy and wet, forget it.)

As far as ski-touring goes, there is arguably no ski area in New Zealand that opens up as much good terrain as The Remarkables. Over the ridge that runs from the top of Sugar Bowl to Double Cone are two valleys – Wye Creek and the right branch of Doolans Creek. Heliski operators have runs in both of these, and the skiing in each can be superb. It can also be very dangerous, so don't go without getting a hazard forecast from ski patrol.

Finally, and perhaps the greatest point in The Remarkables' favour, there are very rarely queues. Even during school holidays you can often ski straight on to a chairlift. The area's number of fans is growing though, and it may not be too long before queuing here reaches the same stage it's at on other ski areas in the region.

# TREBLE CONE

## HISTORY

In 1968, a group of 16 keen skiers from Otago formed a private company, Treble Cone Skifields (Wanaka) Ltd, each investing $1000. Treble Cone, a mountain at the western end of Lake Wanaka, had long been regarded as having great ski slopes. It is close to the main divide (the Southern Alps) with an easterly aspect, meaning that the slopes receive good amounts of snow from the frequent northwest wind, while also remaining reasonably sheltered. In the years preceding the company's

 **Treble Cone**

- *Location:* 19 km from Wanaka.
  90 km from Queenstown.
- *Season:* Usually open by mid-June and closed by early-October.
- *Elevation:* The summit of Treble Cone is 2100 metres.
  The top of Saddle T-bar is 1860 metres.
  The base buildings are at 1250 metres.
- *Vertical drop:* 610 metres.
- *Terrain:* Beginner 20%, Intermediate 45%, Advanced 35%.
- *Snowmaking:* Yes.
- *Groomers:* Four.
- *Road toll:* $7.
- *Lifts:* Two T-bars, a double chairlift, and a platter lift.
  High charge, with child and student reductions.

formation, its founders had made several ski trips to Treble Cone.

At the time of the company's formation, Coronet Peak, run by the Mount Cook Company, was the only ski area in the Queenstown–Wanaka region. Coronet Peak was becoming increasingly busier and the potential for another ski area in the region was huge. This was a fact noted by the Queenstown Mayor, Mr W. Cooper, and Harry Wigley, managing director of the Mount Cook Company, who both agreed that a back-up ski area to Coronet Peak was needed. The Mount Cook Company began searching for suitable areas in 1970, and eventually chose the site of The Remarkables. It also advised the Treble Cone company throughout the early 1970s but would not, although requested, become financially involved in that venture.

 **Treble Cone**

*Ski hire:* Adult full set: $25 (Day); $18 (Half day).
Child full set: $20 (Day); $10 (Half day).

*Specials:* 'Frequent Skiers Card' ($25) gives discounted day passes.

*Ski school:* Group lessons (10:30 am; 1:30 pm): $30 (Adult); $20 (Child).
Private lessons (one hour): $60 (Adult); $50 (Child).
Private lessons at 9:30 am or 12:00 pm: $50 (Adult); $40 (Child).

*Address:* Treble Cone Ski Area, PO Box 206, Wanaka.
Telephone: 0–3–443 7443.

*Snow reports:* Phone the Treble Cone Snowphone on 0900–34444 or listen to Wanaka Radio, 4XO or Resort Radio.

In June 1969, the Treble Cone company used its initial capital to build a shelter and install a rope tow in the northern section of Treble Cone's slopes (where Easy Street is now). Access to the ski area required driving 28 kilometres from Wanaka through the privately owned Cattle Flat farm, and then climbing 500 metres on foot. The ski area was not open to the public, but used mainly by the company founders and members of the Wanaka Ski Club.

In June 1971, directors of Treble Cone Skifields (Wanaka) Ltd announced that it would become a public company. By doing so they were hoping to gain enough capital to purchase an Italian-built cable car to carry people from the valley floor up to the ski

## Getting there

**From Wanaka**

*By car*

Take the road going west towards Glendhu Bay and the mountains. After 15 kilometres you'll arrive at the access road. The road is unsealed from Glendhu Bay. The access road is kept in good shape and, although a little steep in places, is easily negotiated.

*Hitching*

Join the group of people on the corner of the camping ground; they usually congregate from 8:30 am onwards. It's normally no problem catching a ride to the mountain.

*By shuttle*

GoodSports run two trips daily, making pick-ups at 8:30 am and 9:00 am. An adult return fare is $20; a child's (10 and under) is $15. Bookings are essential: 0–3–443 7966.

Edgewater Resorts make a daily trip, starting pick-ups at 8:15 am. An adult return fare is $20; a child's (10 and under) is $15. Bookings are essential: 0–3–443 8311.

slopes. A road up to the area had been ruled out as the terrain it would have to climb through was considered too rugged. The company, however, did not turn public. Potential investors were not interested while there was no guarantee of any return.

Subsequently, in March 1972, under the Government's Tourist Facilities Development Scheme, the company sought a $400,000 Government-backed loan guarantee. Unfortunately, this was unsuccessful, and the cable car was not installed. Had it been, Treble Cone and Wanaka would have been well on their way to becoming the next Coronet Peak and Queenstown equivalent.

It's interesting to note that, while there was unanimous

---

**From Queenstown**

*By car*

Follow the instructions for Cardrona, only keep going to Wanaka. From Wanaka take the road going left toward Glendhu Bay. It's sign-posted the whole way.

*Hitching*

It's a bit ambitious, but you may get there in a day. Follow the instructions for Cardrona, only be on the road by 7:00 am.

*By shuttle*

Danes is the only shuttle company running regular trips to Treble Cone. The shuttle makes pick-ups from 7:45 am. A return trip, plus a day pass (buy from the shop), is $75 (Adult); $55 (Child). The shuttle is back in Queenstown by 6:00 pm. Bookings are essential: 0-3-442 7318.

The other Queenstown-based shuttle companies will make trips to TC, provided enough people are going.

support for the ski area from all sectors – the competition, the Government, and the public – there was little interest from anyone in becoming involved financially.

So, in the ensuing years, the company continued operating on its small, club-like scale, attracting private bookings to use the area from around the country. In 1975, the 16 founders met and formally agreed to become a public company. The shares were almost wholly subscribed for by Otago residents, and with this new capital the company began developing the area. The cable car idea had been abandoned, and early in 1976 a road was constructed up to the area. Climbing some of the most rugged slopes in the country, this road was considered a real feat when completed. Another rope tow was installed above the present one, and an access tow, running from the car park to the bottom of the first lift, was put in.

Treble Cone was officially opened to the public on 14 August 1976. Two hundred skiers showed up on the first day. The season was a success, as was the following one and, in December 1977, the company issued more shares and gained a loan to assist with the purchase of two Doppelmayr T-bars. These replaced the two rope tows and carried skiers to 1770 metres. In the 1978 season, 'TC' was recognised as one of the South Island's 'big four' – along with Coronet Peak, Mount Hutt and Tekapo (which ran from 1972–1990) – and the price of a lift pass increased to $5.

The same year, the Wanaka Ski Club installed an experimental rope tow on the site of the present Saddle Ridge T-bar. The rope tow took skiers to 2012 metres and opened up the huge Saddle Basin area. TC, with its steep, ungroomed slopes, was becoming renowned as the advanced skier's area. In order to cater for beginner skiers, the company bought a groomer, and bulldozed a learners' area beside the access tow.

In 1983, the Deliverance double chairlift was installed from the base lodge up to the top T-bar. Three years later, the learners' tow was replaced with a platter lift. The Helicopter Line purchased the ski area in Febraury 1987. In 1989, the lower T-bar was moved to Saddle Ridge, replacing the rope tow, and giving the area a 610-metre vertical drop.

Today, Treble Cone attracts between 80–100,000 skier visits a year and, with the Waiorau Nordic and Cardrona areas, brings thousands of visitors to Wanaka every winter.

## The Ski Area

Treble Cone is probably best described as a 'skiers' playground'. The variety of terrain is great. There are wide, groomed runs; wide, powder runs; mogul runs, and numerous natural half-pipes. Because the mountain is essentially quite steep, it has, in the past, been regarded as an advanced skiers' area. Things are changing though, and work on the area in recent times has established a number of easier routes. Nowadays, anyone visiting TC will find runs as challenging as they like.

Easy Street and Triple Treat are both good runs for beginners who have skied a day or two. For those who have not skied very much, the beginners' area is perfect. It's a long, wide slope that is really used only by novice skiers. If you're skiing the beginners' area confidently, a run from the top of the chairlift should be your next step. For its progression from the beginners' area, to the chairlift runs, to the many intermediate and advanced runs, Treble Cone could not have been better designed. For someone intent on becoming an advanced skier in the shortest possible time, there is no better place to do so than at TC.

Treble Cone is regarded as having the best views of any ski area in the country. The view of Lake Wanaka, with the township on the far shore, is superb, as are the views up the Matukituki Valley from the Viewpoint and Outer Limits Runs. The 360° panorama from the summit is worth the 15-minute walk, and there always seems to be someone making the trip. Chances are, though, they're making the walk for the ski back down, rather than the views. It's a great ski down Summit Slope into Saddle Basin.

Saddle Basin is a wide slope with two deep gullies running down it. Both gullies are reasonably wide and, when lips form down the sides, the skiing in and out of these can be fantastic. More so if the snow is soft! On a powder day, it can be very difficult stopping at the bottom of Far Out and making the traverse back to the Saddle T-bar; it's very tempting to just carry on down and walk back up. You can ski down to about 100 vertical metres beneath the Saddle T-bar and walk up a cat-track. The run down the left of the Saddle T-bar is suited to beginner skiers, though it is a little steep near the top.

Sundance is a great, long run down a large face: fantastic skiing for advanced skiers who prefer uncrowded, ungroomed slopes. The same could be said for the runs in Matukituki Basin, although there are usually more skiers over there. Snowboarders will enjoy the very long, natural half-pipe/barrel, as well as the artificial half-pipe below Easy Street.

For information on ski-touring routes in the Treble Cone region contact the information centre in Wanaka, or one of the ski shops. Don't make a trip without getting a hazard forecast from ski patrol.

# WAIORAU NORDIC

## HISTORY

In the 1960s and 1970s, New Zealand's rural population was in decline. Cardrona Valley, in which John Lee owned a farm, was feeling the impact of this decline – the school bus service had terminated and the mail delivery was under threat of ceasing.

Lee, determined to put a stop to this, saw two options. His first choice was to put a Nordic ski area on his land in the Pisa Range. His second choice was to put a downhill ski area on Mount Cardrona, which he bought in 1970. At this time there were already over 20 downhill ski areas in the country, and Lee saw the market for a Nordic ski area being larger than that for another downhill area.

The tenure Lee held on Mount Cardrona and Pisa Range differed; he owned Cardrona freehold, while Pisa Range was on Crown land (leased from the Government). In looking into his possibilities, Lee talked to ski area operators and business people around the country. These people informed him of the bureaucracy, time and money required when attempting to develop Crown land. While the operator is interested in financial viability, the Government is not.

As a result, Lee put the Nordic idea on hold for the time being, and in 1977 began developing the Cardrona ski area. All his energies went into Cardrona until 1984. By then, Cardrona was firmly established, so his thoughts turned back to the Nordic idea.

In October 1984, Lee applied for a permit to develop a Nordic ski area on the Pisa Range. There were submissions against his application, and a hearing was held by the Otago

Land Settlement Committee in November 1985. The committee granted the permit, but it came with certain conditions. Lee was not prepared to accept these as they would have seriously hindered the economic viability of the whole project. In May 1986, he was granted a rehearing, but to no avail. The conditions were upheld.

In May 1988, the acting director of Lands, Ian Campbell, acknowledged that the imposed conditions were inappropriate, and deleted them from the permit. Lee now had permission to proceed, provided he gained the Department of Conservation's approval for any earthworks carried out. There were a few small 'communication problems' between Lee and DoC but, by January 1989, the two came to an understanding and began stage one of the development plan.

##  Waiorau Nordic

*Location:* 33 km from Wanaka.
57 km from Queenstown (via Crown Range Road).

*Season:* Opens early July and closes early October.

*Elevation:* Mount Pisa, behind the Bob Lee Hut, is 1926 metres high.
The ski area varies in altitude between 1500 and 1800 metres.

*Vertical drop:* Not applicable.

*Terrain:* Beginner 15%, Intermediate 70%, Advanced 15%.

*Snowmaking:* None.

*Groomers:* Two.

*Road toll:* None.

*Lifts:* One small rope tow used for 'tyre-tube' slope.

*Ski pass:* Adult $20, Child $10.

There was already a good road up to the proposed ski area, as Lee had done some major road upgrading in 1987. It was, however, just a farm road at this stage.

Things went well during trail construction, the only problem being the '$11,000 rock' that required huge amounts of gelignite to remove (Lee has called it 'probably the most expensive corner anyone will ever ski around'.) The prefabricated base buildings were put in place, a new groomer went into action and, on 14 July 1989, the Waiorau Nordic ski area opened for business.

Eight people skied on the first day, with a 100 per cent increase on the second day. And, although a warm spell forced the area to close on 1 August, it attracted 339 skier visits in just 21 days.

## Waiorau Nordic

*Ski hire:* Full set (cross-country): $15 (Adult); $10 (Child).

*Specials:* Group discounts by prior arrangement.

*Ski school:* Group lessons: $15 (Adult); $10 (Child).
Private lessons: $30.

*Accomm:* There are two huts on the ski area – Bob Lee and the Meadow Warming. Both are well-equipped, back-country-style huts. Bring your own sleeping bag. A night's accommodation is in the budget range. For more information, phone 0–3–443 7542, or fax 0–3–443 7541.

*Address:* Waiorau Nordic Ski Area, Cardrona RD 1, Wanaka. Telephone: 0–3–443 7541.

*Snow reports:* Listen to Queenstown's Resort Radio, Wanaka Radio, or Radio 4XO, or phone the ski area on 0–3–443 7544.

These days, Waiorau is still the country's only Nordic ski area, and continues to attract more and more visitors every season. Waiorau is actually the Maori name for the Cardrona area.

## THE SKI AREA

While popularity of Nordic, or cross-country skiing, in New Zealand is growing, it is still very much in its infant stages. Waiorau, however, could quite easily change this.

The ski area is located on the Pisa Range, across Cardrona Valley from the Cardrona ski area. The access road, which is about 15 kilometres long, comes off the Crown Range Road a couple of hundred metres south of Cardrona's access road.

### GETTING THERE

**From Wanaka**

*By car*
Follow the instructions for Cardrona. Waiorau's access road is about a kilometre past Cardrona's, on the left.

*Hitching*
Follow the instructions for Cardrona. If you get a lift with someone going to Cardrona, walk the kilometre to Waiorau's access road. You'll then catch people coming from Queenstown, too.

*By shuttle*
GoodSports run a daily shuttle to Waiorau, making pick-ups around Wanaka at 8:30 am. An adult return fare is $20, a child's (10 and under) is $15. Bookings are essential: 0–3–443 7966.

Edgewater Adventures run a daily shuttle, making pick-ups around Wanaka from 8:15 am. An adult return

Waiorau's road is usually in very good condition, but chains are often required towards the top.

The sport of cross-country skiing is a kind of mix of tramping and downhill skiing, although very different from either. To approach a day at Waiorau with the same kind of hype, and perhaps anxiety, as you do a day's downhill skiing is a mistake. There are few sports as peaceful and pressure-free as cross-country skiing at a recreational level. Add that to the fantastic snow-covered plateau region of Waiorau, and you have the recipe for an unforgettable experience.

While there's some truth to the concept that cross-country skiing can be picked up quicker than downhill skiing, a lesson is still a very good idea. There are groomed tracks (two side by

---

fare is $20; a child's (10 and under) is $15. Bookings are essential: 0–3–443 8311.

**From Queenstown**
*By car*
Follow the instructions for Cardrona, only you'll arrive at Waiorau's access road, on your right, before you reach Cardrona.

*Hitching*
Follow the instructions for Cardrona.

*By shuttle*
Outback Tours run a daily shuttle at 8:30 am, making pick-ups throughout Queenstown (and Arrowtown). Transport, lift pass, lesson, ski hire package: $80 (Adult); $50 (Child). Without lesson: $65; $35. Bookings are essential: 0–3–442 7386.

side) over most of the area and these certainly make the skis more manageable for the novice. Off trail, though, the skiing can be considerably more difficult, but well worthwhile for the thrill of exploring. There are areas on the plateau where the rolling snowfields seem to go on forever and you feel worlds away from anything.

To get accustomed to the skis, have a few runs on the flat in front of the base area. If you're happy with your progress, head out on The Loop track, which is generally reasonably flat and easily negotiated by the novice. The beauty of The Loop is also that it takes you around most of the area, and from it you can go off exploring as temptation takes you. From the Tranquillity area you get great views of Cardrona, Lake Wanaka and surrounding mountains. From here you also get some idea of just how large the area is.

From Tranquillity you can descend to the Roaring Meg River and follow it to the Meadow Warming Hut, a great place for lunch, with gas cookers, bunks and picnic tables. After lunch you can continue alongside the picturesque river to Musterers' Flat and make the short climb, on ski, back up to the base area.

Overnighting at either Meadow Warming Hut or Bob Lee Hut is a fantastic experience, particularly on a moonlit night, when a midnight ski is a must. If you're planning to stay in one of the huts, phone the area first and make sure there are bunks available.

There's a small slope in front of the base area that you can slide down on the inner-tube of a tyre, which can be borrowed from the hire shop. There is also a rope tow (operating in the afternoon only) that will drag you and your tube back to the top of the slope. The joy of screaming down this slope on a tube is experienced by people of all ages, and it often appears to be the parents who enjoy it most.

# QUEENSTOWN

Well before Europeans arrived, a Maori tribe, the Kati-Mamoe, had established a village named Te Kirikiri in Queenstown Bay. But by the time the first explorers reached the region in the mid-1850s, the tribe had long since departed.

The first European to see Lake Wakatipu was Nathaniel Chalmers who, in 1853, travelled from the south with two Maori guides, Reko and Kaikoura. Sighting the lake from the Hector Mountains, he chose not to go to it, and instead descended to the Kawarau River, which he crossed before heading north to Lake Hawea.

The first Europeans to reach the lake were John Chubbin, John Morrison and Malcolm MacFarlane in 1856. No sooner had they reached the lake than Morrison lit his pipe and threw down a match that set fire to the dry undergrowth. The fire became a raging blaze along the lake's shore. The three men and their horses were forced into the lake, where they waited, neck-deep in icy water, for three hours. Once the fire had died down sufficiently for them to pass through the charred vegetation, they returned south, never to venture back to the lake.

Late in 1859, Welshman William Gilbert Rees and Russian Nicholas von Tunzelmann set off from Oamaru in search of pasture land in the central Otago region. Early the next year, they found the perfect land at the eastern tip of Lake Wakatipu. They tossed a coin to see who would settle there. Rees won, and Von Tunzelmann chose to settle on the western shores of the lake. Rees brought his family to the land, built a homestead, and established his run, known as The Camp.

In 1862, Rees hired two shearers, Thomas Arthur and Harry Redfern. It was these men who, on their day off, wandered to the Shotover River and, with just a dish and a knife, collected four ounces of gold. The two made no attempt to keep their findings secret and, within weeks, the area became swamped with miners. By the end of 1862, there were 1500 miners working the Shotover River. At the peak of the gold rush, there were over 10,000 miners in the Wakatipu area.

Rees had brought an old whaling boat to his homestead and used it to get to the southern end of the lake (now Kingston), from where a track led to Invercargill and Dunedin. Supplies could be brought from the cities to the lake and ferried to the homestead. As the miners moved into the area, this service came under more and more demand. A town began forming. Miners built their houses, and shops and 'entertainment halls' began appearing. Rees pulled down one of his woolsheds and built in its place the Queens Arms Hotel. This was replaced in 1874 by the Eichardts Hotel, named after its builder, a Prussian ex-officer, Albert Eichardt. The bar is still in use today.

On New Years Day 1863, a meeting was held and The Camp changed its name to Queenstown. Exactly why is unknown. It may have been named after Queenstown in Ireland (now called Cobh), or it may have been given its name after one miner described the place as 'fit for a Queen'. Rees had originally leased the land for his run and when, in 1863, he applied to buy 32 hectares around his homestead, his application was refused as it was planned to build a town there. So, the haphazard type of settlement that had developed became officially known as Queenstown.

The region had been heavily dredged of gold by the turn of the century, and most miners had moved on, although mining did continue on a smaller scale (and still does). Tourism took over almost as soon as gold mining dwindled, and the beauty of Lake Wakatipu and the Queenstown region began drawing people from all over the world, just as gold had done.

Nowhere in New Zealand caters for tourists the way Queenstown does today and, love it or hate it, there's very little that you can't do from the town – skiing, rafting, bungy jumping, parapenting (parachuting from the top of a hill using a rectangular chute), river surfing, hang gliding, jet boating, climbing, tramping, and so on.

The Queenstown Winter Festival, which is fast becoming renowned throughout the skiing world, is held annually in mid-July. It lasts a week and is packed with events, on and off the mountain. The town's usually crammed with people for the festival, and it really is a great time to visit the place.

## Arrival

### *By air*

Queenstown airport is in Frankton, seven kilometres to the east. From the airport you can either catch a shuttle (0–3–442 9803) to town for $5, or pay about three times as much for a taxi (0–3–442 7788). Shuttles and taxis usually meet each flight.

### *By bus*

Two bus companies have their own depots, and both are very central. The Intercity/Ritchies depot is in the Clock Tower Centre, on the corner of Camp and Shotover Streets. The Mount Cook Landline depot is on Church Street.

### *By car*

There are two ways of getting into Queenstown – via Frankton or via Arrowtown. Both routes take you straight to the centre of town. Your only problem may be finding a car park. If all else fails, head along the Esplanade, past the Park Royal. You're bound to find a spot down there.

## Ski and snowboard shops

*Note:*
- The term 'etc' means that a rental charge gets progressively cheaper per day the longer you hire.
- Only the prices for a full set of equipment (skis, boots and poles) are given. Shops also hire out these items separately.
- Every shop will want some kind of deposit before you can

hire gear. Deposits usually requested are credit-card numbers, car licence-plate numbers, passports, and so on.

**Bad Jelly Skis R'Us** has, over the years, become known as the bargain hire shop. It closes down over summer and seems to reappear at a different address every winter. In the 1994 season, it was on Camp Street beside the Danes Rafting shop. The best way to track the shop down is by asking at the Visitors Information Centre or another ski shop.

*Hire charges:*
Full set of equipment: $20 (day).
Snowboards: $19 (day).
Clothing (jacket and pants): $30 (day).
You may be able to negotiate a multi-day hire rate for three or more days.

**Kiwi Discovery** (0–3–442 7340) is on the corner of Camp and Shotover Streets. The shop has a good range of skis and boots for sale, and will carry out boot-fitting as required.

*Hire charges:*
Full ski gear: $27 (first day); $25 (second day); $23 (third); etc.
Executive gear: $45 (first day); $42 (each additional day).
Insurance for equipment is $2 per day.
Also hired out are clothing and chains.

*Ski repair charges:*
Wax: $10.
Edge and wax: $20.
Full tune: $25–$35.

**Bill Lacheny Ski Shop** (0–3–442 8438) is in The Mall. The shop has a very good range of skis, boots and accessories.

*Hire charges:*
Full set: $23 (day); $19 per day for three or more days.
Executive skis: $34 (day).

*Repair charges:*
Wax: $13.
Edge and wax: $40.
Full tune: $53.

**R&R** (0–3–442 7791), on the corner of Shotover and Rees Streets, usually has the largest selection of second-hand equipment for sale. It also has a fair range of new gear.

*Hire charges:*
Full set: $26 (first day); $24 (second day); $22 (third day); etc.

*Repair charges:*
Wax: $10.
Edge and wax: $20.
Full tune: $25–$35.

**Browns** (0–3–442 4005) at 39 Shotover Street is the largest ski shop in Queenstown. There's a huge selection of skis and boots for sale.

*Hire charges:*
Full set: $28 (day).
Executive gear: $45 (day).
Snowboard and boots: $35 (day).

*Repair charges:*
Wax: $15.
Edge and wax: $25.
Full tune: $45.

**Queenstown Sportsworld** (0–3–442 8452) at 17 Rees Street has a fair selection of new and second-hand equipment.

*Hire charges:*
Full set: $26 (first day); $24 each day thereafter.

*Repair charges:*
Wax: $8.

Edge and wax: $18.
Full tune: $35.

For hiring or buying ski-touring or telemark equipment, check out **Mountain Works** (0–3–442 7329) on Camp Street. It's also the main climbing/guiding centre in Queenstown.

## Snowboard shops

**NZ Shred** (0–3–442 6311) at 19 Shotover Street was the first snowboard shop in Queenstown. There's a huge range of snowboards for sale and hire.

*Hire charges:*
Snowboard and boots: $39 (first day); $35 (second day); $150 (five days); $25 per day thereafter.

*Repair charges:*
Wax: $12.
Edge and wax: $19.
Full tune: $45.

The **Snowboard Shop** (0–3–442 6139) is at 45 Camp Street, beside Mountain Works. Like NZ Shred, there's a huge range of boards for sale.

*Hire charges:*
Snowboard and boots: $40 (first day); $35 (per day thereafter).

*Repair charges:*
Wax: $5–15.
Edge and wax: $19.
Full tune: $30–40.

## Places to stay

The **Youth Hostel** (0–3–442 8413) at 80 Lake Esplanade, about a kilometre from the centre of town, is a huge place, and is very popular with skiers. It has a large kitchen and dining area (moderately priced, cooked meals can be purchased from the small café in the dining room), laundry facilities, a large drying room and a TV room (there's a video played every night). The views down Lake Wakatipu from the kitchen and dining room are great. Beside the reception area is an information and booking office. Twin, double and dormitory-style rooms are available, ranging in cost from budget to low for Youth Hostel Association members. Non-members pay slightly more. Booking is essential over the holidays, and advisable at other times.

**Thomas's Hotel** (0–3–442 7180) at 50 Beach Street has standard hotel and backpackers' rooms. It's ideally located – on the waterfront and very central. It is a four-storey place, the upper two floors having the hotel rooms, which include en suite bathrooms, tea- and coffee-making facilities, a TV, refrigerator and electric blankets. There's a variety of rooms – single, double, twin and triple, and the price is moderate. The backpackers' section consists of four-bed dormitory rooms, and a bunk in one of these is in the low price range. It has a communal kitchen/dining room that has fantastic views of the waterfront and lake. It also has a laundry and a drying room. On the ground floor is Thom and Jerrys, a café/bar that serves good food, all-day breakfasts, and has a happy hour at 5:00 pm. Thomas is actually a resident ginger cat, renowned for its size and slothfulness. Book ahead if possible.

**Mountain View Lodge** (0–3–442 8246) on Frankton Road has a reception building constructed out of empty glass bottles, which makes it very difficult to miss. It's a large hotel, with 57 rooms, 25 of which have cooking facilities. They all have an en suite bathroom, TV, telephone, tea- and coffee-making facilities, and a refrigerator. Every room has good views. It has a good restaurant and in-house bar, which also has great views, as well as a pool table and a large video screen, making it a very popular place to watch any big rugby games. Rooms are in the high price range. The hotel also has a number of 'mini-motel' rooms, some of which are moderately priced. These are bunkrooms, with a shared kitchen/dining area. Bookings are essential.

**Four Seasons Motel** (0–3–442 8953) is at 12 Stanley Street, a five-minute walk from the town centre. It has 15 fully self-contained rooms (TV with in-house videos, and telephone in each room). It has a drying room, a laundry, and a spa pool ($2.50 per person per half hour; non-residents are welcome). Continental breakfasts can be delivered to your room for a low charge. The rooms and facilities are very good, well worth its high price. Bookings are essential.

**Lakeland Hotel** (0–3–442 7600; fax 0–3–442 9653) is on Lake Esplanade, on the northern shore of the lake. From the comfortable lobby, to the excellent 'Clancys' restaurant and 'Maggies' bar, this hotel is all class. The rooms (double, twin, single and triple) have superb views of lake Wakatipu and The Remarkables, and naturally come with all the frills (minibar, TV, tea- and coffee-making facilities, refrigerator and en suite bathrooms). There's a sauna, and a spa pool on the sixth floor that is blessed with what are unquestionably the best views from a spa in town. There are also, of course, drying rooms and ski storage areas. It's difficult not to enjoy a stay even when the charges are at the higher end of high. Bookings are essential.

**Park Royal** (0–3–442 7800; fax 0–3–442 8895), like the Lakeland Hotel just down the Lake Esplanade, is one of those places where guests feel like celebrities. It's just across the road from the lake and a two-minute walk from the town centre. It's a large hotel with 139 rooms, each of which has its own balcony and fantastic views. In the rooms are a TV (in-house video channels), minibar, telephone, tea- and coffee-making facilities, and an en suite bathroom. The hotel caters very well to skiers. It has a ski storage area, a drying room, a sauna, a special ski-menu in the Bentleys Brasserie (excellent food, which has won several awards), complimentary hot chocolate in the Steamers bar at the end of each day, and a winter BBQ night held once a week. It also has its own in-house ski instructor, who can take care of all your ski-school arrangements, and is a great source of local knowledge. Providing you can afford the high charge, you may find it a difficult place to leave! Bookings are essential.

**Quality Hotel Queenstown** (0–3–442 8123; fax 0–3–442 7472) is on the corner of Adelaide Street and Frankton Road, a ten-minute walk from the town centre (there is a complimentary shuttle service). It has 100 rooms – 50 Standard and 50 Premier, these having the better views. All rooms have a minibar, TV, tea- and coffee-making facilities, and an en suite bathroom; charges are high. There's an in-house bar, a very good restaurant (with a special three-course, moderately priced skier's meal), a laundry, a drying room and two great spa pools. Bookings are essential.

**Blue Peaks Lodge** (0–3–442 9224), on the corner of Stanley and Sydney Streets, offers motel-style accommodation. A five-minute walk from the town centre, it has a variety of rooms – from one- to five-person units, with or without kitchens. All rooms have an en suite, TV (in-house videos), telephone, and tea- and coffee-making facilities. Cooked or Continental breakfasts can be delivered to your room. The cost is high, though with more people that can be reduced to the moderate level. Bookings are essential.

**Backpackers Downtown Lodge** (0–3–442 6395) is very central, at 48 Shotover Street. It has mainly dormitory-style rooms, with a few twins and doubles. It's a bit of a labyrinth-type set up, with a kitchen/common-room area on the first floor with interesting views down Rees Street. A night's stay is in the low price range. It can get quite busy so it pays to book ahead, if possible.

**Bumbles Hostel** (0–3–442 6298) at 2 Brunswick Street is a quality backpackers' joint in every sense. Three minutes' walk from the centre of town, it's clean, tidy, offers good beds at low prices, has a laid-back atmosphere, and is very friendly. (The current manager, Joy, is a living legend for her character and hospitality.) It consists of dormitory, twin and double rooms, and has a kitchen/common-room area with great views over the lake. There's a laundry, and a drying and storage room. Discount ski hire and transport deals can be arranged from reception. A large heater in each room ensures that you will always be warm. Bookings are essential.

**Bungy Backpackers** (0–3–442 8725) at 15 Sydney Street is a lively kind of place, five minutes' walk from the town centre. It has dormitory rooms, a good kitchen area, and a large common room with a good, and growing, collection of hub caps on its wall. It has a laundry, drying room and a video library. Book ahead, if possible.

## PLACES TO EAT

**Gourmet Express**, in the Bay Centre on Shotover Street (not far from the Naff Caff), is an American-style coffee shop. It's open from 6:30 am until 9:00 pm, but is best known as a great place to have breakfast. The 'Miners Breakfast' is the largest, and is in the low price range.

**Roaring Megs** (0–3–442 9676), on Shotover Street opposite Gourmet Express, is regarded as one of the finer dining spots in town. It's in an old goldminer's cottage dating from the late 1800s. It has an open fire, a great old coal range, and dining is carried out by candlelight to the tune of classical music. Meals are in the high price range. It's open from 6:30 pm, and reservations can be made by leaving a note in the notebook on the front door or by telephoning.

**The Cow** (open from noon to midnight) is a small pizza restaurant in an old stone building in Cow Lane, and seems to be constantly busy to the point of having patrons milling about waiting to get in (bookings cannot be made). It has become renowned not only for its moderately priced pizzas and great atmosphere, but also for its rude waiters and waitresses. They put on an act that can be very amusing and is not intended to be personal. The fact of the matter is, with so many people waiting to dine, the meals tend to be a little rushed. There's a large open fire with a few stools and, if available, this is the best place to wait for a table. It's BYO. Spaghetti, the alternative, is in the moderate price range.

**Avanti Restaurant & Bar** (0–3–442 8503) is an Italian-style place in The Mall, the Italian theme being supported by the use of empty Chianti bottles as candle-holders, and the fact that everything seems to be red, white or green. The meals, which are pizza or pasta, are of a good size, and moderately priced. It's licensed, with a good wine list, and is open from 7:00 am until late. Breakfasts are served from 7:00 am to 2:00 pm. It's a good idea to book ahead for the evenings.

**Berkels Gourmet Burgers** (0–3–442 6950) at 19 Shotover Street offers some of the best-value meals (if you like hamburgers) in town. There are 12 types of hamburger to choose from, all in the low price range. It's licensed (no BYO), and you can either dine in or take away. The burgers make for a great snack if you've just got off the mountain and have one of those insatiable appetites. It's open from 12:00 pm until late. Book ahead if possible, as it can get busy.

The **Pot au Feu Restaurant** (0–3–442 8333) on Camp Street (opposite KFC) has a menu with a Mediterranean slant. The menu has been written with a touch of dry humour, and any place advertising their coffee as 'the second best in town' must have something going for it. The food, wine list and service are great. The cost of meals ranges from moderate to high. It's open from 6:00 pm until late. Book ahead if possible.

**Solera Vino** (0–3–442 6082) is a small Spanish-style wine bar and restaurant at 25 Beach Street. The decor is truly Spanish, complete with barrel-end tables, whitewash walls and a fine wooden staircase. The wine list is excellent and it's a great spot for a meal (global cuisine), or just a snack and a bottle of wine in front of a roaring fire. Meals are in the high price range. It's open from 5:00 pm until late, and bookings are essential.

**Skyline Restaurant** (0–3–442 7860) at the top of the gondola obviously has the best view in town. The food is very good and, combined with the view (which is at its best in the early evening light), a meal here is an unforgettable experience. The cost of meals is high; the gondola trip is $9. Bookings are essential.

## HAPPENING PLACES

**Naff Caff** at 62 Shotover Street is a coffee-drinker's Mecca, with eight types of coffee, great music, and that special aroma that only a good coffee shop has. There's also a wide choice of herbal teas, and the low to moderately priced meals are good, too. Rivalling the Naff Caff for the best coffee in town is the **Take 5 Expresso & Juice Bar** on the wharf, beside the Fiordland Travel office. Hours are 8:00 am to 10:30 pm Tuesday to Friday, and 9:30 am to 6:00 pm Saturday to Monday.

**Abbey Road** at 66 Shotover Street, beside the Naff Caff, is a bar dedicated to pop music. Walls are covered with photographs of 1960s and 1970s bands (there was once a prize offered to anyone who could name every band, but one photo upstairs stumped everyone). It's open from 12:00 pm until late and is lively most nights, particularly Fridays and Saturdays.

**Red Rock Café** at 48 Camp Street is open from 11:00 am until 3:00 am. Everyone out on the town drifts through this place at some stage of the night. It's quiet during the day, and the occasional midweek night; the rest of the time it's the heart of

Queenstown's nightlife. Loud music, ski videos, and the party atmosphere abound. Meals are large and priced in the low to moderate range.

For the laid-back fireside *après-ski* atmosphere, **McNeills** (0–3–442 9688) at 14 Church Street has little competition. It's built in the traditional Greywacke rock, with floors of worn rimu. For anyone with an interest in New Zealand beers and brewing, a visit is compulsory. The brewing room can be seen through a window behind the bar, and the product has been known to flow in abundance. In a room adjacent to the bar is the restaurant, which serves excellent, moderately priced food in the same relaxed surroundings. Bookings for the restaurant are essential. The place is open from 11:30 am until late.

The **Moa Bar & Café** (0–3–442 8372) in The Mall is probably the most European (some say Auckland) type of bar in Queenstown. It has sophisticated surroundings, with a menu to suit and possibly Queenstown's best wine list. There's no better place to try the local Chard Farm or Gibbston Valley wines. Snacks are in the low price range; meals in the moderate range. It's open from 10:30 am until 1:00 am.

**Lone Star Café** (0–3–442 9995) at 14 Brecon Street consists of a restaurant and a saloon bar. The decor is in a class of its own, particularly in the saloon bar. It's done out in a cowboy-type theme, complete with an old Indian motorbike hanging above the bar. The meals are in the high price range, but they are huge, and you would have to be extremely hungry to finish two courses. There's frequently live music; there's a pool table; and the whole place is set out in such a way that makes it possible to have a quiet fireside drink on one side of the room, while on the other side the floor is teeming with dancing bodies. It's a very popular place so, if you feel a little claustrophobic in a ski-lift queue, avoid this place. It's licensed and open from 4:30 pm until late. Bookings for the restaurant are essential.

**Shannahans Bar** in The Mall is Queenstown's obligatory Irish connection and, should you be struck by an overwhelming desire to do a bit of a jig, this is your place. The Great Irish Potato Famine Relief Party seems to be held on a somewhat erratic basis but it can be worth checking out if on.

**Eichardts Hotel**, next door to Shannahans, is the oldest bar in town. It's still very popular, and is done out in true 'Kiwi pub' style, with lean-tos, a pool table, and beer served in jugs. It's a landmark, a relic, and a great place for a jug of beer and an opportunity to play pool against some of the more accomplished players in the region. Above Eichardts is the **Vilagrad**, probably Queenstown's most popular live music and dance venue. When big bands come to town they play here. It's a huge open-plan place with a few pool tables, pinball games and loud music.

The **Swiss Iglu Restaurant & Bar** (0–3–442 6878) at 27 Shotover Street is a large glass dome in the shape of an igloo, so it's difficult to miss. A popular place, serving 'Eskimo Cider' and 'Penguin Lager', the Iglu must get full marks for concept and design. When full of people the 'igloo' tends to steam up a bit, and works as a fairly reliable indicator of how busy you can expect it to be. The restaurant has a very Swiss influence, particularly the main table, which has a four-metre Swiss horn down its centre. Meals are at the upper end of the moderate range. It's licensed, and open from 12:00 pm until late. Bookings are essential.

**Winnie Bagoes** (0–3–442 8635) is a new restaurant/bar in The Mall. It's an extremely popular 'gourmet pizza bar', with a fantastic timber and brick decor, several open fireplaces, a couple of pool tables, and a balcony overlooking The Mall. The more astute buskers have been known to perform below the balcony, from which bar patrons have the added incentive of trying to throw their coins into a hat or guitar case from a height. The bar is split into a dancing area, a pool-playing area, and a quieter dining area. In springtime, the balcony is the place to be. The food is moderately priced. Book ahead.

**Pig and Whistle** is a terribly, terribly English pub opposite the Village Green, at the top of The Mall. A creek running through the garden bar makes its outside drinking area most definitely the best in Queenstown. It tends to be a quiet pub; with its large open fire, dart boards and very English decor, it is no place for those suffering from Anglophobia. A good place for a quiet ale and a snack, it's open from 11:00 am until late.

## SERVICES

*Medical:* Queenstown Hospital is on Douglas Street in Frankton: 0–3–442 3053. There's no Accident and Emergency Department.
The Queenstown Medical Centre is on the corner of Shotover and Stanley Streets: 0–3–442 7301.
*Police:* The police station is at 11 Camp Street: 0–3–442 7900. In emergencies, phone 111.
*Post Office:* The post office is on Camp Street: 0–3–442 7670.

## INFORMATION

You will never be short of information in Queenstown. Every hostel or hotel reception can provide plenty, as can the many ski and adventure shops around town. There are also newspaper stands containing free local papers all over the place. The official Visitor Information Centre is on the corner of Shotover and Camp Streets: 0–3–442 8238; fax 0–3–442 8907.

## GETTING AROUND

The centre of Queenstown is reasonably small and walking is the best way to get around. In fact, most visitors spend at least a couple of hours just strolling about the shops and cafés.

You can catch a taxi from the stand on Camp Street at the top of The Mall, or you can order one by phoning 0–3–442 7788 or 0–3–442 6666.

Bicycles can be hired from the Bike Shop (0–3–442 6039) at 23 Beach Street.

The Shopper Bus makes a continuous circuit around town, and to its outskirts. For $1, you can get on and off wherever you like.

The Circuit Bus makes a circuit around Queenstown, the Shotover Jet, Arrowtown and the Kawerau Bungy bridge, stopping at each place every 75 minutes. The fare for this varies from $2 to $15, depending on your destination.

There are a number of car rental outfits in Queenstown. Rates and conditions vary, the better-known companies charging a little more than the others. It's an idea to call a few before hiring, and negotiate as you see fit. Listed below are the companies:

AA Host Rental Cars, 37 Stanley Street: 0–3–442 7399.
Avis Rent-a-Car, 16 Beach Street: 0–3–442-7280.
Budget Rent-A-Car, Chester Building, corner Camp and Shotover Streets: 0–3–442 9274.
Hertz New Zealand Ltd, 2 Church Street: 0–3–442 8418.
NZ Rent-a-Car, Information Centre, corner Camp and Shotover Streets: 0–3–442 7465.
Pegasus Rental Cars, 18 Lake Esplanade (Motel Lakeside): 0–3–442 7176.
Rent-a-Dent, 48 Shotover Street: 0–3–442 9922.
Thrifty Rental Cars, 27 Shotover Street: 0–3–442 8100.

## Travelling on

*Domestic airlines*
It's possible to fly with the following airlines to most major centres in New Zealand:

Air New Zealand/Mount Cook Airline, Mount Cook Line Travel Centre, Church Street: 0–3–442 4640.
Ansett New Zealand, 76 Shotover Street: 0–3–442 6161.

Aspiring Air (0–3–443 7414), Wanaka Travel Centre, makes a daily scheduled flight to Wanaka.

*Shuttle and bus*
Atomic Shuttles runs services to Christchurch: 0–3–442 8178.
Catch-A-Bus runs services to Wanaka, Christchurch and Dunedin: 0800–50 8000 (toll-free).
Intercity/Ritchies runs services to destinations throughout New Zealand: 0–3–442 8238.
Kiwi Discovery runs services to Christchurch: 0–3–442 7340.
Mount Cook Landline runs services to destinations throughout New Zealand: 0–3–442 4640.
Southern Link Shuttles runs services to Wanaka and Christchurch: 0–3–442 6666.

# WANAKA

Before Europeans arrived in New Zealand, the Maori used the Haast Pass as a means of getting from Otago to the West Coast. They formed camps at Wanaka and Hawea, and would stay there on their journeys. In 1836, a North Island tribe under the command of Te Rauparaha's lieutenant, Te Puoho, invaded the region, massacring most of the resident Maori. Some managed to escape over the Lindis Pass, and down to the East Coast.

When the first European in the region, Nathaniel Chalmers, arrived in 1853, the Maori had long since gone. Chalmers, who had travelled from the south, and was the first European to see Lake Wakatipu, came down with dysentery soon after reaching Lake Wanaka. His Maori guide, Reko, built a flax raft, and the two of them made their way down the rapids of the Clutha River to the coast.

John Turnball Thomson became the first European to cross Lindis Pass in 1857. He climbed to the top of a mountain he named Grandview and looked over the Hawea flats to Lakes Hawea and Wanaka. He named Mount Aspiring from this point, as well as the Pisa Range (after a rock on the ridge that resembled the famous leaning tower).

In early 1858, 'Big' John McLean stood atop Mount Grandview and, on seeing the Hawea flats, immediately went to Dunedin and made a claim on the land. With a lease granted he returned to the region with a flock of sheep and started the Morven Hills Station. McLean was soon followed by others and, by the end of 1858, there were a number of sheep runs around the two lakes.

William Fox discovered gold in the Arrow River in 1862 and, although he managed to keep it a secret for some time, word eventually got out and miners began swarming to Arrowtown. It was a group of these miners who stumbled across gold in the

Cardrona Valley and subsequently started the Cardrona township. The town, which at one stage had over 1000 people living in it, began declining as the gold ran out in the 1870s. A spring flood in 1878 marked the demise of the settlement.

To get to Arrowtown required crossing the Clutha River, a difficult and dangerous crossing. George Hassing brought a whale boat to the river and made a lot of money from the hundreds of prospectors crossing the river daily. First known as Albert Crossing, it became Albert Town, a busy township with several stores.

In 1867, Theodore Russell built a hotel on the shore of Roys Bay, Lake Wanaka. The site had been surveyed for a future town, Pembroke, in 1863. Russell's hotel was first used largely by miners but, by the 1880s, when the pursuit of gold in Otago was dying down, Russell began encouraging tourism by advertising in Dunedin newspapers. By 1900, the region's centre had shifted from Albert Town to Pembroke.

In the 1930s, the town's neighbour, Queenstown, began its meteoric-like rise to become the South Island's major tourist destination. Pembroke, which changed its name to Wanaka in 1940, was not affected by the zest of tourism like its neighbour, and proceeded at a more sedate rate. By the 1980s, a century after Russell had built the first hotel, the Treble Cone and Cardrona ski areas had opened, making Wanaka a year-round tourist destination.

While free of the busy streets, large hotels, and many 'touristy' shops of Queenstown, Wanaka has a similar setting of snow-capped mountains above a tree-lined lake. Of the two, Wanaka is by far the more tranquil.

## ARRIVAL

*By air*
Wanaka Airport is ten kilometres to the east of the township. Wanaka Taxis (0–3–443 7999), will take you into town for $20.

*By bus*
The Mount Cook Landline buses stop at the Wanaka Travel Centre (99 Ardmore Street), on the lake front. The Intercity/Ritchies buses stop outside The Paper Place at 84 Ardmore Street. Both are virtually in the centre of town, and making your way around from either of them is simple.

*By shuttle*
Shuttle operators will drop you off wherever you want. If you're unsure of where to go, the Travel Centre is a good place to start.

*By car*
There are only two roads into Wanaka – Highway 6 from the east and the Crown Range road from the south. Both take you very close to the town's centre.

## SKI AND SNOWBOARD SHOPS

**Good Sports Sportsworld** (0–3–443 7966), in the Pembroke Mall on Dunmore Street, has a huge selection of ski equipment for sale.

*Hire charges:*
Full set: $23 (first day); $20 (second day); $18 (each of third to fifth day).
Performance skis: $35 (day); with boots $45 (day).
Snowboards: $30 (first day); $25 (each day thereafter).
The shop also hires out clothing, roof racks and snow chains.

*Repair charges:*
Base wax and sharpen: $18.
Full ski tune with crystal glide: $42.
Full snowboard tune: from $40.

**Racers Edge Ski and Sports Ltd** (0–3–443 7882) at 99 Ardmore Street also has a huge range of ski equipment, as well as a good selection of snowboards.

*Hire charges:*
Skiing: $24 to $40 a day, depending on the style of the equipment (sport, performance or executive).
Snowboards with boots: $42 (day).
Discounts are given for more than three days.
Also hired out are clothing, toboggans, chains and roof racks.

*Repair charges:*
Ski wax: $8.
Ski edge and wax: $22.
Snowboard wax: $12.
Snowboard edge and wax: $26.
Full tunes: from $27–$37, depending on damage.

## PLACES TO STAY

**Wanaka Bakpaka** (0–3–443 7837) at 117 Lakeside Road is a five- to ten-minute walk along the northern shore of the lake from the centre of town. It has dormitories, twin and double rooms, and prices vary from budget to low. It has a fantastic lounge/dining room area, with great views over the lake. The lounge has a huge log-burner, with plenty of large beanbags, and a stereo with a huge selection of tapes and CDs. There is no television but there is a spa pool. There's a small charge to use the pool, and non-residents cannot use it. The hostel also has a laundry, drying room and ski storage room. Linen can be hired. Book ahead if possible.

The **Wanaka Youth Hostel** (0–3–443 7405) is at 181 Upton Street, a ten-minute walk from the town centre. It's one of the older youth hostels, and has had buildings added to it over the years. There's a comfortable kitchen/common room area in which everyone seems to mingle, creating a very sociable atmosphere. The stereo seems to be playing constantly, and more often than not the general conversation revolves around the day's 'on-snow' activities. There are dormitory, twin and double rooms. Prices range from budget to low. It has a drying room, a ski-tuning room and a laundry. Booking is advisable.

**Matterhorn South Backpackers** (0–3–443 1119) at 56 Brownston Street, a short stroll from the town centre, consists of two buildings – an older house for backpackers and a new building that has mostly double and twin rooms. The backpackers' dorm is budget-priced; twin and double rooms are in the low price category. It's a well-organised hostel that caters very well to skiers. There's a drying room, a ski storage area, and a great kitchen/dining area with a large log-burner and a few beanbags in which to get comfortable. The new building has a kitchen and a lounge room of its own. The lounge is on the second floor and gets good views of the town and lake. Each room has a TV (with in-house videos), refrigerator, en suite bathroom, and tea- and coffee-making facilities. A room in the new building is excellent value, at the higher end of the low range. Bookings for either places are essential.

**Aspiring Lodge** (0–3–443 7816), on the corner of Dungarvon and Dunmore Streets, is a modern motel two minutes' walk from the town centre. It has 11 rooms, all of which are fully self-contained and include a telephone, TV and radio. The rooms are very comfortable, with two queen-sized beds in each. Three units (one of which is designed specifically as a paraplegic suite) are able to sleep up to six people. Continental (low charge) or cooked breakfasts (moderate charge) can be ordered from reception. An additional bonus is a rental 4WD car, which can be very handy should you happen to over-sleep. Rooms are in the moderate or high price category, depending on how many people are sharing. Bookings are advisable.

The **Alpine Motel** (0–3–443 7950) is at 7 Ardmore Street, on your left as you arrive in Wanaka. It's a short walk from the town centre and has 18 rooms – nine studios, and nine one- and two-bedroom rooms. Each room has a TV (with in-house videos), fridge, electric range, telephone and electric blankets. There's a laundry, a ski storage area and a good ski-tuning area. Cooked or Continental breakfasts can be ordered from reception (whitebait fritters are a speciality). And, if you need some sun, the motel has its own suntanning clinic, 'Alpine Bronze'. Rooms are moderately priced. Book ahead if possible.

**Cliffords of Wanaka Hotel** (0–3–443 7826) in Ardmore Street is on the site of the town's first hotel, built by Theodore Russell in 1867. It's a large hotel with plenty of rooms, a restaurant and an in-house bar. The hotel has hosted the Norwegian national ski team, and teams from Canada and Japan, all of whom have their photographs in the hotel's bar. Some of the world's fastest ski racers have enjoyed a quiet drink in this bar. The hotel rooms all have a TV, telephone, tea- and coffee-making facilities, and an en suite bathroom. The hotel has a laundry, a drying room and a huge ski storage/ski-tuning room. Rooms are moderately priced.

Behind the hotel is the **Cliffords Backpackers' Hostel** (0–3–443 7826). It's a fairly basic hostel with a low-priced dorm and moderately priced twin and double rooms. There's a kitchen/TV/common room area, which has been known to get quite rowdy. Many of the people in the hostel stay for the whole season. If you stay six nights, your seventh is free. Book ahead for hotel and hostel.

**Edgewater Resort Hotel** (0–3–443 8311; fax 0–3–443 8323) is on the southern shore of the lake, a ten-minute walk from town. It's a hotel of real quality, with 100 lakeside rooms, all with great views. The hotel bar, 'Goldminers Daughter', and restaurant, 'Nathaniels', are both superb and open to non-residents. Nathaniels wine list is excellent, as are the high-priced meals. The bar is of the relaxing variety, with an enormous open fire and frequent live jazz. Happy hour is from 6:00 to 7:00 pm.

The hotel has three types of room – studios, one-bedroom

suites, two-bedroom apartments. All have en suite bathroom, direct-dial telephone, refrigerator, small cooking area, TV and in-house video. There's a large drying room, a spa pool and a sauna. It would be difficult not to enjoy a stay at Edgewater. Prices are in the high category. Bookings are essential.

## PLACES TO EAT

**Capriccio Restaurant** (0–3–443 8579) in Pembroke Mall serves a range of New Zealand and international cuisine. The food is in the high price range, and is superb (it has won several awards). It's fully licensed, with an excellent wine list, and opens from 6:00 pm. The view of the lake is great. Booking is usually vital.

**Kai Whaka Pai** (Maori for 'House of great food') (0–3–443 9220) in Pembroke Mall has built up a huge reputation and is highly regarded by 'café connoisseurs' throughout New Zealand. There's a great selection of coffees, all of them good; the Soyacino is worth a try. It's a smallish place, with a laid-back atmosphere and, if the weather's bad, it can become quite busy. The food, for which it has gained its reputation, is excellent and moderately priced. It's open from 6:00 am until late. It's a good idea to book ahead for an evening meal.

**Anatoles** (0–3–443 7872) on Ardmore Street, opposite the post office, serves a variety of cuisines, including Indian, German and French. It has good views of the lake, with an atmosphere to match. Warmed by an open fire, it's a great place to enjoy good food and a bottle of Otago wine (it's BYO). Open from 6:00 pm Tuesdays to Sundays, it is non-smoking throughout. Booking ahead is a good idea.

The **Tuatara Pizza Co** (0–3–443 8186) at 72 Ardmore Street opened in 1994, and is the kind of place Wanaka has always needed. The decor is spot-on: old wooden tables and church pews for seats, pot-belly stove, a good (albeit a little sloped) pool table and a separate small area with table soccer and pinball machines. It caters for all, and the consequent ambience is ideal. The music is good, the coffee is good, the pizza is great, and this place obviously rated pretty highly with the author! There are two sizes of moderately priced pizzas. It's licensed and BYO and open from 5:00 pm until late. Takeaways are available. Book ahead if possible.

**Relishes Café** (0–3–443 9018) at 99 Ardmore Street is open from 9:30 am until late, and serves a good lunch or dinner. Evening meals are in the high price range. The food and service are excellent, and the large open fire is great. It's licensed and BYO. The wine list has a great selection and it is the perfect place to try the local Rippon wines. It has a charming timber decor, and a relaxed atmosphere. Bookings are advisable.

**Ripples Restaurant** (0–3–443 7413) in Premboke Mall offers some of the finest dining in town. The menu itself is written in such lyrical manner that it's sure to entice you into eating there, if its contents don't. Winner of several awards, it's BYO and, because it's on the second floor, views of the lake are very good. Prices are in the high range. It's open from 6:00 pm until late, and bookings are essential.

**Te Kano Café** (0–3–443 7028) at 63 Brownston Street is in a converted old house. A small, intimate place that serves gourmet pizzas, it's in a great setting, nestled amongst trees and a short walk from the centre of town. With its open fire and glühwein, it's the perfect spot following a day's skiing. It's open from 7:00 am until late, and is BYO. There are two sizes of pizza, both moderately priced. Bookings are essential. Takeaway and phone-order pizzas are available.

# HAPPENING PLACES

**Barrows** on Ardmore Street has long been regarded as the most 'happening' of places in Wanaka. It tends to be where everyone congregates following a day's skiing, and there's a certain amicable feel about the place. It's the kind of bar where the jukebox and pool table are constantly busy. There's a restaurant upstairs (open from 6:00 pm); cheaper, moderately priced bar meals are available downstairs.

The **White House Bar and Café** (0–3–443 9595) on Dunmore Street is a very Mediterranean-looking building, and the interior perpetuates the theme with a fine wine list, a superb menu, and classical music over the sound system. A slight compromise to the Mediterranean theme has the restaurant with an open fire. It tends to be a quiet, relaxing type of place (good for a morning or afternoon coffee). It's open from 11:00 am to 11:00 pm, and the food is moderately priced. Bookings are advisable.

**Outback Bar** has an Australian theme, with photos of deserts and big red rocks on its walls. It's a modern place but, true to Aussie outback tradition, the pool table commands the centre of the room. Bar snacks are available for low to moderate prices. Connected to the bar is Munchies Café, a fairly standard cafeteria that serves very good cooked breakfasts and a reasonable cup of coffee (open from 7:00 am).

**Soho Café** (0–3–443 8269) at 72 Ardmore Street has, true to its title, a London theme. Real English ale on tap seals the bar's authenticity, as does a large map of the London Underground. Connected to the bar is a restaurant that serves a variety of cuisine at moderate prices. There is frequently live jazz in the restaurant. Booking for the restaurant is advisable. The bar and restaurant are open from 4:30 pm until late.

The **Cardrona Hotel** (0–3–443 8153) is a 20-minute drive along the Crown Range road from Wanaka. It's usually reasonably quiet, except between 4:00 and 6:00 pm, when what seems like the majority of Cardrona's skiers descend on the small bar and restaurant. Whether a day at Cardrona is complete without a stop here is not an unreasonable question. Originally built in the 1860s, it has been very well restored, and you're unlikely to regret a visit. The restaurant meals are great, and moderately priced. It's fully licensed, and taxis travelling from Wanaka are subsidised by the hotel. Book ahead if possible.

## Services

*Medical:* Wanaka Surgery, 37 Russell Street: 0–3–443 7811.
*Police:* The police station is located on Helwick Street: 0–3–443 7272. In emergencies, phone 111.
*Post Office:* 39 Ardmore Street: 0–3–443 8211.

## Information

Most hostel or hotel receptions will be able to provide you with most general and tourist information. The two ski shops are also a good source of local info. If you require more, try these places:

- Wanaka Travel Centre, 99 Ardmore Street: 0–3–443 7414 or 0–3–443 7277; fax 0–3–443 8876.
- Wanaka Information Centre, Ardmore Street: 0–3–443 1233; fax 0–3–443 7660.

## Getting around

Walking or cycling are really the ways to get around town. Bicycles can be hired from Wanaka Lake Services (0–3–443 7495) at the wharf. If the weather's inclement, or you don't feel like walking or cycling, you can call a taxi from Wanaka Taxis (0–3–443 7999). Lakeside Rentals (0–3–443 7495), also at the wharf, is the only car rental outfit in Wanaka.

# Travelling on

*Domestic airlines*
The Mount Cook Line flies from Wanaka, via Queenstown, to most New Zealand centres. To book, contact the Wanaka Travel Centre, 99 Ardmore Street: 0–3–443 7414.
Aspiring Air has a daily scheduled flight to Queenstown. Bookings can also be made at the Wanaka Travel Centre, or phone: 0–3–443 7943.

*Shuttles and buses*
Catch–A–Bus runs services to Queenstown, Christchurch and Dunedin: 0800–508 000 (toll-free).
Intercity/Ritchies runs services to destinations throughout the South Island: 0–3–443 7885.
Mount Cook Landline runs services to destinations throughout the South Island: 0–3–443 7414 or 0800–800 287 (toll-free).

# HELISKIING

When you ask someone who's been heliskiing what they thought of it, you will invariably get one of two responses. The first, and more common, is a kind of ongoing monologue, full of gasps, and much head-nodding, in which the entire experience is recounted in 'turn for turn' detail. The second is a broad, face-wrinkling smile, sometimes followed by a nonchalant 'Great'.

It doesn't matter how many ski areas you've been to, how many magazines you've read, or how many brochures you've studied, until you've actually been heliskiing you'll never quite understand what it is that makes people respond in such a manner to so simple a question. Within the Southern Alps of New Zealand are some of the largest snowfields in the world. Taking a helicopter into these mountains, landing at the top of a slope, then proceeding to carve tracks – your own – while being surrounded by, and taking in, the awe of the Alps, is regarded throughout the world as being amongst the epitome of skiing/snowboarding experiences.

There are nine heliski operations in New Zealand, of which all but one are based in the South Island. Although the services and packages offered vary between operators, a day generally goes something like this:

❏ First you get picked up and taken to the helipad, where you meet the guides who will give a briefing on safety requirements. (Heliski guides are regarded as the élite of mountain guides, and the safety record of heliskiing in New Zealand is impeccable.)

❏ Next, you'll be split into groups according to skiing/boarding ability, jump in the helicopter and head into the mountains. The guide will choose a slope, which the helicopter then takes you to the top of.

- Once the group is out and the helicopter has departed, the guide will then give a quick briefing on local conditions and the best skiing, before leading you down the run.

- When the group is at the bottom of the slope, the helicopter returns, the guide chooses another run, and the whole procedure is repeated.

- Most operators supply a buffet-style lunch to be enjoyed following the morning runs, prior to embarking for more in the afternoon.

To go heliskiing you should really be of at least an intermediate standard, be reasonably fit and, ideally, have some experience in powder snow. A recent invention – powder skis (also known as 'fat skis') – are shorter and wider than standard skis, and make skiing in powder considerably easier. Most ski shops have a few sets of these for hire, and the heliski operators are usually happy to arrange this for you. Snowboarders are welcomed by all heliski operators.

The following is a list of heliski operators in New Zealand, along with a guide to the packages they offer. Bookings are essential for all trips.

**Boarder Patrol**
37 Shotover Street, Queenstown. PO Box 564.
Phone: 0–3–442 5262. Fax: 0–3–442 5265.

Based in Queenstown, these are the heliboarding specialists. They're well tuned into the snowboarding consciousness, with adrenalin-loaded runs, and helicopters with stereos. (They ask that clients bring their favourite sounds.)

*Packages*
For intermediate boarders:
'Intro Heli-boarding'. Morning spent with an instructor on a local ski area; afternoon spent heliboarding. $459 per person.

For intermediate to expert boarders:
'Heli-Epic'. Maximum of four clients per guide and eight clients per group. A minimum of three runs (7500 vertical feet). $525 per person.

'Fully-Epic'. Maximum of four clients per guide and eight clients per group. A minimum of five runs (12,000 vertical feet). $695 per person. Extra runs (2500 vertical feet) are $75.

For advanced and expert boarders:
'Heli-X-Dream'. Two clients and two guides. 25–30,000 vertical feet in one day. $1500 per person.

**Fox Glacier Heliskiing**
PO Box 38, Fox Glacier, West Coast.
Phone: 0–3–751 0825. Fax: 0–3–751 0857.

Run by Alpine Guides (Westland) Ltd, a day's heliskiing on the Fox involves a flight from the Fox Glacier village to the top of the glacier, followed by a single 10-kilometre (4500 vertical feet) run. $450 per person.

**Harris Mountains Heliskiing**
The Wanaka Travel Centre, 99 Ardmore Street, Wanaka. PO Box 177. Phone: 0–3–443 7930. Fax: 0–3–443 8876.

The Queenstown Info Centre, corner of Shotover and Camp Streets. Phone: 0–3–442 6722.

Harris Mountains is the largest heliski operation outside Canada. It has more than 350 runs, ranging between 2000 and 4000 vertical feet, in six separate mountain ranges. Having operated since the late 1970s, it is also really the pioneer company of heliskiing in New Zealand.

*Packages*

Each package has a Shoulder Season and a High Season price. Shoulder Season is from 29 June–21 July and from 16 September–3 November. High Season is from 22 July–15 September.

For intermediate skiers/boarders:
'Experience'. A three-run day with an introduction to the alpine environment, some 'off-*piste*' instruction, and with emphasis on leisure and fun. Shoulder Season $535 per person; High Season $595.

For intermediate and advanced skiers/boarders:
'Classic'. A five-run day encompassing a variety of terrain in several mountain ranges. Shoulder Season $640 per person; High Season $700.

For advanced skiers/boarders:
'Max Vert'. A seven-run day with an emphasis on skiing/boarding as much as possible. Shoulder Season $750 per person; High Season $810. After the seven runs you can carry on, each extra run costing $70 per person.

Vacation Package:
'Odyssey'. This is a seven-day, seven-night package, and includes accommodation, breakfasts, lunches, two evening dinners, local transfers, ski-area skiing on non-flying days, and 75,000 vertical feet of heliskiing. Shoulder Season $5275 per person; High Season $5520 (based on twin share accommodation).

## Heli Guides New Zealand

27 Shotover Street, Queenstown. PO Box 195.
Phone: 0-3-442 8151. Fax: 0-3-442 8151.

Regarded as the 'boutique' heliski outfit, Heli Guides NZ operates in the mountains north of Queenstown – the Cardrona, Moonlight, Aurum and Temple Ranges – as well as on Tasman and Fox Glaciers. They specialise in two- to seven-day packages.

*Packages*
For first-time heliskiers/boarders:
'Instructional Heliskiing'. Clients are flown by helicopter to Cardrona ski area, where they're met by an instructor, and

spend the morning concentrating on techniques suitable for heliskiing. After lunch, there is a minimum of 7500 vertical feet (about three runs) skied, before being flown back to Queenstown or Wanaka. $595 per person.

For intermediate, advanced, or expert skiers/boarders:
'Classic Heliskiing'. Maximum of three clients to one guide, and a maximum of three clients per helicopter. A minimum of three runs (7500 vertical feet). $595 per person.

For advanced and expert skiers/boarders:
'Wilderness Heliskiing'. Same client–guide ratio as Classic Heliskiing. At least five runs (12,500 vertical feet). $695 per person.

Prince of Wales Private Heliski Area:
This is an area set aside for skiers and boarders wanting their own exclusive ski area. There is no set schedule (client–guide ratio is a maximum of one to three) and the price depends on the amount of flying time. It's the best way to go if you're after maximum vertical feet. Two hours' flying with two clients is $1500 per person; with three clients it's $995. Three hours' flying with four to six clients (two guides) is $995 per person.

Vacation Packages:
'Two Day Voucher'. Two full days of heliskiing with a minimum of 25,000 vertical feet guaranteed. This is a good way of booking ahead and allowing some flexibility in the event of inclement weather. $1750 per person, or $1650 per person for a group of three or more.

'Three Day Voucher'. Three full days, with a minimum of 37,000 vertical feet guaranteed. If conditions permit, one of these days can be spent on the Fox or Tasman Glaciers. $2650 per person, or $2550 per person for a group of three or more.

'All-Inclusive Introductory Heliskiing/boarding'. Includes seven nights' accommodation, breakfasts, lunch and refreshments while heliskiing, seven days' guide service, ski-area passes, use of powder skis, ground transport, and return airport transfers.

Guaranteed minimum of 50,000 vertical feet. $5600 per person, share twin; $5900 per person, single.

'Introductory Heliskiing/boarding Only'. Includes seven days' guide service, use of powder skis, ski-area passes, ground transport and return airport transfers. Guaranteed minimum of 50,000 vertical feet. $4200 per person.

'All-Inclusive Heliski Week'. The same as the All-Inclusive Introductory Heliskiing/boarding package, but with a guaranteed minimum 100,000 vertical feet. $7900 per person, share twin; $8200 per person, single.

'Heliski Week'. The same as the Introductory Heliskiing/boarding Only package, but with a guaranteed minimum 100,000 vertical feet. $6500 per person.

### Heliski Mount Cook
PO Box 32, Mount Cook National Park.
Phone/fax: 0–3–435 1890 or 0800–650 651 (toll-free).

Heliski Mount Cook runs heliski trips into the Ben Ohau Range, south of Mount Cook, as well as skiplane flights on to the Tasman Glacier. A day in the Ben Ohau Range consists of about 10,000 vertical feet, usually completed in three or four runs. $530 per person.

The 'Tasman Glacier One Day Ski Adventure' is suited to intermediate and advanced skiers. Clients are flown by helicopter or skiplane from Mount Cook village to the Tasman Glacier, where they enjoy lunch before embarking on a 12-kilometre run down the glacier. Clients are then picked up and flown back to the village. $395 per person.

### Methven Heliski
Alpine Guides Shop, Forest Drive, Methven. PO Box 123.
Phone: 0–3–302 8108. Fax: 0–3–302 8909.
(November–May): Alpine Guides, PO Box 20, Mount Cook.
Phone: 0–3–435 1834. Fax: 0–3–435 1898.

Methven Heliski runs trips into the Arrowsmith, Ragged and Palmer Ranges, west of Methven and Mount Hutt. It's the closest heliski operation to Christchurch, and daily trips from the city can be made. Suitable for intermediate to expert skiers and boarders, a day involves an average of 10,000 vertical feet (often more), usually completed in four or five runs. $595 per person.

**Mount Hutt Heliski**
No 12 RD, Rakaia.
Phone: 0-3-302 8401. Fax: 0-3-302 8102.

Mount Hutt Heliski is based in the Mount Hutt car park. Operating in the ranges to the north and west of Mount Hutt, with a choice of over 40 runs, it can prove to be a very tempting alternative if you're getting a bit tired of the queues on the ski area. Single runs are available from $45 per person. A half-day is $345 per person.

**Ski the Tasman**
Alpine Guides, PO Box 20, Mount Cook.
Phone: 0-3-435 1834. Fax: 0-3-435 1898.
Mount Cook Line, 47 Riccarton Road, Christchurch.
PO Box 4644. Phone: 0-3-379 0690 or 0800-800 737 (toll-free).

Started in the 1960s following Harry Wigley's invention of the skiplane, skiing the Tasman Glacier is regarded as the classic New Zealand ski run. Recent changes in aviation laws have enabled helicopters to take skiers to the top of the Tasman Glacier, where once only fixed aircraft were permitted.

A day's skiing on the 'Ski the Tasman' package involves two ten-kilometre runs down different parts of the glacier. Groups consist of six to ten people of similar ability and, because runs are open and moderately angled, skiers of an intermediate level will have no problems. High Season (15 July–15 September) $575 per person; Low Season (1 June–14 July; 16 September–15 October) $525 per person.

**Snowrange Heliskiing**
RD 54, Kimbolton.
Phone: 0–6–328 2869 or 0–6–388 1696. Fax: 0–6–388 1011.

The only North Island heliski operation, Snowrange is based in Taihape, about 50 kilometres south of Ohakune. It operates in the Ruahine Range, east of Ruapehu. A day's trip, with 10,000 vertical feet guaranteed is $485 per person. A half-day trip, with 6000 feet guaranteed, is $380 per person.

**Southern Lakes Heliski**
Kawarau Rafts Adventure Centre, 38 Shotover Street, Queenstown. PO Box 426.
Phone: 0–3–442 6222. Fax: 0–3–442 7867.

Southern Lakes operates in the mountains surrounding lake Wakatipu – the Thomson, Hector and Richardson Ranges.

*Packages*

'Explorer'. A three-run day, this is also available as the 'Heli-shred', catering specifically for snowboarders on which you're guaranteed not to be mixed with skiers. $565 per person. Extra runs are available at $75 each.

'Adventurer'. A five-run day, this package has been designed with advanced to expert skiers in mind. $665 per person. Extra runs are available at $75 each.

'Unlimited Day'. Designed for the 'hard-core' heliski enthusiasts, this is basically an exercise in fitting as many runs into the day as possible. The more runs you do, the cheaper they become. Price depends on the number of runs skied.